CONTEMPORARY
AMERICAN CRITICISM

SELECTED AND ARRANGED
By
JAMES CLOYD BOWMAN, A. M., LITT. D.
EDITOR OF *Essays for College English*, ETC.

NEW YORK
HENRY HOLT AND COMPANY

COPYRIGHT, 1926,
BY
HENRY HOLT AND COMPANY

PRINTED IN THE
UNITED STATES OF AMERICA

PREFACE

The present volume of essays is the outgrowth of the editor's experience in conducting classes in Contemporary Literature. He very soon discovered that there is to-day much heated discussion and much uncontrolled enthusiasm *in vacuo*. There is too little attempt at a clear understanding of the present conflicting philosophies of life and their resulting literary movements. Much of the fervency, indeed, as well as much of the distrust is then and futile. This volume is intended as a first aid to those who wish to acquire perspective.

The editor here gratefully acknowledges the courtesy of publishers and authors in allowing the reprint of copyrighted material. Specific mention is made of this kindness in footnotes at proper places throughout the volume.

J. C. B.

TABLE OF CONTENTS

INTRODUCTION

INTRODUCTION

The so-called 'poetic Renaissance' of the past two decades has been followed closely by an era of the most significant literary criticism that we have had in America. The new styles in writing have necessarily attracted those who would explain, disparage, or justify.

In these recent years, America has never been richer than in the outlook of maturing youth. Its ideals—instead of being stereotyped and conventional—have been exotic and colorful. Iconoclasts have not been wanting to break with cherished dogma and tradition. The various ensuing clashes of opinion have uncovered many a hidden mystery of the art of literature. They have kept authors alive; they have made experiments fascinating and attractive.

The purpose of this volume of essays is to present a discussion of the various conflicts that have arisen recently in American literary criticism. Each point of view is allowed—as far as space will permit—to have its full say. No effort is made to coerce opinion or to attract disciples: rather, the hope is held that these essays will supply a concise and somewhat inclusive background for the intelligent understanding of the various aspects of literature in general, but more especially of contemporary American literature.

The earliest of these critical controversies, in point of time, began as a discussion of the part nationality should play in American literature. Most of the New England authors, whose ancestry and breeding were traditionally English, naturally thought of American literature as the tender scion from the English parent tree. The revolt, however, came in good earnest with Emerson and Whitman. Longfellow and Lowell maintained the conservative point of view. Emerson and Whitman argued that the growing democracy should produce literature which would express its own unique individuality. This was but the beginning. Much of the discord among contemporary writers and critics to-day grows out of the disagreement over the place of nationality and tradition. It is thus important, first of all, to understand both sides of this argument.

Another controversy has been waged over the purpose of criticism itself. The radical idealists and romanticists, who hold to the supremacy of mind over matter, have naturally maintained that all the formal and traditional approaches to criticism should be disregarded. They have argued that the purpose of the critic is solely to interpret the self-expression of the writer. Mr. Spingarn, in recently giving emphatic approval to this point of view, has drawn hot fire from various sources, and has brought about one of the most vigorous clashes of opinion in contemporary criticism.

Still another controversy has been fought over the moral aspect of literature. Whether the world of literature is a world of moral values, or whether its values are purely æsthetic, has brought on one of the sharpest battles in the entire warfare of recent criticism. The word, 'Puritan,' with varying connotations, has been flung hither and yon, with an ever widening chasm of discord. Mencken, with his rattling barrage of biting epithets, has aroused many. He has, perhaps, found his readiest opponent in Sherman. Many able defenders have joined forces with these leaders, and so the battle goes merrily on.

A different disagreement still has resulted from the general misunderstanding of the field of realism. Many readers are unaware of the distinction between philosophic realism and matter-of-fact realism. Many seem unable to distinguish between fact and truth. Until there is a general clearing of the misconception over the seeming connection between the impression of actuality in realism and the established facts of science, literature cannot hope to go forward to its highest accomplishment.

Another controversy has arisen around the importance of beauty of form in literature. Poe was the first American writer to explain the exquisite deftness with which patterns in literature can be woven. His uncanny self-scrutiny in analyzing the processes of his own mind coupled with his nice precision in actually creating perfection of form in his own writing, has won for him a strong following, especially among those who believe in formal designs and external beauty. In the recent revolt, however, many strange and grotesque patterns have been attempted in the effort to attain freedom and to attract attention in the midst of the babel of voices.

Other subjects also find discussion. The futility of the use of present day commercial methods in the attempt to stimulate literature is brilliantly explained. The aim and accomplishment of contemporary poets and novelists is appraised. The relation of book reviewing to pure criticism is surveyed. A final essay lends courage to those who believe that literature is no superfluous will-o'-the-wisp, but a powerful voice calling civilization from the wilderness of the actual into the too long delayed promised land of the imagination.

BIBLIOGRAPHICAL NOTE

The following volumes contain excellent bibliographical material.

The Cambridge History of American Literature, edited by William Peterfield Trent, John Erskine, Stuart P. Sherman, and Carl Van Doren; 4 vols., Putman, 1917–21.

> Very full bibliographical material on almost every subject in the general field of American Poetry. Does not include the most recent movements.

A History of American Literature Since 1870, by Fred Lewis Pattee; Century, 1915.

> Much bibliographical material covering practically all the movements in American literature down to 1900.

Anthology of American Poetry, edited by Percy H. Boynton, Scribner, 1918.

> Useful bibliographical material covering the major poets down to 1910.

From Whitman to Sandburg in American Poetry, by Bruce Weirick; Macmillan, 1924.

> A carefully selected bibliography of the various movements and also of the various individual authors down to 1924.

The New Poetry, edited by Harriet Monroe and Alice Corbin Henderson; Macmillan, 1923.

> The bibliography gives a complete list of practically all the volumes of verse published in America

between 1900 and 1923. It also gives a list of critical volumes published by these same poets for the same period.

The Little Book of Modern Verse, and also *The Second Book of Modern Verse*, edited by Jessie B. Rittenhouse; Houghton Mifflin, 1917; 1920.
Brief information concerning the lives of the authors whose work is included in the anthologies.

The following volumes contain indispensable critical material covering the recent authors and literary movements.

Tendencies in Modern American Poetry, by Amy Lowell; Macmillan, 1917.
A keen analysis of the recent movements.

The New Era in American Poetry, by Louis Untermeyer; Henry Holt, 1919.
Much information concerning the contemporary movements and also concerning individual authors.

America's Coming of Age, by Van Wyck Brooks; Huebsch.
Entertaining and penetrating.

Convention and Revolt in Poetry, by John Livingston Lowes; Houghton Mifflin, 1919.
A scholarly analysis of the contemporary movements in relation to the conflicts of past movements.

Midwest Portraits, by Harry Hansen; Harcourt, Brace, 1923.
A very full account of the few authors whose work is discussed.

Poetry Magazine, Chicago, beginning 1912.
Current movements and current authors brilliantly criticised.

The Way of the Makers, by Marguerite Wilkinson; Macmillan, 1925.

> A criticism of poetry from the point of view of the creative impulse of the poets themselves. Many of the contemporary poets are quoted.

A Study of Poetry and also *A Study of Prose Fiction*, by Bliss Perry; Houghton Mifflin.

> A study of the traditional generics. Indispensable for those who lack a grasp of the fundamental principles of literary art.

A Modern Book of Criticisms, edited by Ludwig Lewisohn; Boni and Liveright, 1919.

> A collection of French, German, and American critical essays, selected to show the unity of the recent radical movement in literature. A decidedly interesting volume.

Contemporary American Literature, by John Matthews Manly and Edith Rickert; Harcourt, Brace, 1922.

> A volume of bibliographies and outline studies. Includes practically all known contemporary authors. Gives suggestive outline summary of work of each together with suggestive bibliography.

CONTEMPORARY AMERICAN
CRITICISM

PREFACE

In Lowell's day, America had not yet won a national intellectual independence as far as other countries were concerned. Foreigners practiced a certain condescension in thinking of American literature. They considered American writers, at best, but servile imitators of foreign authors of established fame.

There was, however, the stirring of revolt against this point of view. America was full of the independence of youth. There were those addicted to tall talk. Whenever anything was produced in America, it was praised lustily by these cheer leaders.

Lowell easily took a middle ground. He maintained that literature was literature, wherever produced. He explained that nationality is not important—at least not in the sense that content and style are important.

Lowell contributed much to the poise of the generation in which he was acclaimed the Dean of American Critics. His wide knowledge of the Romance languages and literatures as well as of modern political institutions made him a citizen, not only of America, but of Western Civilization. He was at home in the society of gentlemen anywhere.

It is fashionable to-day for the younger generation to sniff when Lowell's name is mentioned. It should be remembered, however, that his general scholarship, his success in diplomacy, his acclaim as a poet and editor, as well as his personal good breeding, did much to dignify American literature at home and abroad in an age when the need for dignity was sorely pressing.

"Nationality in Literature" first appeared as a book review of Longfellow's *Kavanagh*, in 1849. The portion of the essay dealing with Longfellow, is here omitted.

2

NATIONALITY IN LITERATURE

By James Russell Lowell

Time is figured with scythe, hourglass, wallet, and slippery forelock. He is allegorized as the devourer of his own offspring. But there is yet one of his functions, and that not the least important, which wants its representative among his emblems. To complete his symbolical outfit, a sieve should be hung at his back. Busy as he must be at his mowing, he has leisure on his hands, scents out the treacherous saltpeter in the columns of Thebes, and throws a handful of dust over Nineveh, that the mighty hunter Nimrod may not, wanting due rites of sepulture, wander, a terrible shadow, on this side the irrepassable river. A figurative personage, one would say, with quite enough to do already, without imposing any other duty upon him. Yet it is clear that he finds opportunity also thoroughly to sift men and their deeds, winnowing away with the untired motion of his wings, monuments, cities, empires, families, generations, races, as chaff.

We must go to the middle of a child's bunch of cherries to be sure of finding perfect fruit. The outer circles will show unripened halves, stabs of the robin's bill, and raincracks, so soon does the ambition of quantity deaden the nice conscience of quality. Indeed, with all of us, men as well as children, amount passes for something of intrinsic value. But Time is more choice, and makes his sieve only the coarser from age to age. One book, one man, one action, shall often be all of a generation busy with sword, pen, and trowel, that has not slipped irrevocably through the ever-widening meshes.

3

We are apt to forget this. In looking at the literature of a nation, we take note only of such names as Dante, Shakespeare, Goethe, not remembering what new acres have been added to the wide chaff-desert of Oblivion, that we may have these great kernels free from hull and husk. We overlook the fact that contemporary literature has not yet been put into the sieve, and quite gratuitously blush for the literary shortcomings of a whole continent. For ourselves, we have long ago got rid of this national (we might call it hemispherical) sensitiveness, as if there were anything in our Western half-world which stimulated it to produce great rivers, lakes, and mountains, mammoth pumpkins, Kentucky giants, two-headed calves, and what not, yet at the same time rendered it irremediably barren of great poets, painters, sculptors, musicians, and men generally. If there be any such system of natural compensations, whereby geological is balanced against human development, we may, at least, console ourselves with the anticipation, that America can never (from scientifically demonstrable inability) incur the odium of mothering the greatest fool.

There is, nevertheless, something agreeable in being able to shift the responsibility from our own shoulders to the broader ones of a continent. When anxious European friends inquire after our Art and our Literature, we have nothing to do but to refer them to Mount Washington or Lake Superior. It is their concern, not ours. We yield them without scruple to the mercies of foreign reviewers. Let those generously solicitous persons lay on and spare not. There are no such traitors as the natural features of a country which betray their sacred trusts. They should be held strictly to their responsibilities, as, in truth, what spectacle more shameful than that of a huge, lubberly mountain, hiding its talent under a napkin, or a repudiating river? Our geographers should look to it, and instill proper notions on this head. In stating the heights of our mountains and the lengths of our rivers, they should take care to graduate the scale of reproach with a scrupulous regard to every additional foot and mile. They should say, for example, that such a peak is six thousand three hundred feet high, and has never yet produced a poet; that the river so-and-so is a thousand miles long, and has wasted its energies in the manufacture of alligators and flatboatmen. On the other hand, they should remember to the credit of the Mississippi, that, being the longest river in the world, it has very properly produced the longest painter, whose single work would overlap by a mile or two the pictures of all the old masters stitched together. We can only hope that it will never give birth to a poet long in proportion.

Since it seems to be so generally conceded, that the form of an author's work is entirely determined by the shape of his skull, and that in turn by the peculiar configuration of his native territory, perhaps a new system of criticism should be framed in accordance with these new developments of science. Want of sublimity would be inexcusable in a native of the mountains, and sameness in one from a diversified region, while flatness could not fairly be objected to a dweller on the prairies, nor could eminent originality be demanded of a writer bred where the surface of the country was only hilly or moderately uneven. Authors, instead of putting upon their title-pages the names of previous works, or of learned societies to which they chance to belong, should supply us with an exact topographical survey of their native districts. The Himalaya mountains are, we believe, the highest yet discovered, and possibly society would find its account in sending the greater part of our poets thither, as to a university, either by subscription or by a tax laid for the purpose. How our literature is likely to be affected by the acquisition of the mountain ranges of California, remains to be seen. Legislators should certainly take such matters into consideration in settling boundary lines, and the General Court of Massachusetts should weigh well the responsibility it may incur to posterity, before transferring to New York the lofty nook of Boston Corner with its potential Homers and Miltons.

But perhaps we have too hastily taken the delinquency of our physical developments for granted. Nothing has hitherto been demanded of rivers and lakes in other parts of the world, except fish and mill privileges, or, at most, a fine waterfall or a pretty island. The received treatises on mountainous obstetrics give no hint of any parturition to be expected, except of mice. So monstrous a conception as that of a poet is nowhere on record; and what chloroform can we suggest to the practitioner who should be taken unawares by such a phenomenon?

At least, before definite sentence be passed against us, the period of gestation which a country must go through, ere it bring forth a great poet, should be ascertained with scientific exactness. Let us not be in any hurry to resort to a Cæsarean operation. Poets, however valuable in their own esteem, are not, after all, the most important productions of a nation. If we can frame a commonwealth in which it shall not be a misfortune to be born, in which there shall never be a pair of hands nor a mouth too much, we shall be as usefully employed as if we should flower with a Dante or so, and remain a bony stalk forever after. We can, in the meantime, borrow a great poet when we want one, unless the pleasure and profit which we derive from the works of a great master, depend upon the proprietary right in him secured to us by compatriotism. For ourselves, we should be strongly inclined to question any exclusive claim to Shakespeare on the part of our respected relative, John Bull, who could do nothing better than look foolish when the great dramatist was called *bizarre*, and who has never had either the taste or the courage to see a single one of his most characteristic plays acted as he wrote it.

The feeling that it was absolutely necessary to our respectability that we should have a literature, has been a material injury to such as we have had. Our criticism has oscillated between the two extremes of depreciation and overpraise. On the one hand, it has not allowed for the variations of the magnetic needle of taste, and on the other, it has estimated merit by the number of degrees west from Greenwich. It seems never to have occurred to either sect of critics, that there were such things as principles of judgment immutable as those of mathematics. One party has been afraid to commend lest an English Reviewer might afterward laugh; the other has eulogized because it considered so terrible a catastrophe probable. The Stamp Act and the Boston Port Bill scarcely produced a greater excitement in America than the appalling question, *Who reads an American book?* It is perfectly true, that the amount of enlightenment which a reader will receive from a book depends upon the breadth of surface which he brings within its influence, for we never get *something* for *nothing;* but we would deferentially suggest for the relief of many a still trembling soul, repeating to itself the *quid sum miser tunc dicturus* to that awful question from the Edinburgh judgment seat, that it is barely possible that the *power* of a book resides in the book itself, and that real books somehow compel an audience without extraneous intervention. From the first, it was impossible that Art should show here the successive stages of growth which have characterized it in the Old World. It is only geographically that we can call ourselves a new nation. However else our literature may avoid the payment of its liabilities, it can surely never be by a plea of infancy. Intellectually, we were full-grown at the start. Shakespeare had been dead five years, and Milton was eleven years old, when Mary Chilton leaped ashore on Plymouth Rock.

In looking backward or forward mentally, we seem to be infected with a Chinese incapacity of perspective. We forget the natural foreshortening, taking objects as they are reflected upon our retina, and neglecting to supply the proper interstices of time. This is equally true whether we are haruspicating the growth of desired opinions and arts, or are contemplating those which are already historical. Thus, we know statistically the amount which any race or nation has stored in its intellectual granaries, but make no account of the years of scarcity, of downright famine even, which have intervened between every full harvest. There is an analogy between the successive stages of a literature and those of a plant. There is, first of all, the seed, then the stalk, and then the seed again. What a length of stalk between Chaucer and Spenser, and again between Milton and Wordsworth! Except in India, perhaps, it would be impossible to affirm confidently an indigenous literature. The seed has been imported, accidentally or otherwise, as the white-seed and Hessian fly into America. Difference of soil, climate, and exposure will have their legitimate influence, but characteristics enough ordinarily remain for the tracing of the pedigree. The locality of its original production is as indisputable as that of the garden of Eden. Only this is certain, that our search carries us farther and farther eastward.

No literature, of which we have authentic record or remains, can be called national in this limited and restricted sense. Nor, if one could be found, would the calling it so be commendation. The best parts of the best authors in all languages can be translated; but, had they this element of exclusive nationality, the idea would demand a lexicon as well as the language which enveloped it. This shell within a shell would give more trouble in the cracking than any author can safely demand of his readers. Only a Dante can compel us to take an interest in the petty local politics of his day. No grubs were ever preserved in such amber. No Smiths and Browns were ever elevated upon so sublime and time-defying pinnacles of love, horror, and pity. The key by which we unlock the great galleries of Art is their common human interest. Nature supplies us with lexicon, commentary, and glossary to the great poems of all ages.

It would be hard to estimate the immediate indebtedness of Grecian literature; easier to reckon how much must have been due to the indirect influence of a religion and philosophy, whose esoteric ideas were of Egyptian derivation. Aristophanes is perhaps the only Grecian poet who is characterized by that quality of nationality of which we are speaking. Nay, it is something intenser than mere nationality in which his comedy is steeped. It is not the spirit of Greece, not even of Attica, but of Athens. It is cockneyism, not nationality. But his humor is more than Athenian. Were it not so, it would be dreary work enough deciphering jokes, as it were, in a mummypit, by the dim light of the scholiast's taper, too choked with dust and smoke to do anything but cough when we are solemnly assured that we have come to the point.

There is a confusion in men's minds upon this subject. Nationality and locality are not distinguished from one another; and were this jumble fairly cleared up, it would appear that there was a still farther confounding of truth to nature with fidelity of local coloring. Mere nationality is no more nor less than so much provincialism, and will be found but a treacherous antiseptic for any poem. It is because they are men and women, that we are interested in the characters of Homer. The squabbles of a score of petty barbarian chiefs, and the siege of a city which never existed,[1] would have been as barren and fruitless to us as a Welsh genealogy, had the foundations of the Iliad been laid no wider and deeper than the Troad. In truth, the only literature which can be called purely national is the Egyptian. What poetry, what philosophy, the torch of the Arab has fruitlessly lighted up for European eyes, we as yet know not; but that any ideas valuable to mankind are buried there, we do not believe. These are not at the mercy of sand, or earthquake, or overflow. No race perishes without intellectual heirs, but whatever was locally peculiar in their literature, their art, or their religious symbols, becomes in time hieroglyphical to the rest of the world, to be, perhaps, painfully deciphered for the verification of useless history, but incapable of giving an impulse to productive thought. Literature survives, not because of its nationality, but in spite of it.

After the United States had achieved their independence, it was forthwith decided that they could not properly be a nation without a literature of their own. As if we had been without one! As if Shakespeare, sprung from the race and the class which colonized New England, had not been also ours! As if we had no share in the puritan and republican Milton, we who had cherished in secret for more than a century the idea of the great puritan effort, and at last embodied it in a living commonwealth! But this ownership in common was not enough for us, and, as partition was out of the question, we must have a drama and an epos of our own. It must be national, too; we must have it all to our-

---

[1] Written before Schliemann's discoveries.—Ed.

selves. Other nations kept their poets, and so must we.
We were to set up a literature as people set up a carriage, in
order to be as good as our neighbors. It was even seriously
proposed to have a new language. Why not, since we could
afford it? Beside, the existing ones were all too small to
contain our literature whenever we should get it. One
enthusiast suggested the ancient Hebrew, another a fire-new
tongue of his own invention. Meanwhile, we were busy
growing a literature. We watered so freely, and sheltered
so carefully, as to make a soil too damp and shaded for anything but mushrooms; wondered a little why no oaks came
up, and ended by voting the mushroom an oak, an American
variety. Joel Barlow made the lowest bid for the construction of our epos, got the contract, and delivered in due
season the Columbiad, concerning which we can only regret
that it had not been entitled to a still higher praise of nationality by being written in one of the proposed new languages.

One would think that the Barlow experiment should have
been enough. But we are still requested by critics, both
native and foreign, to produce a national literature, as if it
were some school exercise in composition to be handed in by
a certain day. The sharp struggle of a day or a year may
settle the question of a nation's political independence, but
even for that, there must be a long moral preparation. The
first furrow drawn by an English plow in the thin soil of
Plymouth was truly the first line in our Declaration of
Independence. Jefferson was not the prophet looking forth
into the future, but the scribe sitting at the feet of the past.
But nationality is not a thing to be won by the sword. We
may safely trust to the influence of our institutions to produce all of it that is valuable. Let us be content that, if we
have been to blame for a Columbiad, we have also given

form, life, and the opportunity of entire development to social ideas ever reacting with more and more force upon the thought and the literature of the Old World.

The poetry and romance of other nations are assumed to be national, inasmuch as they occupy themselves about local traditions or objects. But we, who never had any proper youth as a nation, never had our mythic period either. We had no cradle and no nursery to be haunted with such bugaboos. One great element of external and immediate influence is therefore wanting to our poets. They cannot, as did Goethe in his "Faust," imbue an old legend, which already has a hold upon the fancy and early associations of their countrymen, with a modern and philosophical meaning which shall make it interesting to their mature understandings and cultivated imaginations. Whatever be the cause, no race into whose composition so large a Teutonic element has entered, is divided by such an impassable chasm of oblivion and unbelief from the ancestral mythology as the English. Their poets accordingly are not popular in any true sense of the word, and have influenced the thought and action of their countrymen less than those of any other nation except those of ancient Rome. Poets in other countries have mainly contributed to the creating and keeping alive of national sentiment; but the English owe theirs wholly to the sea which islands them. Chaucer and Spenser are Normans, and their minds open most fairly southward. Skelton, the Swift of his day, a purely English poet, is forgotten. Shakespeare, thoroughly English as he is, has chosen foreign subjects for the greatest of his dramas, as if to show that genius is cosmopolitan. The first thorough study, criticism, and consequent appreciation of him we owe to the Germans; and he can in no sense be called national except by accident of birth. Even if we grant that he drew his fairy mythology from any then living faith among his coun-trymen, this formed no bond of union between him and them, and was even regarded as an uncouthness and barbarism till long after every vestige of such faith was obliterated. If we concede any nationality to Milton's great poem, we must at the same time allow to the English an exclusive title to the localities where the scene is laid, a title which they would hardly be anxious to put forward in respect, at least, to one of them. When he was meditating a national poem, it was, he tells us, on the legend of Arthur, who, if he had ever existed at all, would have been English only in the same sense that Tecumseh is American. Coleridge, among his thousand reveries, hovered over the same theme, but settled at last upon the siege of Jerusalem by Titus as the best epical subject remaining. Byron, in his greatest poem, alludes only to England in a rather contemptuous farewell. Those strains of Wordsworth, which have entitled his name to a place on the selecter list of English poets, are precisely the ones in which England has only a common property with the rest of mankind. He could never have swum over Lethe with the sonnets to the river Duddon in his pocket. Whether we look for the cause in the origin of the people, or in their insular position, the English mind has always been character-ized by an emigrating tendency. Their most truly national epic was the colonizing of America.

If we admit that it is meritorious in an author to seek for a subject in the superstitions, legends, and historical events of his own peculiar country or district, yet these (unless delocalized by their own intrinsic meaning) are by nature ephemeral, and a wide tract of intervening years makes them as truly foreign as oceans, mountains, or deserts could. Distance of time passes its silent statute of outlawry and alienage against them, as effectually as distance of space.

Indeed, in that strictness with which the martinets of nationality use the term, it would be a hard thing for any people to prove an exclusive title to its myths and legends. Take, for example, the story of Wayland the Smith, curious as furnishing the undoubted original of the incident of Tell and the apple, and for its analogies with the Grecian fable of Dædalus. This, after being tracked through the *folklore* of nearly all the nations of Northern Europe, was at last, to the great relief of the archæologic mind, supposed to be *treed* in Scandinavia, because the word *voelund* was found to mean smith among the Icelanders. Yet even here we cannot rest secure that this piece of mythical property has been restored to its rightful owners. As usual in such cases, investigation points Asia-ward, and the same word is found with the same signification in Ceylon. However unsatisfying in other respects, the search has at least turned up a euphonious synonym for the name Smith, which might be assumed by any member of that numerous patronymic guild desirous of attaining a nearer approach to individuality.

But even the most indisputable proof of original ownership is of no great account in these matters. These tools of fancy cannot be branded with the name of any exclusive proprietor. They are his who can use them. Poor Peter Claus cries out in vain that he has been robbed of himself by the native of a country undiscovered when he took his half-century's nap on the Kypphauser mountains. *Caret vate sacro*, and nobody gives him the least heed. He has become the shadow, and Rip Van Winkle the substance. Perhaps he has made up his mind to it by this time, and contrives to turn an honest penny among the shades by exhibiting himself as the *Original* Rip Van Winkle. We trust, for the honor of our country, that Rip brazens it out there, and denounces the foreign impostor in the purest—

American, we were going to say; but here another nationality interposes its claim, and we must put up with Low Dutch.

The only element of permanence which belongs to myth, legend, or history, is exactly so much of each as refuses to be circumscribed by provincial boundaries. When once superstitions, customs, and historic personages are dead and buried in antiquarian treaties or county annals, there is no such thing as resurrection for them. The poet who encumbers himself with them takes just that amount of unnecessary burthen upon his shoulders. He is an antiquary, not a creator, and is writing what posterity will read as a catalogue rather than a poem. There is a homeliness about great genius which leads it to glorify the place of its "kindly engendure," (as Chaucer calls it,) either by a tender allusion, or by images and descriptions drawn from that fairest landscape in the gallery of memory. But it is a strange confusion of thought to attribute to a spot of earth the inspiration whose source is in a universal sentiment. It is the fine humanity, the muscular sense, and the generous humor of Burns which save him from being merely Scotch, like a score of rhymesters as national as he. The Homers of Little Pedlington die, as their works died before them, and are forgotten; but let a genius get born there, and one touch of his nature shall establish even for Little Pedlington an immortal consanguinity which the whole world shall be eager to claim. The field-mouse and the mountain-daisy are not Scotch, and Tam o' Shanter died the other day within a mile of where we are writing. Measuring Burns by that which is best in him, and which insures to him a length of life coincident with that of the human heart, he is as little national as Shakespeare, and no more an alien in Iowa than in Ayrshire. There is a vast difference between truth to nature and truth to fact; an impassable gulf between genius, which deals only with the true, and that imitative faculty which patiently and exactly reproduces the actual. This makes the distinction between the works of Fielding, which delight and instruct forever, and those of Smollett, which are of value as affording a clear insight into contemporaneous modes of life, but neither warm the heart nor impregnate the imagination. It is this higher and nobler kind of truth which is said to characterize the portraits of Titian, which gives an indefinable attraction to those of Page, and which inspires the busts of Powers. This excuses meagerness of color and incorrectness of drawing in Hogarth, who was truly rather a great dramatist than a great painter, and gives them that something which even indifferent engraving cannot destroy, any more than bad printing can extinguish Shakespeare.

This demand for a nationality bounded historically and geographically by the independent existence and territory of a particular race or fraction of a race, would debar us of our rightful share in the past and the ideal. It was happily illustrated by that parochially national Gascon, who would have been edified by the sermon had it been his good fortune to belong to the parish. Let us be thankful that there is no court by which we can be excluded from our share in the inheritance of the great poets of all ages and countries, to which our simple humanity entitles us. No great poet has ever sung but the whole human race has been, sooner or later, the wiser and better for it. Above all, let us not tolerate in our criticism a principle which would operate as a prohibitory tariff of ideas. The intellect is a diœcious plant, and books are the bees which carry the quickening pollen from one to another mind. It detracts nothing from Chaucer that we can trace in him the influences of Dante and Boccaccio; nothing from Spenser that he calls Chaucer master;

nothing from Shakespeare that he acknowledges how dear Spenser was to him; nothing from Milton that he brought fire from Hebrew and Greek altars. There is no degradation in such indebtedness. Venerable rather is this apostolic succession, and inspiring to see the *vitai lampada* passed thus from consecrated hand to hand.

Nationality, then, is only a less narrow form of provincialism, a sublimer sort of clownishness and ill-manners. It deals in jokes, anecdotes, and allusions of such purely local character that a majority of the company are shut out from all approach to an understanding of them. Yet so universal a demand must have for its basis a more or less solid substratum of truth. There are undoubtedly national, as truly as family, idiosyncrasies, though we think that these will get displayed without any special schooling for that end. The substances with which a nation is compelled to work will modify its results, as well intellectual as material. The still renewing struggle with the unstable desert sands gave to the idea of durability in the Egyptian imagination a preponderance still further increased by the necessity of using granite, whose toughness of fiber and vagueness of coloring yielded unwillingly to fineness of outline, but seemed the natural helpmates of massiveness and repose. The out-of-door life of the Greeks, conducing at once to health and an unconscious education of the eye, and the perfection of physical development resulting from their palæstral exercises and constantly displayed in them, made the Greeks the first to perceive the noble symmetry of the human figure, for embodying the highest types of which Pentelicus supplied the fittest material. Corporeal beauty and strength, therefore, entered largely into their idea of the heroic, and perhaps it was rather policy than dandyism which hindered Alcibiades from learning to play the flute. With us, on the other hand, clothed to the chin in the least graceful costume ever invented by man, and baked half the year with stoves and furnaces, beauty of person has gradually receded from view, and wealth or brain is the essential of the modern novelist's hero. It may not be fanciful to seek in climate, and its resultant effects upon art, the remote cause of that fate-element which entered so largely into the Greek drama. In proportion as sculpture became more perfect, the images of the gods became less and less merely symbolical, and at last presented to the popular mind nothing more than actual representations of an idealized humanity. Before this degradation had taken place, and the divinities had been vulgarized in marble to the common eye, the ideas of the unseen and supernatural came to the assistance of the poet in giving interest to the struggles or connivances between heroes and gods. But presently a new and deeper chord of the imagination must be touched, and the unembodiable shadow of Destiny was summoned up, to move awe and pity as long as the human mind is incapable of familiarizing by precise definition the fearful and the vague. In that more purely objective age, the conflict must be with something external, and the struggles of the mind with itself afforded no sufficient theme for the poet. With us introspection has become a disease, and a poem is a self-dissection.

That Art in America will be modified by circumstances, we have no doubt, though it is impossible to predict the precise form of the moulds into which it will run. New conditions of life will stimulate thought and give new forms to its expression. It may not be our destiny to produce a great literature, as, indeed, our genius seems to find its kindliest development in practicalizing simpler and more perfect forms of social organization. We have yet many problems of this kind to work out, and a continent to subdue with the plow and the railroad, before we are at leisure for æsthetics. Our spirit of adventure will first take a material and practical direction, but will gradually be forced to seek outlet and scope in unoccupied territories of the intellect. In the meantime we may fairly demand of our literature that it should be national to the extent of being as free from outworn conventionalities, and as thoroughly impregnated with humane and manly sentiment, as is the idea on which our political fabric rests. Let it give a true reflection of our social, political, and household life. The "Poems on Man in the Republic," by Cornelius Mathews, disfigured as they were by gross faults of dialect and meter, had the great merit of presenting the prominent features of our civilization in an American light. The story of "Margaret" is the most emphatically *American* book ever written. The want of plan and slovenliness of construction are characteristic of a new country. The scenery, character, dialect, and incidents mirror New England life as truly as Fresh Pond reflects the sky. The moral, also, pointing forward to a new social order, is the intellectual antitype of that restlessness of disposition, and facility of migration which are among our chief idiosyncrasies. This mistake of our imaginative writers generally is that, though they may take an American subject, they *costume* it in a foreign or antique fashion. The consequence is a painful vagueness and unreality. It is like putting Roman drapery upon a statue of Washington, the absurdity of which does not strike us so forcibly because we are accustomed to it, but which we should recognize at once were the same treatment applied to Franklin. The old masters did exactly the reverse of this. They took ancient or foreign subjects, but selected their models from their own immediate neighborhood. When Shakespeare conceived his Athenian mechanics, he did not cram with

Grecian antiquities in order to make them real in speech and manners. Their unconscious prototypes were doubtless walking Stratford streets, and demonstrating to any one who had clear enough eyes, that stupidity and conceit were precisely the same things on the banks of the Avon and those of the Ilissus. Here we arrive at the truth which is wrapped up and concealed in the demand for nationality in literature. It is neither more nor less than this, that authors should use their own eyes and ears, and not those of other people. We ask of them human nature as it appears in man, not in books; and scenery not at second hand from the canvas of painter or poet, but from that unmatched landscape painted by the Great Master upon the retina of their own eyes. Though a poet should make the bobolink sing in Attica, the *anachronism* is nothing, provided he can only make it truly sing so that we can hear it. He will have no difficulty in making his peace with posterity. The error of our advocates of nationality lies in their assigning geographical limits to the poet's range of historical characters as well as to his natural scenery. There is no time or place in human nature, and Prometheus, Coriolanus, Tasso and Tell are ours if we can use them, as truly as Washington or Daniel Boone. Let an American author make a living character, even if it be antediluvian, and nationality will take care of itself. The newspaper, the railroad, and the steamship are fast obliterating the externals of distinct and hostile nationality. The Turkish soldier has shrunk into coat and pantaloons, and reads Dickens. But human nature is everywhere the same, and everywhere inextinguishable. If we only insist that our authors shall be good, we may cease to feel nervous about their being national. Excellence is an alien nowhere. And even if, as we hear it lamented, we have no literature, there are a thousand other ways of making ourselves useful. If the bobolink and mocking-bird find no poet to sing them, they can afford, like Kepler, to wait; and in the meantime they themselves will sing as if nothing had happened. For ourselves, we confess, we have hopes. The breed of poets is not extinct, nor has Apollo shot away all the golden, singing arrows in his quiver. We have a very strong persuasion, amounting even to faith, that eyes and ears will yet open on this Western Continent, and find adequate utterance. If some of our birds have a right to feel neglected, yet other parts of our natural history have met with due civility; and if the pine tree complain of the tribute which Emerson has paid it, we surrender it to the lumberer and the saw-mill without remorse. It must be an unreasonable tree, wooden at head and heart.

Nay, how are we to know what is preparing for us at this very moment? What herald had Chaucer, singing the matins of that grand cathedral-service whose vespers we have not yet heard, in England? What external circumstance controlled the sweet influence of Spenser? Was Gorboduc a prologue that should have led us to expect Hamlet? Did the Restoration furnish the score for those organ-strains of Milton, breaking in with a somewhat unexpected voluntary to drown the thin song of pander and parasite with its sublime thunders of fervor and ascription? What collyrium of nationality was it that enabled those pleasant Irish eyes of Goldsmith to pierce through the artificial tinsel and frippery of his day to that little clump of roses at Wakefield? England had long been little better than a province of France in song when Wordsworth struck the note of independence, and led the people back to the old worship. While we are waiting for our literature, let us console ourselves with the following observation with which Dr. Newman commences his History of the Hebrew Monarchy. "Few nations," he says, "which have put forth a wide and enduring influence upon others, proclaim themselves to have been indigenous on the land of their celebrity." Or, if the worst come, we can steal a literature like the Romans, and thus acquire another point of similarity to that remarkable people, whom we resemble so much, according to the Quarterly Review, in our origin. . . .

PREFACE

No understanding of the controversy over America's intellectual independence can be had without a knowledge of Whitman's point of view. Whitman maintained that America is unique, both in its form of Government and in its Population. What the world at large had been striving through the ages to attain was at last being realized in America. All past civilizations were coming to their fullest fruitage in the Democracy of the United States. He was filled, also, with the Transcendental doctrine as regards the Individual.

Whitman believed emphatically that it should be the purpose of American literature to express this God-given uniqueness. The youthful vivacious civilization of the West but awaited the voice of its poets. And since America's uniqueness is the greatest, the literature that expresses it is also to be the greatest literature that the world has ever known.

Whitman was early recognized abroad as the most representative of American Poets. At home he has had to wait until the past two decades for full recognition. At present his acclaim is becoming almost universal. He is, for many, the father of the contemporary movement.

Democratic Vistas, Whitman's most important prose work, appeared first in 1870. Those who are interested in the part of the essay here presented will do well to read the parts which, for want of space, are omitted. The reader should also become familiar with Emerson's *American Scholar* and *Self-Reliance*. These and other utterances of Emerson served as early guides for Whitman.

23

DEMOCRATIC VISTAS

By Walt Whitman

As the greatest lessons of Nature through the universe are
perhaps the lessons of variety and freedom, the same present
the greatest lessons also in New World politics and progress.
If a man were asked, for instance, the distinctive points con-
trasting modern European and American political and other
life with the old Asiatic cultus, as lingering-bequeathed yet
in China and Turkey, he might find the amount of them in
John Stuart Mill's profound essay on Liberty in the Future,
where he demands two main constituents, or substrata, for
a truly grand nationality—1st, a large variety of character—
and 2nd, full play for human nature to expand itself in
numberless and even conflicting directions—(seems to be
for general humanity much like the influences that make up,
in their limitless field, that perennial health-action of the air
we call the weather—an infinite number of currents and
forces, and contributions, and temperatures, and cross-pur-
poses, whose ceaseless play of counterpart upon counterpart brings constant restoration and vitality). With this
thought—and not for itself alone, but all it necessitates, and
draws after it—let me begin my speculations.

America, filling the present with greatest deeds and problems, cheerfully accepting the past, including feudalism (as,
indeed, the present is but the legitimate birth of the past,
including feudalism), counts, as I reckon, for her justification
and success (for who, as yet, dare claim success?) almost
entirely on the future. Nor is that hope unwarranted. To-
day, ahead, though dimly yet, we see, in vistas, a copious,

sane, gigantic offspring. For our New World I consider far
less important for what it has done, or what it is, than for
results to come. Sole among nationalities, these States have
assumed the task to put in forms of lasting power and practicality, on areas of amplitude rivaling the operations of the
physical kosmos, the moral political speculations of ages,
long, long deferred, the democratic republican principle, and
the theory of development and perfection by voluntary
standards, and self-reliance. Who else, indeed, except the
United States, in history, so far, have accepted in unwitting
faith, and, as we now see, stand, act upon, and go security
for, these things?

But preluding no longer, let me strike the keynote of the
following strain. First premising that, though the passages
of it have been written at widely different times (it is, in fact,
a collection of memoranda, perhaps for future designers, com-
prehenders), and though it may be open to the charge of one
part contradicting another—for there are opposite sides to the
great question of democracy, as to every great question—I
feel the parts harmoniously blended in my own realization
and convictions, and present them to be read only in such
oneness, each page and each claim and assertion modified
and tempered by the others. Bear in mind, too, that they are
not the result of studying up in political economy, but of the
ordinary sense, observing, wandering among men, these
States, these stirring years of war and peace. I will not gloss
over the appalling dangers of universal suffrage in the United
States. In fact, it is to admit and face these dangers I am
writing. To him or her within whose thought rages the battle, advancing, retreating, between democracy's convictions,
aspirations, and the people's crudeness, vice, caprices, I
mainly write this essay. I shall use the words American and
democracy as convertible terms. Not an ordinary one is the

issue. The United States are destined either to surmount
the gorgeous history of feudalism, or else prove the most
tremendous failure of time. Not the least doubtful am I on
any prospects of their material success. The triumphant
future of their business, geographic and productive departments, on larger scales and in more varieties than ever, is
certain. In those respects the republic must soon (if she does
not already) outstrip all examples hitherto afforded, and
dominate the world.[1]

[1] "From a territorial area of less than nine hundred thousand square
miles, the Union has expanded into over four millions and a half—
fifteen times larger than that of Great Britain and France combined—
with a shore-line, including Alaska, equal to the entire circumference of
the earth, and with a domain within these lines far wider than that of
the Romans in their proudest days of conquest and renown. With a
river, lake, and coastwise commerce estimated at over two thousand
millions of dollars per year; with a railway traffic of four to six thousand
millions per year, and the annual domestic exchanges of the country
running up to nearly ten thousand millions per year; with over two
thousand millions of dollars invested in manufacturing, mechanical,
and mining industry; with over five hundred millions of acres of land
in actual occupancy, valued, with their appurtenances, at over seven
thousand millions of dollars, and producing annually crops valued at
over three thousand millions of dollars; with a realm which, if the density
of Belgium's population were possible, would be vast enough to include
all the present inhabitants of the world; and with equal rights guaranteed
to even the poorest and humblest of our forty millions of people—we
can, with a manly pride akin to that which distinguished the palmiest
days of Rome, claim," etc., etc., etc.—*Vice-President Colfax's Speech,
July* 4, 1870.

LATER—*London Times (Weekly), June 23, '82.*
"The wonderful wealth-producing power of the United States defies
and sets at naught the grave drawbacks of a mischievous protective
tariff, and has already obliterated, almost wholly, the traces of the
greatest of modern civil wars. What is especially remarkable in the
present development of American energy and success is its wide and
equable distribution. North and south, east and west, on the shores of
the Atlantic and the Pacific, along the chain of the great lakes, in the
valley of the Mississippi, and on the coasts of the Gulf of Mexico, the
creation of wealth and the increase of population are signally exhibited.

Admitting all this, with the priceless value of our political institutions, general suffrage (and fully acknowledging the latest, widest opening of the doors), I say that, far deeper than these, what finally and only is to make of our western world a nationality superior to any hither known, and out-topping the past, must be vigorous, yet unsuspected Literatures, perfect personalities and sociologies, original, transcendental, and expressing (what, in highest sense, are not yet expressed at all) democracy and the modern. With these, and out of these, I promulgate new races of Teachers, and of perfect Women, indispensable to endow the birth-stock of a New World. For feudalism, caste, the ecclesiastic traditions, though palpably retreating from political institutions, still hold essentially, by their spirit, even in this country, entire possession of the more important fields, indeed the very subsoil, of education, and of social standards and literature.

I say that democracy can never prove itself beyond cavil, until it founds and luxuriantly grows its own forms of art, poems, schools, theology, displacing all that exists, or that has been produced anywhere in the past, under opposite influences. It is curious to me that while so many voices, pens, minds, in the press, lecture-rooms, in our Congress, etc., are discussing intellectual topics, pecuniary dangers, legislative problems, the suffrage, tariff and labor questions, and the various business and benevolent needs of America, with

It is quite true, as has been shown by the recent apportionment of population in the House of Representatives, that some sections of the Union have advanced, relatively to the rest, in an extraordinary and unexpected degree. But this does not imply that the States which have gained no additional representatives or have actually lost some have been stationary or have receded. The fact is that the present tide of prosperity has risen so high that it has overflowed all barriers, and had filled up the backwaters, and established something like an approach to uniform success."

propositions, remedies, often worth deep attention, there is one need, a hiatus the profoundest, that no eye seems to perceive, no voice to state. Our fundamental want to-day in the United States, with closest, amplest reference to present conditions, and to the future, is of a class, and the clear idea of a class, of native authors, literatures, far different, far higher in grade, than any yet known, sacerdotal, modern, fit to cope with our occasions, lands, permeating the whole mass of American mentality, taste, belief, breathing into it a new breath of life, giving it decision, affecting politics far more than the popular superficial suffrage, with results inside and underneath the elections of Presidents or Congresses—radiating, begetting appropriate teachers, schools, manners, and, as its grandest result, accomplishing (what neither the schools nor the churches and their clergy have hitherto accomplished, and without which this nation will no more stand, permanently, soundly, than a house will stand without a substratum), a religious and moral character beneath the political and productive and intellectual bases of the States. (For know you not, dear, earnest reader, that the people of our land may all read and write, and may all possess the right to vote—and yet the main things may be entirely lacking?—and this to suggest them.)

Viewed, to-day, from a point of view sufficiently overarching, the problem of humanity all over the civilized world is social and religious, and is to be finally met and treated by literature. The priest departs, the divine literatus comes. Never was anything more wanted than, to-day, and here in the States, the poet of the modern is wanted, or the great literatus of the modern. At all times, perhaps, the central point in any nation, and that whence it is itself really swayed the most, and whence it sways others, is its national literature, especially its archetypal poems. Above all previous lands, a great original literature is surely to become the justification and reliance (in some respects the sole reliance) of American democracy.

Few are aware how the great literature penetrates all, gives hue to all, shapes aggregates and individuals, and, after subtle ways, with irresistible power, constructs, sustains, demolishes at will. Why tower, in reminiscence, above all the nations of the earth, two special lands, petty in themselves, yet inexpressibly gigantic, beautiful, columnar? Immortal Judah lives, and Greece immortal lives, in a couple of poems.

Nearer than this. It is not generally realized, but it is true, as the genius of Greece, and all the sociology, personality, politics, and religion of those wonderful states, resided in their literature or æsthetics, that what was afterwards the main support of European chivalry, the feudal, ecclesiastical, dynastic world over there—forming its osseous structure, holding it together for hundreds, thousands of years, preserving its flesh and bloom, giving it form, decision, rounding it out, and so saturating it in the conscious and unconscious blood, breed, belief, and intuitions of men, that it still prevails powerful to this day, in defiance of the mighty changes of time —was its literature, permeating to the very marrow, especially that major part, its enchanting songs, ballads, and poems.[1]

---

[1] See, for hereditaments, specimens, Walter Scott's Border Minstrelsy, Percy's collection, Ellis's early English Metrical Romances, the European continental poems of Walter of Aquitania, and the Nibelungen, of pagan stock, but monkish-feudal redaction; the history of the Troubadours, by Fauriel; even the far-back cumbrous old Hindu epics, as indicating the Asian eggs out of which European chivalry was hatched; Ticknor's chapters on the Cid, and on the Spanish poems and poets of Calderon's time. Then always, and, of course, as the superbest poetic culmination-expression of feudalism, the Shakespearean dramas, in the attitudes, dialogue, characters, etc., of the princes, lords, and gentlemen, the pervading atmosphere, the implied and expressed standard of manners, the high port and proud stomach, the regal embroidery of style, etc.

To the ostent of the senses and eyes, I know, the influences which stamp the world's history are wars, uprisings or downfalls of dynasties, changeful movement of trade, important inventions, navigation, military or civil governments, advent of powerful personalities, conquerors, etc. These of course play their part; yet, it may be, a single new thought, imagination, abstract principle, even literary style, fit for the time, put in shape by some great literatus, and projected among mankind, may duly cause changes, growths, removals, greater than the longest and bloodiest war, or the most stupendous merely political, dynastic, or commercial overturn.

In short, as, though it may not be realized, it is strictly true, that a few first-class poets, philosophs, and authors have substantially settled and given status to the entire religion, education, law, sociology, etc., of the hitherto civilized world, by tingeing and often creating the atmospheres out of which they have arisen, such also must stamp, and more than ever stamp, the interior and real democratic construction of this American continent, to-day, and days to come. Remember also this fact of difference, that, while through the antique and through the mediæval ages, highest thoughts and ideals realized themselves, and their expression made its way by other arts, as much as, or even more than by, technical literature (not open to the mass of persons, or even to the majority of eminent persons), such literature in our day and for current purposes is not only more eligible than all the other arts put together, but has become the only general means of morally influencing the world. Painting, sculpture, and the dramatic theater, it would seem, no longer play an indispensable or even important part in the workings and mediumship of intellect, utility, or even high æsthetics. Architecture remains, doubtless with capacities, and a real future. Then music, the combiner, nothing more spiritual, nothing more sensuous, a god, yet completely human, advances, prevails, holds highest place; supplying in certain wants and quarters what nothing else could supply. Yet in the civilization of to-day it is undeniable that, over all the arts, literature dominates, serves beyond all—shapes the character of church and school—or, at any rate, is capable of doing so. Including the literature of science, its scope is indeed unparalleled.

Before proceeding further, it were perhaps well to discriminate on certain points. Literature tills its crops in many fields, and some may flourish, while others lag. What I say in these Vistas has its main bearing on imaginative literature, especially poetry, the stock of all. In the department of science, and the speciality of journalism, there appear, in these States, promises, perhaps fulfillments, of highest earnestness, reality and life. These, of course, are modern. But in the region of imaginative, spinal and essential attributes, something equivalent to creation is, for our age and lands, imperatively demanded. For not only is it not enough that the new blood, new frame of democracy shall be vivified and held together merely by political means, superficial suffrage, legislation, etc., but it is clear to me that, unless it goes deeper, gets at least as firm and as warm a hold in men's hearts, emotions and belief, as, in their days, feudalism or ecclesiasticism, and inaugurates its own perennial sources, welling from the center forever, its strength will be defective, its growth doubtful, and its main charm wanting. I suggest, therefore, the possibility, should some two or three really original American poets (perhaps artists or lecturers) arise, mounting the horizon like planets, stars of the first magnitude, that, from their eminence, fusing contributions, races, far localities, etc., together, they would give more compaction and more moral identity (the quality to-day most needed) to these States, than all its Constitutions, legislative and judicial ties, and all its hitherto political, warlike, or materialistic experiences. As, for instance, there could hardly happen anything that would more serve the States, with all their variety of origins, their diverse climes, cities, standards, etc., than possessing an aggregate of heroes, characters, exploits, sufferings, prosperity or misfortune, glory or disgrace, common to all, typical of it all—no less, but even greater would it be to possess the aggregation of a cluster of mighty poets, artists, teachers, fit for us, national expressers, comprehending and effusing for the men and women of the States, what is universal, native, common to all, inland and seaboard, northern and southern. The historians say of ancient Greece, with her ever-jealous autonomies, cities and states, that the only positive unity she ever owned or received, was the sad unity of a common subjection, at the last, to foreign conquerors. Subjection, aggregation of that sort, is impossible to America; but the fear of conflicting and irreconcilable interiors, and the lack of a common skeleton, knitting all close, continually haunts me. Or, if it does not, nothing is plainer than the need, a long period to come, of a fusion of the States into the only reliable identity, the moral and artistic one. For, I say, the true nationality of the States, the genuine union, when we come to a mortal crisis, is, and is to be, after all, neither the written law, nor (as is generally supposed) either self-interest, or common pecuniary or material objects—but the fervid and tremendous IDEA, melting everything else with resistless heat, and solving all lesser and definite distinctions in vast, indefinite, spiritual, emotional power.

It may be claimed (and I admit the weight of the claim) that common and general worldly prosperity, and a populace well-to-do, and with all life's material comforts, is the main thing, and is enough. It may be argued that our republic is, in performance, really enacting to-day the grandest arts, poems, etc., by beating up the wilderness into fertile farms, and in her railroads, ships, machinery, etc. And it may be asked, Are these not better, indeed, for America, than any utterances even of greatest rhapsode, artist, or literatus?

I too hail those achievements with pride and joy: then answer that the soul of man will not with such only—nay, not with such at all—be finally satisfied; but needs what (standing on these and on all things, as the feet stand on the ground) is addressed to the loftiest, to itself alone.

Out of such considerations, such truths, arises for treatment in these Vistas the important question of character, of an American stock-personality, with literatures and arts for outlets and return-expressions, and, of course, to correspond, within outlines common to all. To these, the main affair, the thinkers of the United States, in general so acute, have either given feeblest attention, or have remained, and remain, in a state of somnolence.

For my part, I would alarm and caution even the political and business reader, and to the utmost extent, against the prevailing delusion that the establishment of free political institutions, and plentiful intellectual smartness, with general good order, physical plenty, industry, etc. (desirable and precious advantages as they all are), do, of themselves, determine and yield to our experiment of democracy the fruitage of success. With such advantages at present fully, or almost fully, possessed—the Union just issued, victorious, from the struggle with the only foes it need ever fear (namely, those within itself, the interior ones), and with unprecedented materialistic advancement—society, in these States, is cankered, crude, superstitious and rotten. Political, or law-made society is, and private, or voluntary society, is also. In any vigor, the element of the moral conscience, the most important, the verteber to State or man, seems to me either entirely lacking, or seriously enfeebled or ungrown.

I say we had best look our times and lands searchingly in the face, like a physician diagnosing some deep disease. Never was there, perhaps, more hollowness at heart than at present, and here in the United States. Genuine belief seems to have left us. The underlying principles of the States are not honestly believed in (for all this hectic glow, and these melodramatic screamings), nor is humanity itself believed in. What penetrating eye does not everywhere see through the mask? The spectacle is appalling. We live in an atmosphere of hypocrisy throughout. The men believe not in the women, nor the women in the men. A scornful superciliousness rules in literature. The aim of all the *littérateurs* is to find something to make fun of. A lot of churches, sects, etc., the most dismal phantasms I know, usurp the name of religion. Conversation is a mass of badinage. From deceit in the spirit, the mother of all false deeds, the offspring is already incalculable. An acute and candid person, in the revenue department in Washington, who is led by the course of his employment to regularly visit the cities, north, south, and west, to investigate frauds, has talked much with me about his discoveries. The depravity of the business classes of our country is not less than has been supposed, but infinitely greater. The official services of America, national, state, and municipal, in all their branches and departments, except the judiciary, are saturated in corruption, bribery, falsehood, maladministration; and the judiciary is tainted. The great cities reek with respectable as much as nonrespectable robbery and scoundrelism. In fashionable life, flippancy, tepid amours, weak infidelism, small aims, or no aims at all, only to kill time. In business (this all-devouring modern word, business), the one sole object is, by any means, pecuniary gain. The magician's serpent in the fable ate up all the other serpents; and money-making is our magician's serpent, remaining to-day sole master of the field. The best class we show, is but a mob of fashionably dressed speculators and vulgarians. True, indeed, behind this fantastic farce, enacted on the visible stage of society, solid things and stupendous labors are to be discovered, existing crudely and going on in the background, to advance and tell themselves in time. Yet the truths are none the less terrible. I say that our New World democracy, however great a success in uplifting the masses out of their sloughs, in materialistic development, products, and in a certain highly-deceptive superficial popular intellectuality, is, so far, an almost complete failure in its social aspects, and in really grand religious, moral, literary, and æsthetic results. In vain do we march with unprecedented strides to empire so colossal, outvying the antique, beyond Alexander's, beyond the proudest sway of Rome. In vain have we annexed Texas, California, Alaska, and reach north for Canada and south for Cuba. It is as if we were somehow being endowed with a vast and more thoroughly-appointed body, and then left with little or no soul.

Let me illustrate further, as I write, with current observations, localities, etc. The subject is important, and will bear repetition. After an absence, I am now again (September, 1870) in New York city and Brooklyn, on a few weeks' vacation. The splendor, picturesqueness, and oceanic amplitude and rush of these great cities, the unsurpassed situation, rivers and bay, sparkling sea-tides, costly and lofty new buildings, façades of marble and iron, of original grandeur and elegance of design, with the masses of gay color, the preponderance of white and blue, the flags flying, the endless ships, the tumultuous streets, Broadway, the heavy, low, musical roar, hardly ever intermitted, even at night; the jobbers' houses, the rich shops, the wharves, the great Central Park, and the Brooklyn Park of hills (as I wander among them this beautiful fall weather, musing, watching, absorbing)—the assemblages of the citizens in their groups, conversations, trades, evening amusements, or along the by-quarters—these, I say, and the like of these, completely satisfy my senses of power, fullness, motion, etc., and give me, through such senses and appetites, and through my æsthetic conscience, a continued exaltation and absolute fulfillment. Always and more and more, as I cross the East and North rivers, the ferries, or with the pilots in their pilot-houses, or pass an hour in Wall Street, or the Gold Exchange, I realize (if we must admit such partialisms) that not Nature alone is great in her fields of freedom and the open air, in her storms, the shows of night and day, the mountains, forests, seas—but in the artificial, the work of man too is equally great—in this profusion of teeming humanity—in these ingenuities, streets, goods, houses, ships—these hurrying, feverish, electric crowds of men, their complicated business genius (not least among the geniuses), and all this mighty, many-threaded wealth and industry concentrated here.

But sternly discarding, shutting our eyes to the glow and grandeur of the general superficial effect, coming down to what is of the only real importance, Personalities, and examining minutely, we question, we ask, Are there, indeed, *men* here worthy the name? Are there athletes? Are there perfect women, to match the generous material luxuriance? Is there a pervading atmosphere of beautiful manners? Are there crops of fine youths, and majestic old persons? Are there arts worthy freedom and a rich people? Is there a

great moral and religious civilization—the only justification
of a great material one? Confess that to severe eyes, using
the moral microscope upon humanity, a sort of dry and flat
Sahara appears, these cities, crowded with petty grotesques,
malformations, phantoms, playing meaningless antics. Confess that everywhere, in shop, street, church, theater, bar-
room, official chair, are pervading flippancy and vulgarity,
low cunning, infidelity—everywhere the youth puny, im-
pudent, foppish, prematurely ripe—everywhere an abnormal
libidinousness, unhealthy forms, male, female, painted,
padded, dyed, chignoned, muddy complexions, bad blood,
the capacity for good motherhood decreasing or deceased,
shallow notions of beauty, with a range of manners, or rather
lack of manners (considering the advantages enjoyed),
probably the meanest to be seen in the world.[1]

Of all this, and these lamentable conditions, to breathe into
them the breath recuperative of sane and heroic life, I say a
new-founded literature, not merely to copy and reflect existing surfaces, or pander to what is called taste—not only to
amuse, pass away time, celebrate the beautiful, the refined,
the past, or exhibit technical, rhythmic, or grammatical
dexterity—but a literature underlying life, religious, con-

[1] Of these rapidly-sketched hiatuses, the two which seem to be most
serious are, for one, the condition, absence, or perhaps the singular abey-
ance, of moral conscientious fiber all through American society; and, for
another, the appalling depletion of women in their powers of sane ath-
letic maternity, their crowning attribute, and ever making the woman,
in loftiest spheres, superior to the man.

I have sometimes thought, indeed, that the sole avenue and means of
a reconstructed sociology depended, primarily, on a new birth, elevation,
expansion, invigoration of woman, affording, for races to come (as the
conditions that antedate birth are indispensable), a perfect motherhood.
Great, great, indeed, far greater than they know, is the sphere of women.
But doubtless the question of such new sociology all goes together, in-
cludes many varied and complex influences and premises, and the man
as well as the woman, and the woman as well as the man.

sistent with science, handling the elements and forces with competent power, teaching and training men—and, as perhaps the most precious of its results, achieving the entire redemption of woman out of these incredible holds and webs of silliness, millinery, and every kind of dyspeptic depletion— and thus insuring to the States a strong and sweet Female Race, a race of perfect Mothers—is what is needed.

And now, in the full conception of these facts and points, and all that they infer, pro and con—with yet unshaken faith in the elements of the American masses, the composites, of both sexes, and even considered as individuals—and ever recognizing in them the broadest bases of the best literary and æsthetic appreciation—I proceed with my speculations, Vistas. . . .

PREFACE

The clash in American criticism that has arisen over nationality is not more important than the clash over the relation of the author to his writing. This clash in literature has its origin in the conflict between the two outstanding systems of philosophy of the modern world—Idealism and Materialism.

The Idealist reasons that man's contact with the outside world is determined largely by his own mental processes. Each individual recreates the world anew for himself. The only reality in the world is, therefore, the sacred reality of the soul's experiences. The Materialist maintains just as stoutly that the world of Nature is a real world, that man is only great to the extent that he sees and feels the world as it actually is. Idealism gives rise to Romanticism, Expressionism, and Primitivism in literature; Materialism, to Realism.

Mr. Spingarn's present essay is a statement of robustuous Idealism in terms of literature. Literature can mean nothing except as a revelation of the author's own personality. Benedetto Croce, upon whose critical theory the essay is, in a general way, based, is one of the world's leading exponents of Idealism among philosophers of the present age.

"The New Criticism" was first given as a lecture in 1910, when the author was a professor at Columbia University. It was later incorporated as a chapter in *Creative Criticism: Essays on the Unity of Genius and Taste*, Holt, 1917. The essay is here reprinted in its revised form from *Criticism in America: Its Function and Status*, Harcourt, Brace, 1924.

THE NEW CRITICISM [1]

By J. E. Spingarn

"What droll creatures these college professors are when-ever they talk about art," wrote Flaubert in one of his letters, and voiced the world's opinion of academic criticism. For the world shares the view of the Italian poet that "monks and professors cannot write the lives of poets," and looks only to those rich in literary experience for its opinions on literature. But the poets themselves have had no special grudge against academic criticism that they have not felt equally for every other kind. For the most part, they have objected to all criticism, since what each mainly seeks in his own case is not criticism, but uncritical praise. "Kill the dog, he is a reviewer," cried the young Goethe; and in an age nearer our own William Morris expressed his contempt for those who earn a livelihood by writing their opinions of the works of others. Fortunately for Criticism, it does not live by the grace of poets, to whom it can be of small service at its best, but by the grace of others who have neither the poet's genius nor the critic's insight. I hope to persuade you this evening that the poets have been mistaken in their very con-ception of the critic's craft, which lives by a power that poets and critics share together. The secret of this power has come to men slowly, and the knowledge they have gained by it has transformed their idea of Criticism. What this secret is, and into what new paths Criticism is being led by it, is the subject of my lecture to-night.

[1] Reprinted with permission of Harcourt, Brace & Company and of the author from *Criticism in America: Its Function and Status*.

I

At the end of the last century, France once more occupied the center of that stage whose auditors are the inheritors of European civilization. Once more all the world listened while she talked and played, and some of the most brilliant of her talk was now on the question of the authority of Criticism. It is not my purpose to tell you (what you know already) with what sober and vigorous learning the official critics of the *Revue des deux Mondes* espoused the cause of old gods with the new weapons of science, and with what charm and tact, with what grace and suppleness of thought, Jules Lemaître and Anatole France, to mention no others, defended the free play of the appreciative mind. Some of the sparks that were beaten out on the anvil of controversy have become fixed stars, the classical utterances of Criticism, as when Anatole France described the critic not as a judge imposing sentence, but as a sensitive soul detailing his "adventures among masterpieces."

To have sensations in the presence of a work of art and to express them, that is the function of Criticism for the impressionistic critic. His attitude he would express somewhat in this fashion: "Here is a beautiful poem, let us say Shelley's *Prometheus Unbound*. To read it is for me to experience a thrill of pleasure. My delight in it is itself a judgment, and what better judgment is it possible for me to give? All that I can do is to tell how it affects me, what sensations it gives me. Other men will derive other sensations from it, and express them differently; they too have the same right as I. Each of us, if we are sensitive to impressions and express ourselves well, will produce a new work of art to replace the work which gave us our sensations. That is the art of Criticism, and beyond that Criticism cannot go."

We shall not begrudge this exquisite soul the pleasure of his sensations or his cult of them, nor would he be disconcerted if we were to point out that the interest has been shifted from the work of art to his own impressions. Let us suppose that you say to him: "We are not interested in you, but in *Prometheus Unbound.* To describe the state of your health is not to help us to understand or to enjoy the poem. Your criticism constantly tends to get away from the work of art, and to center attention on yourself and your feelings."

But his answer would not be difficult to find: "What you say is true enough. My criticism tends to get farther and farther from the work of art and to cast a light upon myself; but all criticism tends to get away from the work of art and to substitute something in its place. The impressionist substitutes himself, but what other form of criticism gets closer to *Prometheus Unbound?* Historical criticism takes us away from it in a search of the environment, the age, the race, the poetic school of the artist; it tells us to read the history of the French Revolution, Godwin's *Political Justice,* the *Prometheus Bound* of Æschylus, and Calderón's *Mágico Prodigioso.* Psychological criticism takes me away from the poem, and sets me to work on the biography of the poet; I wish to enjoy *Prometheus Unbound,* and instead I am asked to become acquainted with Shelley the man. Dogmatic criticism does not get any closer to the work of art by testing it according to rules and standards; it sends me to the Greek dramatists, to Shakespeare, to Aristotle's *Poetics,* possibly to Darwin's *Origin of Species,* in order that I may see how far Shelley has failed to give dramatic reality to his poem, or has failed to observe the rules of his *genre;* but that means the study of other works, and not of *Prometheus Unbound.* Æsthetics takes me still farther afield into speculations on art and beauty. And so it is with every form of Criticism.

im personal

Do not deceive yourself. [All criticism tends to shift the interest from the work of art to something else.] The other critics give us history, politics, biography, erudition, metaphysics. [As for me, I re-dream the poet's dream, and if I seem to write lightly, it is because I have awakened, and smile to think I have mistaken a dream for reality.] I at least strive to replace one work of art by another, and art can only find its *alter ego* in art."

It would be idle to detail the arguments with which the advocates of the opposing forms of Criticism answered these questionings. Literary erudition and evolutionary science were the chief weapons used to fight this modern heresy, but the one is an unwieldy and the other a useless weapon in the field of æsthetic thought. On some sides, at least, the position of the impressionists was impregnable; but two points of attack were open to their opponents. They could combat the notion that taste is a substitute for learning, or learning a substitute for taste, since both are vital for Criticism; and they could maintain that the relativity of taste does not in any sense affect its authority. In this sense impressionistic Criticism erred only less grievously than the "judicial" Criticism which opposed it. Each in its own way was inadequate and incomplete.

But these arguments are not my present concern; what I wish to point out is that the objective and dogmatic forms of Criticism were fighting no new battle against impressionistic Criticism in that decade of controversy. It was a battle as old as the earliest reflection on the subject of poetry, if not as old as the sensitiveness of poets. Modern literature begins with the same doubts, with the same quarrel. In the sixteenth century the Italians were formulating that classical code which imposed itself on Europe for two centuries, and which, even in our generation, Brunetière has merely disguised under the trappings of natural science. They evolved the dramatic unities, and all those rules which the poet Pope imagined to be "Nature still but Nature methodized." But at the very moment when their spokesman Scaliger was saying that "Aristotle is our emperor, the perpetual dictator of all the fine arts," another Italian, Pietro Aretino, was insisting that there is no rule except the whim of genius and no standard of judgment beyond individual taste.

The Italians passed on the torch to the French of the seventeenth century, and from that day to this the struggle between the two schools has never ceased to agitate the progress of Criticism in France. Boileau against Saint-Evremond, Classicists against Romanticists, dogmatists against impressionists,—the antinomy is deep in the French nature, indeed in the nature of Criticism itself. Listen to this: "It is not for the purpose of deciding on the merit of this noble poet [Vergil], nor of harming his reputation, that I have spoken so freely concerning him. The world will continue to think what it does of his beautiful verses; and as for me, I judge nothing, I only say what I think, and what effect each of these things produces on my heart and mind." Surely these words are from the lips of Lemaître himself! "I judge nothing; I only say what I feel." But no, these are the utterances of the Chevalier de Méré, a wit of the age of Louis XIV, and he is writing to the secretary of that stronghold of authority, the French Academy. For some men, even in the age of Boileau, Criticism was nothing but an "adventure among masterpieces."

No, it is no new battle; it is the perpetual conflict of Criticism. In every age impressionism (or enjoyment) and dogmatism (or judgment) have grappled with one another. They are the two sexes of Criticism; and to say that they flourish in every age is to say that every age has its masculine

as well as its feminine criticism,—the masculine criticism
that may or may not force its own standards on literature,
but that never at all events is dominated by the object of its
studies; and the feminine criticism that responds to the lure
of art with a kind of passive ecstasy. In the age of Boileau
it was the masculine type which gave the tone to Criticism;
in our own, outside of the universities, it has certainly been
the feminine. But they continue to exist side by side, ever
falling short of their highest powers, unless mystically mated,
—judgment erecting its edicts into arbitrary standards and
conventions, enjoyment lost in the mazes of its sensuous
indecision.

Yet if we examine these opposing forms of Criticism in our
own age, we shall find, I think, that they are not wholly without a common ground to meet on; that, in fact, they are
united in at least one prepossession which they do not share
with the varying forms of Criticism in any of the earlier
periods of its history. The Greeks conceived of literature,
not as an inevitable expression of creative power, but as a
reasoned "imitation" or re-shaping of the materials of life;
for Aristotle, poetry is the result of man's imitative instinct,
and differs from history and science in that it deals with the
probable or possible rather than with the real. The Romans
conceived of literature as a noble art, intended (though
under the guise of pleasure) to inspire men with high ideals
of life. The classicists of the sixteenth and seventeenth
centuries accepted this view in the main; for them, literature
was a kind of exercise,—a craft acquired by study of the
classics, and guided in the interpretation of nature by the
traditions of Greek and Roman art. For these men literature
was as much a product of reason as science or history. The
eighteenth century complicated the course of Criticism by
the introduction of vague and novel criteria, such as "imag-

ination," "sentiment," and "taste," yet it was only in part able to liberate itself from the older tradition.

But with the Romantic Movement there developed the new idea which coördinates all Criticism in the nineteenth century. Very early in the century, Mme. de Staël and others formulated the idea that literature is an "expression of society"—a phrase that is merely a half-truth if "society" is interpreted in terms of the narrow circle of the individual poet's life instead of in terms of the society which is commensurate with the spirit of man. Victor Cousin enunciated "the fundamental rule, that expression is the supreme law of art," and, as the meaning of expression was gradually misunderstood and narrowed, became the unwitting parent of the mechanical theories of the French school of "art for art's sake." Later, Sainte-Beuve developed and illustrated his theory that literature is an expression of personality— another misleading half-truth, if by personality is meant, not the artistic personality which unfolds itself in the work of art, but the complex of external traits which the artist exhibits in his practical life. Still later, under the influence of natural science, Taine took a hint from Hegel and elaborated the idea that literature is an expression of race, age, and environment. The extreme impressionists prefer to think of art as the exquisite expression of delicate and fluctuating sensations or impressions of life. But for all these critics and theorists, literature is an expression of something, of experience or emotion, of the external or internal, of the man himself or something outside the man; yet it is always conceived of as an art of expression. The objective, the dogmatic, the impressionistic critics of our day may set for themselves very different tasks, but the idea of expression is implicit in all they write.

French criticism has been leaning heavily on the idea of

expression for a century or more, but no attempt has been
made in France to understand its æsthetic content, except
for a few vague echoes of German thought.   For the first
to give philosophic precision to the theory of expression, and
to found a method of Criticism based upon it, were the Germans of the age that stretches from Herder to Hegel.   All
the forces of philosophical thought were focused on this
central concept, while the critics enriched themselves from
out this golden store.   I suppose you all remember the
famous passage in which Carlyle describes the achievement
of German criticism in that age.   "Criticism," says Carlyle,
"has assumed a new form in Germany.   It proceeds on other
principles and proposes to itself a higher aim.   The main
question is not now a question concerning the qualities of
diction, the coherence of metaphors, the fitness of sentiments,
the general logical truth in a work of art, as it was some half
century ago among most critics, neither is it a question
mainly of a psychological sort to be answered by discovering
and delineating the peculiar nature of the poet from his
poetry, as is usual with the best of our own critics at present;
but it is, not indeed exclusively, but inclusively, of its two
other questions, properly and ultimately a question of the
essence and peculiar life of the poetry itself. . . . The problem is not now to determine by what mechanism Addison
composed sentences and struck out similitudes, but by what
far finer and more mysterious mechanism Shakespeare organized his dramas and gave life and individuality to his
Ariel and his Hamlet.   Wherein lies that life; how have they
attained that shape and individuality?   Whence comes that
empyrean fire which irradiates their whole being, and pierces,
at least in starry gleams, like a diviner thing, into all hearts?
Are these dramas of his not verisimilar only, but true; nay,
truer than reality itself, since the essence of unmixed reality

is bodied forth in them under more expressive similes? What is this unity of pleasures; and can our deeper inspection discern it to be indivisible and existing by necessity because each work springs as it were from the general elements of thought and grows up therefrom into form and expansion by its own growth? Not only who was the poet and how did he compose, but what and how was the poem, and why was it a poem and not rimed eloquence, creation and not figured passion? These are the questions for the critic. Criticism stands like an interpreter between the inspired and the uninspired; between the prophet and those who hear the melody of his words, and catch some glimpse of their material meaning, but understand not their deeper import."

I am afraid that no German critic wholly realized this ideal; but it was at least the achievement of the Germans that they enunciated the doctrine, even if they did not always adequately illustrate it in practice. It was they who first realized that art has performed its function when it has expressed itself; it was they who first conceived of Criticism as the study of expression. "There is a destructive and a creative or constructive criticism," said Goethe; the first measures and tests literature according to mechanical standards, the second answers the fundamental questions: "What has the writer proposed to himself to do? and how far has he succeeded in carrying out his own plan?" Carlyle, in his essay on Goethe, almost uses Goethe's own words, when he says that the critic's first and foremost duty is to make plain to himself "what the poet's aim really and truly was, how the task he had to do stood before his eye, and how far, with such materials as were afforded him, he has fulfilled it."

This has been the central problem, the guiding star, of all modern criticism. From Coleridge to Pater, from Sainte-Beuve to Lemaître, this is what critics have been striving for, even when they have not succeeded; yes, even when they have been deceiving themselves into thinking that they were striving for something else. This was not the ideal of the critics of Aristotle's day, who, like so many of their successors, censured a work of art as "irrational, impossible, morally hurtful, self-contradictory, or contrary to technical correctness." This was not Boileau's standard when he blamed Tasso for the introduction of Christian rather than pagan mythology into epic poetry; nor Addison's, when he tested *Paradise Lost* according to the rules of Le Bossu; nor Dr. Johnson's, when he lamented the absence of poetic justice in *King Lear*, or pronounced dogmatically that the poet should not "number the streaks of the tulip." What has the poet tried to do, and how has he fulfilled his intention? What is he striving to express and how has he expressed it? What vital and essential spirit animates his work, what central impression does it leave on the receptive mind, and how can I best express this impression? Is his work true to the laws of its own being rather than to laws formulated by others? These are the questions that modern critics have been taught to ask when face to face with the work of a poet. Only one *caveat* must be borne in mind when attempting to answer them; the poet's aim must be judged at the moment of the creative act, that is to say, by the art of the poem itself, and not by the vague ambitions which he imagines to be his real intentions before or after the creative act is achieved. For to create a work of art is the goal of every artist; and all questions in regard to his achievement resolve themselves into this: Has he or has he not created a work of art?

II

The theory of expression, the concept of literature as an art of expression, is the common ground on which critics have met for a century or more. Yet how many absurdities, how many complicated systems, how many confusions have been superimposed on this fundamental idea; and how slowly has its full significance become the possession of critics! To accept the naked principle is to play havoc with these confusions and complications; and no one has seen this more clearly, or driven home its inevitable consequences with more intelligence and vigor, than an Italian thinker and critic of our own day, Benedetto Croce, who has been gaining ground in the English-speaking world from the day when Mr. Balfour several years ago gave him a kind of official introduction in his Romanes Lecture. But I for one needed no introduction to his work; under his banner I enrolled myself long ago, and here reënroll myself in what I now say. He has led æsthetic thought inevitably from the concept that art is expression to the conclusion that all expression is art. Time does not permit, nor reason ask, that we should follow this argument through all its *pros* and *cons*. If this theory of expression be once and for all accepted, as indeed it has been partly though confusedly accepted by all modern critics, the ground of Criticism is cleared of its dead lumber and its weeds. I propose now merely to point out this dead lumber and these weeds. In other words, we shall see to what conclusions the critical thought and practice of a century have been inevitably converging, and what elements of the old Criticism and the old literary history are disappearing from the new.

In the first place, we have done with all the old Rules. The very conception of "rules" harks back to an age of magic, and reminds the modern of those mysterious words which the heroes of the fairy-tales are without reason forbidden to utter; the rules are a survival of the savage *taboo*. We find few arbitrary rules in Aristotle, who limited himself to empirical inductions from the experience of literature;

but they appear in the later Greek rhetoricians; and in the Romans, empirical induction has been hardened into dogma. Horace lays down the law to the prospective playwright in this manner: "You must never have more than three actors on the stage at any one time; you must never let your drama have more or less than five acts." It is unnecessary to trace the history of these rules, or to indicate how they increased in number, how they were arranged into a system by the classicists of the sixteenth and seventeenth centuries, and how they burdened the creative art of that period. They were never without their enemies. We have seen how Aretino was pitted against Scaliger, Saint-Evremond against Boileau; and in every age the poets have astounded the critics by transgressing rules without the sacrifice of beauty; but it was not until the end of the eighteenth century that the Romanticists banished them from the province of Criticism. The pedantry of our own day has borrowed "conventions" from history and "technique" from science as substitutes for the outworn formulæ of the past; but these are merely new names for the old mechanical rules; and they too will go, when Criticism clearly recognizes in every work of art a spiritual creation governed by its own law.

We have done with the *genres*, or literary kinds. Their history is inseparably bound up with that of the classical rules. Certain works of literature have a general resemblance and are loosely classed together (for the sake of convenience) as lyric, comedy, tragedy, epic, pastoral, and the like; the classicists made of each of these divisions a fixed norm governed by inviolable laws. The separation of the *genres* was a consequence of this law of classicism: comedy should not be mingled with tragedy, nor epic with lyric. But no sooner was the law enunciated than it was broken by an artist impatient or ignorant of its restraints, and the critics have been obliged to explain away these violations of their laws, or gradually to change the laws themselves. But if art is organic expression, and every work of art is to be interrogated with the question, "What has it expressed, and how completely?" there is no place for the question whether it has conformed to some convenient classification of critics or to some law derived from this classification. The lyric, the pastoral, the epic, are abstractions without concrete reality in the world of art. Poets do not really write epics, pastorals, lyrics, however much they may be deceived by these false abstractions; they express themselves, and this expression is their only form. There are not, therefore, only three, or ten, or a hundred literary kinds; there are as many kinds as there are individual poets. But it is in the field of literary history that this error is most obvious. Shakespeare wrote *King Lear*, *Venus and Adonis*, and a sequence of sonnets. What becomes of Shakespeare, the creative artist, when these three works are separated from one another by the historian of poetry; when they lose their connection with his single creative soul, and are classified with other works with which they have only a loose and vague relation? To slice up the history of English literature into compartments marked comedy, tragedy, lyric, and the like, is to be guilty of a complete misunderstanding of the meaning of Criticism; and literary history becomes a logical absurdity when its data are not organically related but cut up into sections, and placed in such compartments as these. Only in one sense has any of these terms any profound significance, and that is the use of the word "lyric" to represent the free expressiveness of art. All art is lyrical,—the *Divine Comedy*, *King Lear*, Rodin's "Thinker," the Parthenon, a Corot landscape, a Bach fugue, or Isadora Duncan's dancing, as much as the songs of Heine or Shelley.

definitions of

We have done with the comic, the tragic, the sublime, and an army of vague abstractions of their kind. These have grown out of the generalizations of the Alexandrian critics, acquiring a new lease of life in the eighteenth century. Gray and his friend West corresponded with each other on the subject of the sublime; later, Schiller distinguished between the naïve and the sentimental; Jean Paul defined humor, and Hegel defined the tragic. If these terms represent the content of art, they may be relegated to the same category as joy, hate, sorrow, enthusiasm; and we should speak of the comic in the same general way in which we might speak of the expression of joy in a poem. If, on the other hand, these terms represent abstract classifications of poetry, their use in Criticism sins against the very nature of art. Every poet reëxpresses the universe in his own way, and every poem is a new and independent expression. The tragic does not exist for Criticism, but only Æschylus and Calderón, Shakespeare and Racine. There is no objection to the use of the word tragic as a convenient label for somewhat similar poems, but to find laws for the tragic and to test creative artists by such laws as these is simply to give a more abstract form to the outworn classical conception of dramatic rules.

We have done with the theory of style, with metaphor, simile, and all the paraphernalia of Græco-Roman rhetoric. These owe their existence to the assumption that style is separate from expression, that it is something which may be added or subtracted at will from the work of art, a flourish of the pen, an external embellishment, instead of the poet's individual vision of reality, the music of his whole manner of being. But we know that art *is* expression, that it is complete in itself, that to alter it is to create another expression and therefore to create another work of art. If the poet, for example, says of springtime that " 'Tis now the blood runs gold," he has not employed a substitute for something else, such as "the blood tingles in our veins"; he has expressed his thought in its completeness, and there is no equivalent for his expression except itself.

> " Each perfect in its place; and each content
> With that perfection which its being meant."

Such expressions are still called metaphors in the textbooks; but metaphor, simile, and all the old terms of classical rhetoric are signs of the zodiac, magical incantations, astrological formulæ, interesting only to antiquarian curiosity. To Montaigne they suggested "the prattle of chambermaids"; to me they suggest rather the drone and singsong of many schoolmistresses. We still hear talk of the "grand style," and essays on style continue to be written, like the old "arts of poetry" of two centuries ago. But the theory of styles has no longer a real place in modern thought; we have learned that it is no less impossible to study style as separate from the work of art than to study the comic as separate from the work of the comic artist.

We have done with all moral judgment of art as art. Horace said that pleasure and profit are the function or end of poetry, and for many centuries the critics quarreled over the terms "pleasure" and "profit." Some said that poetry was meant to instruct; some, merely to please; some, to do both. Romantic criticism first enunciated the principle that art has no aim except expression; that its aim is complete when expression is complete; that "beauty is its own excuse for being." It is not the inherent function of poetry to further any moral or social cause, any more than it is the function of bridge-building to further the cause of Esperanto. The historian, the philosopher, the legislator, may consider a work of art, not as a work of art, but as a social document, just as the quarryman may consider a statue merely as so many pounds of marble, but in so doing they ignore its essential purpose and the fundamental source of its power. For if the achievement of the poet be to express any material he may select, and to express it with a completeness that we recognize as perfection, obviously morals can play no part in the judgment which Criticism may form of this artistic achievement. To say that poetry, as poetry, is moral or immoral is as meaningless as to say that an equilateral triangle is moral and an isosceles triangle immoral, or to speak of the immorality of a musical chord or a Gothic arch. It is only conceivable in a world in which dinner-table conversation runs after this fashion: "This cauliflower would be good if it had only been prepared in accordance with international law." "Do you know why my cook's pastry is so good? Because he has never told a lie or seduced a woman." We do not concern ourselves with morals when we test the engineer's bridge or the scientist's researches; indeed we go farther, and say that it is the moral duty of the scientist to disregard any theory of morals in his search for truth. Beauty's world is remote from both these standards; she aims neither at morals nor at truth. Her imaginary creations, by definition, make no pretense to reality, and cannot be judged by reality's tests. The poet's only moral duty, as a poet, is to be true to his art, and to express his vision of reality as well as he can. If the ideals enunciated by poets are not those which we admire most, we must blame not the poets but ourselves: in the world where morals count we have failed to give them the proper material out of which to rear a nobler edifice. In so far as this is inherent in the nature of our humanity, it is not affected by the special conditions of any single society in space and time: though art is a symbol of the eternal conflict between aspiration and reality, it must at the same time remain forever a symbol of mortal imperfection. Critics everywhere except in America have ceased to test literature by the standards of ethics, and recognize in art an inevitable expression of a side of man's nature that can find no other realization except in it.

We have done with the confusion between the drama and the theater which has permeated dramatic criticism for over half a century. The theory that the drama is not a creative art, but a mere product of the physical exigencies of the theater, is as old as the sixteenth century. An Italian scholar of that age was the first to maintain that plays are intended to be acted on a stage, under certain restricted physical conditions, and before a large and heterogeneous crowd; dramatic performance has developed out of these conditions, and the test of its excellence is therefore the pleasure it gives to the mixed audience that supports it. This idea was taken hold of by some of the German romanticists, for the purpose of justifying the Shakespearean drama in its apparent divergence from the classical "rules." Shakespeare cannot be judged by the rules of the Greek theater (so ran their argument), for the drama is an inevitable product of theatrical conditions; these conditions in Elizabethan England were not the same as those of Periclean Athens; and it is therefore absurd to judge Shakespeare's practice by that of Sophocles. Here at least the idea helped to bring Shakespeare home to many new hearts by ridding the age of mistaken prejudices, and served a useful purpose, as a specious argument may persuade men to contribute to a noble work, or a mad fanatic may rid the world of a tyrant. But with this achievement its usefulness but not its life was ended. It has been developed into a system, and become a dogma of dramatic critics; it is our contemporary equivalent for the "rules" of seventeenth-century pedantry. As a matter of fact, the dramatic artist is to be judged by no other standard than that applied to any other creative artist: what has he tried to express, and how has he expressed it? It is true that the theater is not only an art but a business, and the so-called "success" of a play is of vital interest to the theater in so far as it is a commercial undertaking. "The success may justify the playwright," said an old French critic, "but it may not be so easy to justify the success." The test of "success" is an economic test, and concerns not art or the criticism of art, but political economy. Valuable contributions to economic and social history have been made by students who have investigated the changing conditions of the theater and the vicissitudes of taste on the part of theatrical audiences; but these have the same relation to Criticism, and to the drama as an art, that a history of the publisher's trade and its influence on the personal fortunes of poets would bear to the history of poetry.

We have done with technique as separate from art. It has been pointed out that style cannot be disassociated from art; and the false air of science which the term "technique" seems to possess should not blind us to the fact that it too involves the same error. "Technique is really personality; that is the reason why the artist cannot teach it, why the pupil cannot learn it, and why the æsthetic critic cannot understand it," says Oscar Wilde, in a dialogue on "The Critic as Artist," which, amid much perversity and paradox, is illumined by many flashes of strange insight. The technique of poetry cannot be separated from its inner nature. Versification cannot be studied by itself, except loosely and for convenience; it remains always an inherent quality of the single poem. No two poets ever write in the same meter. Milton's line:—

" These my sky-robes spun out of Iris' woof "

is called an iambic pentameter; but it is not true that artistically it has something in common with every other line possessing the same succession of syllables and accents; in this sense it is not an iambic pentameter; it is only one thing; it is the line:—

"These my sky-robes spun out of Iris' woof."

We have done with the history and criticism of poetic themes. It is possible to speak loosely of the handling of such a theme as Prometheus by Æschylus and by Shelley, of the story of Francesca da Rimini by Dante, Stephen Phillips, and D'Annunzio, or the story of King Arthur by Malory and Tennyson; but strictly speaking, they are not employing the same theme at all. Each artist is expressing a certain material and labeling it with an historic name. For Shelley Prometheus is only a label; he is expressing his artistic conception of life, not the history of a Greek Titan. It is the vital flame he has breathed into his work that makes it what it is, and with this vital flame (and not with labels) the critic should concern himself in the works of poets. The same answer must be given to those critics who insist on the use of contemporary material in poetry, and praise the poets whose subjects are drawn from the life of our own time. But even if it were possible for critics to determine in advance the subject matter of poetry or to impose subjects on poets, how can a poet deal with anything but contemporary material? How can a twentieth-century poet, even when he imagines that he is concerned with Greek or Egyptian life, deal with any subject but the life of his own time, except in the most external and superficial detail? Cynics have said since the first outpourings of men's hearts, "There is nothing new in art; there are no new subjects." But the very reverse is true. There are no old subjects; every subject is new as soon as it has been transformed by the imagination of the poet.

We have done with the race, the time, the environment of a poet's work as an element in Criticism. To study these phases of a work of art is to treat it as an historic or social document, and the result is a contribution to the history of culture or civilization, with only a subsidiary interest for the history of art. We are not here concerned with the value of such studies as empirical preparations or concomitants, but only in their relation to the essential and inherent nature of the critical act. "Granted the times, the environment, the race, the passions of the poet, what has he done with his materials, how has he converted poetry out of reality?" To answer this question of the Italian De Sanctis as it refers to each single work of art is to perform what is truly the critic's vital function; this is to interpret "expression" in its rightful sense, and to liberate æsthetic Criticism from the vassalage to *Kulturgeschichte* imposed on it by the school of Taine.

We have done with the "evolution" of literature. The concept of progress was first applied to literature in the seventeenth century, but at the very outset Pascal pointed out that a distinction must here be made between science and art; that science advances by accumulation of knowledge, while the changes of art cannot be reduced to any theory of progress. As a matter of fact, the theory involves the ranking of poets according to some arbitrary conception of their value; and the ranking of writers in order of merit has become obsolete, except in the "hundred best books" of the last decade and the "five-foot shelves" of yesterday. The later nineteenth century gave a new air of verisimilitude to this old theory by borrowing the term "evolution" from science; but this too involves a fundamental misconception of the

free and original movement of art. A similar misconception
is involved in the study of the "origins" of art; for art has
no origin separate from man's life.

> "In climes beyond the solar road,
>   Where shaggy forms o'er ice-built mountains roam,
>   The Muse has broke the twilight-gloom";

but though she wore savage raiment, she was no less the
Muse. Art is simple at times, complex at others, but it is
always art. The simple art of early times may be studied
with profit; but the researches of anthropology have no
vital significance for Criticism, unless the anthropologist
studies the simplest forms of art in the same spirit as its
highest; that is, unless the anthropologist is an æsthetic
critic.

Finally, we have done with the old rupture between genius
and taste. When Criticism first propounded as its real concern the oft-repeated question: "What has the poet tried to
express and how has he expressed it?" Criticism prescribed
for itself the only possible method. How can the critic
answer this question without becoming (if only for a moment of supreme power) at one with the creator? That is to
say, taste must reproduce the work of art within itself in
order to understand and judge it; and at that moment
æsthetic judgment becomes nothing more nor less than creative art itself. The identity of genius and taste is the final
achievement of modern thought on the subject of art, and
it means that fundamentally, in their most significant moments, the creative and the critical instincts are one and the
same. From Goethe to Carlyle, from Carlyle to Arnold,
from Arnold to Symons, there has been much talk of the
"creative function" of Criticism. For each of these men
the phrase held a different content; for Arnold it meant

merely that Criticism creates the intellectual atmosphere of the age,—a social function of high importance, perhaps, yet wholly independent of æsthetic significance. But the ultimate truth toward which these men were tending was more radical than that, and plays havoc with all the old platitudes about the sterility of taste. Criticism at last can free itself of its age-long self-contempt, now that it may realize that æsthetic judgment and artistic creation are instinct with the same vital life. This identity does not sum up the whole life of the complex and difficult art of Criticism; but it is this identity which has been lost sight of and needs most emphasis now, for without it Criticism would really be impossible. "Genius is to æsthetics what the ego is to philosophy, the only supreme and absolute reality," said Schelling; and without subduing the mind to this transcendental system, it remains true that what must always be inexplicable to mere reflection is just what gives power to poetry; that intellectual curiosity may amuse itself by asking its little questions of the silent sons of light, but they vouchsafe no answer to art's pale shadow, thought; the gods are kind if they give up their secret in another work of art, the art of Criticism, that serves as some sort of mirror to the art of literature, only because in their flashes of insight taste and genius are one.

PREFACE

Mr. Mencken is an Idealist in his own personal aims and methods as a Critic. In his "Footnote on Criticism" he writes: "The critic is trying to arrest and challenge a sufficient body of readers, to make them pay attention to him, to impress them with the charm and novelty of his ideas, to provoke them into an agreeable (or shocked) awareness of him, and he is trying to achieve thereby for his own inner ego the grateful feeling of a function performed, a tension relieved, a *katharsis* attained which Wagner achieved when he wrote 'Die Walküre,' and a hen achieves every time she lays an egg." Instead of merely reporting ideas and points of view, the Critic should express his own individual uniqueness. Charm with Mr. Mencken is a million times more to be desired than truth.

Mr. Mencken has enjoyed a very widespread notoriety during the past decade. He has succeeded in making disciples and also enemies to an extent enjoyed by few contemporary critics. If the reader cares to know the worst that can be said against Mr. Mencken, he should read "A Critic in C. Major" by Fred Lewis Pattee from *Sidelights on American Literature* or the various sword thrusts administered by Stuart P. Sherman. About the best that can be said for Mr. Mencken is to be found in his own delightful series of *Prejudices*. Mr. Ernest Boyd, in his slender volume, *H. L. Mencken*, presents the charming side of his friend.

Mr. Mencken is at present the editor of *The American Mercury*. The present essay was chosen for this volume because of its treatment of Mr. Spingarn's "The New Criticism." "Criticism of Criticism of Criticism" was first published in the New York *Evening Mail*, July 1, 1918. It is here reprinted, in the revised form, from *Prejudices, First Series*, 1919.

CRITICISM OF CRITICISM OF CRITICISM [1]

By H. L. Mencken

Every now and then, a sense of the futility of their daily
endeavors falling suddenly upon them, the critics of Christen-
dom turn to a somewhat sour and depressing consideration
of the nature and objects of their own craft. That is to say,
they turn to criticizing criticism. What is it in plain words?
What is its aim, exactly stated in legal terms? How far can
it go? What good can it do? What is its normal effect upon
the artist and the work of art?

Such a spell of self-searching has been in progress for
several years past, and the critics of various countries have
contributed theories of more or less lucidity and plausibility
to the discussion. Their views of their own art, it appears,
are quite as divergent as their views of the arts they more
commonly deal with. One group argues, partly by direct
statement and partly by attacking all other groups, that the
one defensible purpose of the critic is to encourage the virtu-
ous and oppose the sinful—in brief, to police the fine arts
and so hold them in tune with the moral order of the
world. Another group, repudiating this constabulary function,
argues hotly that the arts have nothing to do with morality
whatsoever—that their concern is solely with pure beauty.
A third group holds that the chief aspect of a work of art,
particularly in the field of literature, is its aspect as psychological document—that if it doesn't help men to know them-

[1] Originally published in the New York *Evening Mail*, July 1, 1918;
reprinted with considerable revision in 1919 in *Prejudices, First Series*,
and here reprinted by special arrangement with Alfred A. Knopf, Inc.,
authorized publishers.

selves it is nothing. A fourth group reduces the thing to an exact science, and sets up standards that resemble algebraic formulæ— this is the group of metrists, of contrapuntists and of those who gabble of light-waves. And so, in order, follow groups five, six, seven, eight, nine, ten, each with its theory and its proofs.

Against the whole corps, moral and æsthetic, psychological and algebraic, stands Major J. E. Spingarn, U. S. A. Major Spingarn lately served formal notice upon me that he had abandoned the life of the academic grove for that of the armed array, and so I give him his military title, but at the time he wrote his *Creative Criticism* he was a professor in Columbia University, and I still find myself thinking of him, not as a soldier extraordinarily literate, but as a professor in rebellion. For his notions, whatever one may say in opposition to them, are at least magnificently unprofessorial—they fly violently in the face of the principles that distinguish the largest and most influential group of campus critics. As witness: "To say that poetry is moral or immoral is as meaningless as to say that an equilateral triangle is moral and an isosceles triangle immoral." Or, worse: "It is only conceivable in a world in which dinner-table conversation runs after this fashion: ' This cauliflower would be good if it had only been prepared in accordance with international law.' " One imagines, on hearing such atheism flying about, the amazed indignation of Prof. Dr. William Lyon Phelps, with his discovery that Joseph Conrad preaches "the axiom of the moral law" ; the "Hey, what's that!" of Prof. Dr. W. C. Brownell, the Amherst Aristotle, with his eloquent plea for standards as iron-clad as the Westminster Confession; the loud, patriotic alarm of the gifted Prof. Dr. Stuart P. Sherman, of Iowa, with his maxim that Puritanism is the official philosophy of America, and that all who dispute it are enemy aliens and should be deported. Major Spingarn, in truth, here performs a treason most horrible upon the reverend order he once adorned, and having achieved it, he straightway performs another and then another. That is to say, he tackles all the antagonistic groups of orthodox critics seriatim, and knocks them about unanimously—first the aforesaid agents of the sweet and pious; then the advocates of unities, meters, all rigid formulæ; then the experts in imaginary psychology; then the historical comparers, pigeonholers and makers of categories; finally, the professors of pure æsthetic. One and all, they take their places upon his operating table, and one and all they are stripped and anatomized.

But what is the anarchistic ex-professor's own theory?— for a professor must have a theory, as a dog must have fleas. In brief, what he offers is a doctrine borrowed from the Italian, Benedetto Croce, and by Croce filched from Goethe —a doctrine anything but new in the world, even in Goethe's time, but nevertheless long buried in forgetfulness —to wit, the doctrine that it is the critic's first and only duty, as Carlyle once put it, to find out "what the poet's aim really and truly was, how the task he had to do stood before his eye, and how far, with such materials as were afforded him, he has fulfilled it." For poet, read artist, or, if literature is in question, substitute the Germanic word *Dichter*—that is, the artist in words, the creator of beautiful letters, whether in verse or in prose. Ibsen always called himself a *Digter*, not a *Dramatiker* or *Skuespiller*. So, I dare say, did Shakespeare. . . . Well, what is this generalized poet trying to do? asks Major Spingarn, and how has he done it? That, and no more, is the critic's quest. The morality of the work does not concern him. It is not his business to determine whether it heeds Aristotle or flouts Aristotle. He passes no judgment on its rhyme scheme, its

length and breadth, its iambics, its politics, its patriotism,
its piety, its psychological exactness, its good taste. He
may note these things, but he may not protest about them—
he may not complain if the thing criticized fails to fit into
a pigeonhole. Every sonnet, every drama, every novel is
sui generis; it must stand on its own bottom; it must be judged
by its own inherent intentions. "Poets," says Major Spingarn, "do not really write epics, pastorals, lyrics, however
much they may be deceived by these false abstractions;
they express *themselves, and this expression is their only form.*
There are not, therefore, only three or ten or a hundred
literary kinds; there are as many kinds as there are individual poets." Nor is there any valid appeal *ad hominem.*
The character and background of the poet are beside the
mark; the poem itself is the thing. Oscar Wilde, weak and
swine-like, yet wrote beautiful prose. To reject that prose
on the ground that Wilde had filthy habits is as absurd as
to reject *What Is Man?* on the ground that its theology is
beyond the intelligence of the editor of the New York *Times.*

This Spingarn-Croce-Carlyle-Goethe theory, of course,
throws a heavy burden upon the critic. It presupposes that
he is a civilized and tolerant man, hospitable to all intelligible ideas and capable of reading them as he runs. This
is a demand that at once rules out nine-tenths of the grown-up
sophomores who carry on the business of criticism in
America. Their trouble is simply that they lack the intellectual resilience necessary for taking in ideas, and particularly new ideas. The only way they can ingest one is by
transforming it into the nearest related formula—usually
a harsh and devasting operation. This fact accounts for
their chronic inability to understand all that is most personal and original and hence most forceful and significant
in the emerging literature of the country. They can get down

what has been digested and redigested, and so brought into forms that they know, and carefully labeled by predecessors of their own sort—but they exhibit alarm immediately they come into the presence of the extraordinary. Here we have an explanation of Brownell's loud appeal for a tightening of standards—*i. e.*, a larger respect for precedents, patterns, rubber-stamps—and here we have an explanation of Phelps's inability to comprehend the colossal phenomenon of Dreiser, and of Boynton's childish nonsense about realism, and of Sherman's effort to apply the Espionage Act to the arts, and of More's querulous enmity to romanticism, and of all the fatuous pigeonholing that passes for criticism in the more solemn literary periodicals.

As practiced by all such learned and diligent but essentially ignorant and unimaginative men, criticism is little more than a branch of homiletics. They judge a work of art, not by its clarity and sincerity, not by the force and charm of its ideas, not by the technical virtuosity of the artist, not by his originality and artistic courage, but simply and solely by his orthodoxy. If he is what is called a "right thinker," if he devotes himself to advocating the transient platitudes in a sonorous manner, then he is worthy of respect. But if he lets fall the slightest hint that he is in doubt about any of them, or, worse still, that he is indifferent, then he is a scoundrel, and hence, by their theory, a bad artist. Such pious piffle is horribly familiar among us. I do not exaggerate its terms. You will find it running through the critical writings of practically all the dull fellows who combine criticism with tutoring; in the words of many of them it is stated in the plainest way and defended with much heat, theological and pedagogical. In its baldest form it shows itself in the doctrine that it is scandalous for an artist—say a dramatist or a novelist—to depict vice as attractive. The fact that vice, more often than not, undoubtedly *is* attractive—else why should it ever gobble any of us?—is disposed of with a lofty gesture. What of it? say these birchmen. The artist is not a reporter, but a Great Teacher. It is not his business to depict the world as it is, but as it ought to be.

Against this notion American criticism makes but feeble headway. We are, in fact, a nation of evangelists; every third American devotes himself to improving and lifting up his fellow-citizens, usually by force; the Messianic delusion is our national disease. Thus the moral *Privatdozenten* have the crowd on their side, and it is difficult to shake their authority; even the vicious are still in favor of crying vice down. "Here is a novel," says the artist. "Why didn't you write a tract?" roars the professor—and down the chute go novel and novelist. "This girl is pretty," says the painter. "But she has left off her undershirt," protests the headmaster—and off goes the poor dauber's head. At its mildest, this balderdash takes the form of the late Hamilton Wright Mabie's *White List of Books;* at its worst, it is comstockery, an idiotic and abominable thing. Genuine criticism is as impossible to such inordinately narrow and cocksure men as music is to a man who is tone-deaf. The critic, to interpret his artist, even to understand his artist, must be able to get into the mind of his artist; he must feel and comprehend the vast pressure of the creative passion; as Major Spingarn says, "Esthetic judgment and artistic creation are instinct with the same vital life." This is why all the best criticism of the world has been written by men who have had within them, not only the reflective and analytical faculty of critics, but also the gusto of artists—Goethe, Carlyle, Lessing, Schlegel, Sainte-Beuve, and, to drop a story or two, Hazlitt, Hermann Bahr, Georg Brandes and James Huneker. Huneker, tackling *Also sprach Zarathustra*, revealed its content

CRITICIS... flashes. But tackled by Paul Elmer More,
in illuminating ... e than a dull student's exercise, ill-naturedly
it became no mor...
corrected. ... theory of Major J. E. Spingarn, U. S. A.,
So much for the ... mparative literature in Columbia Univer-
late professor of co... is a far sounder and more stimulating
sity. Obviously, it ... those cherished by the other professors.
theory than any of ... critic be a man of intelligence, of tolera-
It demands that the ...tion, of genuine hospitality to ideas,
tion, of wide informa... y demand that he have learning,
whereas the others on... arning that has been said before.
and accept anything as le... doctrine, the ingenious ex-pro-
But once he has stated his ... ately begins to corrupt it by
fessor, professor-like, immedi... ing laid and hatched, so to
claiming too much for it. Hav... ll highly nourishing eggs,
speak, his somewhat stale but sti... esultant flamingo is
he begins to argue fatuously that the ... the fact is, of
the whole mustering of the critical *Aves*. Bu... needs fall
course, that criticism, as humanly practiced, must ... eauty,
a good deal short of this intuitive recreation of b... one
and what is more, it must go a good deal further. For ...
thing, it must be interpretation in terms that are not only
exact but are also comprehensible to the reader, else it will
leave the original mystery as dark as before—and once interpretation comes in, paraphrase and transliteration come
in. What is recondite must be made plainer; the transcendental, to some extent at least, must be done into common
modes of thinking. Well, what are morality, trochaics,
hexameters, movements, historical principles, psychological maxims, the dramatic unities—what are all these save
common modes of thinking, short-cuts, rubber stamps, words
of one syllable? Moreover, beauty as we know it in this
world is by no means the apparition *in vacuo* that Mr. Spingarn seems to see. It has its social, its political, even its moral

implications. The finale of Beethoven's C
is not only colossal as music; it is also o   minor symphony
it says something against something. Yet   olossal as revolt;
of beauty are not within itself alone, nor ev   more, the springs
but often in things without. Brahms w   en in genius alone,
Requiem, not only because he was a g   rote his Deutsches
because he was a good German. And i   reat artist, but also
times when the divine afflatus takes   n Nietzsche there are
spirochætæ have the floor.   a back seat, and the

Major Spingarn himself seems
this limitation on his doctrine.   to harbor some sense of
poet's intention must be judge   e gives warning that "the
tive act"—which opens the do   d at the moment of the crea-
to creep in. But limited o   or enough for many an ancient
of moldy rubbish, and ge   r not, he at least clears off a lot
of his former collea   s further toward the truth than any
ries that onl   gues. They waste themselves upon theo-
more dil   conceal the poet's achievement the more, the
hims   gently they are applied; he, at all events, grounds
sp   elf upon the sound notion that there should be free
    eech in art, and no protective tariffs, and no *a priori* as-
sumptions, and no testing of ideas by mere words. The safe
ground probably lies between the contestants, but nearer
Spingarn. The critic who really illuminates starts off much
as he starts off, but with a due regard for the prejudices and
imbecilities of the world. I think the best feasible practice
is to be found in certain chapters of Huneker, a critic of vastly
more solid influence and of infinitely more value to the arts
than all the prating pedagogues since Rufus Griswold. Here,
as in the case of Poe, a sensitive and intelligent artist recreates the work of other artists, but there also comes to the
ceremony a man of the world, and the things he has to say
are apposite and instructive too. To denounce moralizing
out of hand is to pronounce a moral judgment. To dispute

the categories is to set up a new anti-categorical category. And to admire the work of Shakespeare is to be interested in his handling of blank verse, his social aspirations, his shot-gun marriage and his frequent concessions to the bombastic frenzy of his actors, and to have some curiosity about Mr. W. H. The really competent critic must be an empiricist. He must conduct his exploration with whatever means lie within the bounds of his personal limitation. He must produce his effects with whatever tools will work. If pills fail, he gets out his saw. If the saw won't cut, he seizes a club.

Perhaps, after all, the chief burden that lies upon Major Spingarn's theory is to be found in its label. The word "creative" is a bit too flamboyant; it says what he wants to say, but it probably says a good deal more. In this emergency, I propose getting rid of the misleading label by pasting another over it. That is, I propose the substitution of "catalytic" for "creative," despite the fact that "catalytic" is an unfamiliar word, and suggests the dog-Latin of the seminaries. I borrow it from chemistry, and its meaning is really quite simple. A catalyzer, in chemistry, is a substance that helps two other substances to react. For example, consider the case of ordinary cane sugar and water. Dissolve the sugar in the water and nothing happens. But add a few drops of acid and the sugar changes into glucose and fructose. Meanwhile, the acid itself is absolutely unchanged. All it does is to stir up the reaction between the water and the sugar. The process is called catalysis. The acid is a catalyzer.

Well, this is almost exactly the function of a genuine critic of the arts. It is his business to provoke the reaction between the work of art and the spectator. The spectator, untutored, stands unmoved; he sees the work of art, but it fails to make any intelligible impression on him; if he were spontaneously sensitive to it, there would be no need for criticism. But now comes the critic with his catalysis. He makes the work of art live for the spectator; he makes the spectator live for the work of art. Out of the process comes understanding, appreciation, intelligent enjoyment—and that is precisely what the artist tried to produce.

PREFACE

After a reading of Mr. Spingarn and Mr. Mencken, it is interesting to turn to a different type of mind, and to look at literature from a more conservative point of view. Mr. Brownell's mind is saturated with the most widely heralded ideals and theories of historical criticism. He has assimilated the best that has been thought and said in the world, and this has influenced his own outlook. He discusses the field of criticism, and its function, and then explains its method.

Mr. Brownell was born in New York and educated at Amherst. From 1879 to 1881, he served on the staff of the New York *Nation*. For the past thirty-five years, he has been a literary adviser for Charles Scribner's Sons. He has received honorary degrees from Amherst and from Columbia University. He is a member of the American Academy of Arts and Letters, and is everywhere recognized as one of the most scholarly of our literary critics. The following works should be familiar to all students of literature: *Victorian Prose Writers; American Prose Writers; Criticism; Standards; The Genius of Style*. The present essay is taken from the volume entitled *Criticism*.

CRITICISM[1]

By W. C. BROWNELL

I. *Field and Function*

Criticism itself is much criticized—which logically establishes its title. No form of mental activity is commoner, and, where the practice of anything is all but universal, protest against it is as idle as apology for it should be superfluous. The essentially critical character of formularies alleging the inferiority to books of the books about books that Lamb preferred, finding the genesis of criticism in creative failure, and so on, should of itself demonstrate that whatever objection may be made to it in practice there can be none in theory. In which case the only sensible view is that its practice should be perfected rather than abandoned. However, it is probably only in—may one say?—"uncritical circles," notoriously as skeptical about logic as about criticism, that it encounters this fundamental censure. "Nobody here," Lord Morley remarked, addressing the English Association, "will undervalue criticism or fall into the gross blunder of regarding it as a mere parasite of creative work." And, indeed, it would be slighting just proportion and intellectual decorum to lay any particular stress on the aspersions of the sprightly sciolists of the studios, such as, for example, the late Mr. Whistler, and of brilliant literary adventurers, such as, for another instance, the late Lord Beaconsfield.

[1] From a volume entitled *Criticism*, published by Charles Scribner's Sons. Of the four chapters in that volume, on "Field and Function," "Equipment," "Criterion," and "Method," the first and the last are here reprinted. Copyright, 1914, by Charles Scribner's Sons. By permission of the publishers.

As a matter of fact these two rather celebrated disparagers of criticism were greatly indebted to the critical faculty, very marked in each of them. It is now becoming quite generally appreciated, I imagine,—thanks to criticism,—that Degas's admonition to Whistler about his conduct cheapening his talent, which every one will remember, embodied a slight misconception. Whistler's achievements in painting, however incontestable their merits, would certainly have enjoyed less of the vogue he so greatly prized had his prescription that work should be "received in silence" been followed in his own case by himself. And it was certainly the critical rather than the creative element in Disraeli's more serious substance that gave it the interest it had for his contemporaries, and has now altogether lost.

More worth while recalling than Disraeli's inconsistency, however, is the fact that in plagiarizing he distorted Coleridge's remark, substituting "critics" for "reviewers" as those who had failed in creative fields. The substitution is venial in so far as in the England of that day the critics were the reviewers. But this is what is especially noteworthy in considering the whole subject: namely, that in England, as with ourselves, the art of criticism is so largely the business of reviewing as to make the two, in popular estimation at least, interconvertible terms. They order the matter differently in France. Every one must have been struck at first by the comparative slightness of the reviewing in French journalism. One's impression at first is that they take the business much less seriously than one would expect in a country with such an active interest in art and letters. The papers, even the reviews, concern themselves with the current product chiefly in the "notice" or the *compte rendu*, which aims merely to inform the reader as to the contents of the book or the contributions to the exposition, whatever it may

be, with but a meager addition of comment either courteous
or curt. The current art criticism even of Gautier, even of
Diderot for that matter, is largely descriptive. In the literary
revues what we should call the reviewing is apt to be consigned
to a few back pages of running *chronique*, or a supplementary
leaflet.

Of course one explanation is that the French public reads
and sees for itself too generally to need or savor extensive
treatment of the essentially undifferentiated. The practice
of reviewing scrupulously all the output of the novel factories,
exemplified by such periodicals as even the admirable *Athe-
næum*, would seem singular to it. But with us, even when the
literature reviewed is eminent and serious, it is estimated,
when it is reviewed with competence, by the anonymous
expert, who confines himself to the matter in hand and de-
livers a kind of bench decision in a circumscribed case. And
in France this is left to subsequent books or more general
articles, with the result of releasing the critic for more personal
work of larger scope. Hence, there are a score of French
critics of personal quality for one English or American. Even
current criticism becomes a province of literature instead of
being a department of routine. Our own current criticism,
anonymous or other, is, I need not say, largely of this routine
character, when it has character, varied by the specific expert
decision in a very few quarters, and only occasionally by a
magazine *article de fond* of a real synthetic value. This last
I should myself like to see the Academy, whose function
must be mainly critical, encourage by every means open to it,
by way of giving more *standing* to our criticism, which is
what I think it needs first of all.

For the antipathy to criticism I imagine springs largely
from confounding it with the reviewing—which I do not
desire to depreciate, but to distinguish from criticism of a

Par

more personal order and a more permanent appeal. The tradition of English reviewing is impressive, and it is natural that Coleridge should have spoken of reviewers as a class, and that Mr. Birrell should have them exclusively in mind in defining the traits of the ideal critic. And we ourselves are not without journals which review with obvious resources of scholarship and skill, and deliver judgments with the tone, if not always with the effect, of finality. But of course, taking the country as a whole, reviewing is the least serious concern of the journalism that seems to take so many things lightly. And it is this reviewing that I fancy the authors and artists have in mind when they disparage criticism. They disparage it in the main, however, as insufficiently expert, but though I dare say this is often just, the objection to it which is apparently not considered, but which I should think even more considerable, is its tendency to monopolize the critical field and establish this very ideal of specific expertness, which its practice so frequently fails to realize, as the ideal of criticism in general. This involves, I think, a restricted view of the true critic's field, and an erroneous view of his function. Virtually it confines his own field to that of the practice he criticizes; and his function to that of estimating any practice with reference to its technical standards. In a word, expert criticism is necessarily technical criticism, and, not illogically, those whose ideal it is insist that the practitioner himself is the only proper critic of his order of practice.

This was eminently the view of the late Russell Sturgis, who had an inexhaustible interest in technic of all kinds and maintained stoutly that only artists should write about art. And though his own practice negatived his principle so far as painting and sculpture are concerned, that was perhaps because the painters and sculptors were themselves so remiss in lending a hand to the work he deemed it important to have done. They were surely excusable, in many cases, since they could allege preoccupation with what they could do even better, in proportion as they were either satisfactorily good at it or successful with it. Sturgis's theory was that art should be interpreted from the artist's point of view, assuming of course the existence of such a point of view. As a matter of fact there is none, and when it is sought what is found is either *an* artist's point of view, which is personal and not professional, or else it is that of every one else sufficiently educated in the results which artists could hardly have produced for centuries without, sooner or later, at least betraying what it is their definite aim distinctly to express. The esoteric in their work is a matter, not of art,—the universal language in which they communicate,—but of science; it does not reside in the point of view, but in the process.

All artistic accomplishment divides itself naturally, easily, and satisfactorily, however loosely, into the two categories, moral and material. The two certainly overlap, and this is particularly true of the plastic arts, whose peculiarity— or whose distinction, if you choose—is to appeal to the senses as well as to the mind. A certain technic therefore—that is to say, the science of their material side—is always to be borne in mind. But a far less elaborate acquaintance with this than is vital to the practitioner is ample for the critic, who may in fact easily have too much of it if he have any inclination to exploit rather than to subordinate it. He may quite conceivably profit by Arnold's caution: "To handle these matters properly, there is needed a poise so perfect that the least overweight in any direction tends to destroy the balance . . . even erudition may destroy it. Little as I know therefore, I am always apprehensive, in dealing with poetry, lest even that little should [quoting a remark by the Duke of Wellington] 'prove too much for my abilities.'"

The artist who exacts more technical expertness from the critic than he finds is frequently looking in criticism for what it is the province of the studio to provide; he requires of it the educational character proper to the classroom, or the qualifications pertinent to the hanging committee. Now, even confined within its proper limits, this esoteric criticism suffers from its inherent concentration on technic. Artistic innovation meets nowhere with such illiberal hostility as it encounters in its own hierarchy, and less on temperamental than on technical grounds. On the other hand, a painter like Bouguereau may systematically invert the true relations of conception and execution, employing the most insipid conventionalities to express his exquisite drawing, and remain for a generation the head of the professional corner in a school edifice where the critical faculty seems sometimes paralyzed by the technical criterion. And of course in technical circles such a criterion tends to establish itself. Millet, who refused to write about a fellow painter's work for the precise reason that he was a painter himself and therefore partial to his own different way of handling the subject, was a practitioner of exceptional breadth of view, and would perhaps have agreed with Aristotle, who, as Montaigne says, "will still have a hand in everything," and who asserts that the proper judge of the tiller is not the carpenter but the helmsman. Indeed, "The wearer knows where the shoe pinches" is as sound a maxim as "Ne sutor ultra crepidam"; and the authority of the latter itself may be invoked in favor of leaving criticism to critics. The classics of æsthetic criticism constitute an impressive body of literature, which has been of immense interpretative service to art, and to which the only practicing contributor of signal importance, it is worth bearing in mind, was himself a littérateur—even a novelist and a poet. Nor does it seem singular that, as a rule and in proportion to his seriousness, the practitioner should be engrossed by practice.

It is true that we have in America—possibly in virtue of our inevitable eclecticism—a considerable number of practicing artists who also write distinguished criticism. But to ascribe its excellence to their technical expertness, rather than to their critical faculty and literary ability, would really be doing an injustice to the felicity with which they subordinate in their criticism all technical parade beyond that which is certainly too elementary to be considered esoteric. Certainly some of them would be indisposed to measure work by their own practice, and in that case what critical title does this practice in itself confer? As a rule indeed, I think, they rather help than hinder the contention that criticism is a special province of literature with, in fact, a technic of its own in which they show real expertness, instead of a literary adjunct of the special art with which it is variously called upon to concern itself. And in this special province, material data are far less considerable than moral—with which latter, accordingly, it is the special function of criticism to deal. Every one is familiar with plastic works of a perfection that all the technical talk in the world would not explain, as no amount of technical expertness could compass it. However young the artist might have begun to draw, or model, or design, whatever masters he might have had, however long he might have practiced his art, whatever his skill, native or acquired, whatever his professional expertness, in a word, no artist could have achieved the particular result in question without those *qualities* which have controlled the result, and which it is the function of criticism to signalize, as it is the weakness of expert evaluation to neglect.

Criticism, thus, may not inexactly be described as the statement of the concrete in terms of the abstract. It is its function to discern and characterize the abstract qualities informing the concrete expression of the artist. Every important piece of literature, as every important work of plastic art, is the expression of a personality, and it is not the material of it, but the mind behind it, that invites critical interpretation. Materially speaking, it is its own interpretation. The concrete absorbs the constructive artist whose endeavor is to give substance to his idea, which until expressed is an abstraction. The concern of criticism is to measure his success by the correspondence of his expression to the idea it suggests and by the value of the idea itself. The critic's own language, therefore, into which he is to translate the concrete work he is considering, is the language of the abstract; and as in translation what is needed is appreciation of the foreign tongue and expertness in one's own, it is this language that it behooves him especially to cultivate.

As it is the *qualities* of the writer, painter, sculptor, and not the *properties* of their productions, that are his central concern, as his function is to disengage the moral value from its material expression,—I do not mean of course in merely major matters, but in minutiæ as well, such as even the lilt of a verse or the drawing of a wrist, the distinction being one of kind, not of rank,—qualities, not properties, are the very substance and not merely the subject of the critic's own expression. The true objects of his contemplation are the multifarious elements of truth, beauty, goodness, and their approximations and antipodes, underlying the various phenomena which express them, rather than the laws and rules peculiar to each form of phenomenal expression; which, beyond acquiring the familiarity needful for adequate appreciation, he may leave to the professional didacticism of each. And in thus confining itself to the art and eschewing the science of whatever forms its subject—mindful mainly of no science, indeed, except its own—criticism is enabled to extend its field while restricting its function, and to form a distinct province of literature, while relinquishing encroachments upon the territory of more exclusively constructive art.

Of course thus individualizing the field and the function of criticism neither predicates universal capacity in nor prescribes universal practice to the individual critic, who however, will specialize all the more usefully for realizing that both his field and his function are themselves as special as his faculty is universally acknowledged to be.

II. *Method*

A rational criterion implies a constructive method. In itself analysis reaches no conclusion, which is the end and aim of reason. Invaluable as is its service in detail, some rational ideal must underlie its processes, and if those are to be fruitful they must determine the relations of the matter in hand to this ideal, and even in dissection contribute to the synthesis that constitutes the essence of every work of any individuality. The weak joint in Sainte-Beuve's armor is his occasional tendency to rest in his analysis. It is the finer art to suggest the conclusion rather than to draw it, no doubt, but one should at least do that; and I think Sainte-Beuve, in spite of his search for the *faculté maîtresse* and his anticipation of the race, the *milieu*, and the moment theory so hard worked by Taine, occasionally fails to justify his analysis in this way; so that his result is both artistically and philosophically inconclusive. Now and then he pays in this way for his aversion to pedantry and system, and the excessive disinterestedness of his curiosity.

It would certainly be pedantry to insist on truly constructive criticism in every *causerie du lundi* in which a great critic may quite pardonably vary his more important work with the play for which he has a *penchant*. But on the other hand truly constructive criticism does not of necessity involve rigidity. It implies not a system, but a method—to employ the distinction with which Taine defended his procedure but which assuredly he more or less conspicuously failed to observe. It prescribes, in every work of criticism, a certain independence of its subject, and imposes on it the same constructive obligations that it in turn requires of its theme. A work of criticism is in fact as much a thesis as its theme, and the same thematic treatment is to be exacted of it. And considered in this way as a thesis, its unity is to be secured only by the development in detail of some central conception preliminarily established and constantly referred to, however arrived at, whether by intuition or analysis. The detail thus treated becomes truly contributive and constructive in a way open to no other method. We may say indeed that all criticism of moment, even impressionist criticism, has this synthetic aspect at least, as otherwise it must lack even the appearance of that organic quality necessary to effectiveness. And when we read some very interesting and distinguished criticism—such as the agglutinate and amorphous essays of Lowell, for example—and compare it with concentric and constructive work,—such as *par excellence* that of Arnold,—we can readily see that its failure in force is one of method as well as of faculty.

On the other hand, the constructive method is peculiarly liable to excess. If the central conception it is concerned with is followed out in detail without the checks and rectifications of analysis—the great verifying process—we have the partisanship of Carlyle, the inelasticity of Taine, the prescriptive formulary of Brunetière. The spirit of system

stifles freedom of perception and distorts detail. Criticism
becomes theoretic. And though theoretic criticism may be,
and in fact is not unlikely to be, artistically effective, it is
fatally untrustworthy, because it is bent on illustrating
its theory in its analysis, instead of merely verifying such
features of its central conception as analysis will confirm.
Against such intuitive extravagance as Carlyle's the advantages of remarkable insight may fairly be set off. The academic prescriptions of Brunetière, too, have a distinct
educational value—the results of a high-class literary scholiast
are always technically instructive, however lacking they may
be in the freedom and impressionability sanctioned by a criterion less rigid for being purely rational, and committed
to no body of doctrine, traditional or other.

It is, however, the historical method of criticism that
chiefly illustrates constructive excess. This method has at
present probably the center of the stage; and though there is
in France a distinct reaction from the supremacy of Taine
and in favor of Sainte-Beuve's sinuous plasticity, the method
itself maintains its authority. Taine was an historian and a
philosopher rather than a critic, and his criticism is accordingly not so much criticism illuminated by history and philosophy as philosophic history. The data of literature and
art under his hand become the "documents" of history, of
which in a scientific age we hear so much. His thesis once
established, however, as historical rather than literary or æsthetic, too much I think can hardly be said for his treatment.
Classification has the advantage of clearing up confusion,
and the value of a work like the *History of English Literature*
appears when one recognizes its paramount merit as resident
in the larger scope and general view of history in which of
necessity purely individual traits are to some extent blurred
if not distorted. These indeed may very well be left to pure

criticism whose precise business they are. But the historic
method in pure criticism is held quite independently of
Taine's authority. Scherer, for example, arguing against
"personal sensations" in criticism, maintains that from the
study of a writer's character and of his period the right understanding of his work issues spontaneously. This is excellent
prescription for the impressionist, although Scherer doubtless
means by "personal sensations," personal *judgment* also, and
thus minimizes or indeed obliterates perhaps the most essential element of all in criticism, the critic's own personality.
Scherer's practice, precisely owing to his personality, far
excelled his theory, as to which Arnold reminded him of
Macaulay, who certainly knew his writers and their period,
but in whose mind a right understanding of their works
occasionally failed spontaneously to issue.

In fine, the historic method, great as have been its services
to criticism and truly constructive as it is, has two erroneous
tendencies. It tends generally to impose its historical theory
on the literary and æsthetic facts, to discern their historical
rather than their essential character; and, as inelastically
applied, at all events, it tends specifically to accept its "documents" as final rather than as the very *subjects* of its concern.
Taine furnishes a striking instance of the latter practice. I
have never myself been able to agree with those of his opponents, who, like Brunetière, rested in the comfortable
assurance that his whole theory was overthrown by the fact
that the ordinary Venetian gondolier of the period was the
product of the influences that also produced Tintoretto. One
might as well hold that immunity in some cases is not the
result of the vaccine that fails to take in others; the causes
of such differences in either physiology or history being perhaps, so far as they are not obvious, too obscure for profitable
discussion compared with the causes of resemblances. But

from the critical point of view it *is* a legitimate objection to his rigorous application of his method that he is led by it to consider so disproportionately *causes*, which are the proper subject of history, rather than *characteristics*, which are the true subject of criticism; to deem the business finished, so to say, when it is explained, and, comparatively speaking, to eschew its estimation.

As to the other tendency, that of imposing historical theory on critical data, it is a commonplace that history itself, which has been luminously called philosophy teaching by examples, sometimes suffers from the submergence of its examples by its philosophy. In criticism the result is more serious because, viewed in the same light, its "examples" have a far more salient importance. They are themselves differentiated philosophically in a high degree, and it is correspondingly difficult successfully to treat them merely as pieces of some vaster mosaic. On large lines and in an elementary way, this may of course be usefully done, but the work belongs in general I think rather to the classroom than to the forum of criticism. In the latter place their traits call for a treatment at once more individually searching and more conformed to an abstract, ideal, independent, and rational standard—for the application to the data they furnish of the *ideas* they suggest, not the theory they fit.

Now, in the true critical field of independent judgment, however enlightened by culture and fortified by philosophic training, we know very well that theory means preconception. And, carried into any detail of prescription, preconception is as a matter of fact constantly being confuted by performance. Divorced from the ideas proper to each performance, reposing on a formula derived in its turn from previous performance become accepted and consecrate, it is continually disconcerted. New schools with new formulæ arise as if by some inherent law, precisely at the apogee of old ones. And pre-conception, based as it perforce is upon some former crystal-lization of the diverse and undulating elements of artistic expression, is logically inapplicable at any given time—*except* as it draws its authority from examples of permanent value and enduring appeal, in which case no one would think of calling it preconception at all. It may be said, to be sure, that philosophically this view, in excluding theory, degrades criticism to an altogether ancillary station—the business of merely furnishing data for an historical synthesis. But I am disinclined to accept this implication until the possibility of an historical synthesis at all comparable in exactness with the critical determination of the data for it is realized or shown to be realizable. The monument that Sainte-Beuve's critical essays constitute is, in spite of their dispro-portionate analysis, far otherwise considerable than the fascinating historical and evolutionary framework within which Taine's brilliant synthesis so hypnotizes our critical faculty.

In general effect, moreover, Sainte-Beuve's work is itself markedly synthetic. What a complete picture it presents, at the same time continually illustrating the truth that the wiser business of criticism is to occupy itself with examples and the ideas they evoke, not with theories and the systems they threaten! For with examples we have the essential element of unity "given"; it is actual, not problematical. And—impersonal theses of course aside—in criticism of the larger kind as distinct from mere reviewing or expert com-mentary, by examples we mean, practically, personalities. That is to say, not *Manfred*, but Byron, not the Choral Symphony, but Beethoven. I mean, naturally, so far as personality is expressed in work, and do not suggest invasion of the field of biography except to tact commensurable with

that which so notably served Sainte-Beuve. There is here
ample scope for the freest exercise of the synthetic method.
For personality is the most concrete and consistent entity
imaginable, mysteriously unifying the most varied and complicated attributes. The solution of this mystery is the end
of critical research. To state it is the crown of critical achievement. The critic may well disembarrass himself of theoretical
apparatus, augment and mobilize his stock of ideas, sharpen
his faculties of penetration, and set in order all his constructive
capacity, before attacking such a complex as any personality,
worthy of attention at all, presents at the very outset. If he
takes to pieces and puts together again the elements of its
composition, and in the process or in the result conveys a
correct judgment as well as portrait of the original thus interpreted, he has accomplished the essentially critical part of a
task demanding the exercise of all his powers.

And I think he will achieve the most useful result in following the line I have endeavored to trace in the work of the true
masters of this branch of literature, the born critics whose
practice shows it to be a distinctive branch of literature, having a function, an equipment, a criterion, and a method of its
own. This practice involves, let me recapitulate, the initial
establishment of some central conception of the subject,
gained from specific study illuminated by a general culture,
followed by an analysis of detail confirming or modifying
this, and concluding with a synthetic presentation of a
physiognomy whose features are as distinct as the whole they
compose—the whole process interpenetrated by an estimate
of value based on the standard of reason, judging the subject
freely after the laws of the latter's own projection, and
not by its responsiveness to either individual whim or formulated prescription. This, at all events, is the ideal illustrated, with more or less closeness, by not only such critics

as Sainte-Beuve, Scherer, and Arnold, but such straight forward apostles of pure good sense as Sarcey and Émile Faguet.

How the critic conducts his criticism will of course depend upon his own personality, and the ranks of criticism contain perhaps as great a variety of types and individuals as is to be found in any other field of artistic expression. For, beyond denial, criticism is itself an art; and, as many of its most successful products have been entitled "portraits," sustains a closer analogy at its best with plastic portraiture than with such pursuits as history and philosophy, which seek system through science. One of Sainte-Beuve's studies is as definitely a portrait as one of Holbein's; and on the other hand a portrait by Sargent, for example, is only more obviously and not more really a critical product than are the famous "portraits" that have interpreted to us the generations of the great. More exclusively imaginative art the critic must, it is true, forego. He would wisely, as I have contended, confine himself to portraiture and eschew the panorama. In essaying a "School of Athens" he is apt, rather, to produce a "Victory of Constantine." His direct aim is truth even in dealing with beauty, forgetting which his criticism is menaced with transmutation into the kind of poetry that one "drops into" rather than attains.

I have dwelt on the æsthetic as well as the literary field in the province of criticism, and insisted on the æsthetic element as well as the historic in the culture that criticism calls for, because in a very true and fundamental sense art and letters are one. They are so at all events in so far as the function of criticism is concerned, and dictate to this the same practice. Current philosophy may find a pragmatic sanction for a pluralistic universe, but in the criticism of art, whether plastic or literary, we are all "monists." The end of our effort is a

true estimate of the data encountered in the search for that
beauty which from Plato to Keats has been virtually identi-
fied with truth, and the highest service of criticism is to secure
that the true and the beautiful, and not the ugly and the false,
may in wider and wider circles of appreciation be esteemed
to be the good.

PREFACE

Idealism, as it reveals itself in Literature, has had many critics. One of the most alert of these has been Irving Babbitt. Professor Babbitt views contemporary Idealism through eyes that have long reveled in Ancient Grecian Æsthetics. The Greek conception of the beautiful has fascinated many humanists through the ages. It attained a perfection which the years have not dimmed; a rounded proportion that has never been rivaled.

Looked at through spectacles already captivated by Greek symmetry and perfection, modern Romance and Expressionism and Primitivism seem crude and actually ugly. They lack restraint; they are erratic in their vapid emotionalism; they but caricature true beauty. Professor Babbitt has done much in this age of revolt and sentimentalism to interpret the Classical beauty of Grecian Art to America.

Mr. Babbitt has been Professor of French Literature at Harvard University since 1912. He was a lecturer at the Sorbonne in 1923. Students of contemporary literature will find two of his books, *Literature and the American College*, 1908, and *Rousseau and Romanticism*, 1919, decidedly interesting. "Genius and Taste" first appeared in *The Nation*, February 7, 1918.

GENIUS AND TASTE[1]

By Irving Babbitt

I

In *Roderick Random* (1748), the poet Melopoyn, confined in the Marshalsea for debt, stalks forth "wrapped in a dirty rug tied about his loins with two pieces of list of different colors," and, making a profound bow to the assembled prisoners, pronounces before them "with great significance of voice and gesture a very elegant and ingenious discourse upon the difference between genius and taste." Mr. Spingarn's views on genius and taste, in his *Creative Criticism*, like so many other views that are being put forth as ultra-modern, take us back to this period in the eighteenth century. A new movement began to gain head about that time, a movement in the midst of which we are still living, and the opposition between this movement and traditional conceptions appears nowhere more clearly, perhaps, than in its reinterpretation of such words as genius and taste. In one of his most conservative moods Voltaire defined genius as only "judicious imitation"; which meant in practice the imitation of the approved models according to certain rules and conventions. But to imitate thus is to be merely orthodox, and Voltaire maintains that after all mere orthodoxy, though necessary, does not suffice. In any one who hopes to achieve literary salvation good works must be supplemented by grace, and grace is accorded to but few. If Voltaire is to the last degree astringent and restrictive in his attitude towards

[1] Reprinted by permission from *The Nation* of February 7, 1918.

literary genius, he is hardly less so in his attitude towards taste. The critic, too, he holds, must have a special tact and intuition that cannot be acquired. Voltaire estimates that in the whole world there are only a few thousand men of taste—mainly settled about Paris. In short, genius and taste as Voltaire views them are very vivid and vital things, but operate within the limits imposed by the neoclassic doctrine of imitation, a doctrine that suffered from the start from a taint of formalism.

Those who sought to purge literature of this taint began towards the middle of the eighteenth century to oppose to the neoclassical harping on judgment and imitation a plea for imagination and originality. The enthusiast and original genius who emerged at this time and arrayed himself against the wit and man of the world had from the outset a strong leaning towards primitivism. For example, Edward Young's *Conjectures on Original Composition* (1759) will be found in its attacks on imitation, and its exaltation of spontaneity and free expression, to anticipate surprisingly the gospel of recent primitivists like Mr. Spingarn and his master, Benedetto Croce. According to the older school, art aims not at the expression of the individual, but at the universal—the "grandeur of generality." On the contrary, says Young, genius resides in one's ultimate idiosyncrasy, that ineffable something that makes every man different from his fellows. If one wishes to be a creator and not a mechanical imitator, one should simply be one's temperamental self, and above all submit to no constraint upon one's imagination. "In the fairyland of fancy genius may wander wild; there it has a creative power and may reign arbitrarily over its own empire of chimeras." (The empire of chimeras was later to become the tower of ivory.) If one is not to be contaminated by imitation, it is an advantage, Young insinuates, to be ignorant and brainless. "Many a genius probably there has been which could neither write nor read." This advantage, the primitivist soon came to argue, was enjoyed especially in the early stages of society before originality had been crushed beneath a superincumbent weight of artificial culture, and before critics had begun their pernicious activities. This primitivistic view of genius received a great stimulus from the publication of the Ossianic poems. "Genius," says Diderot, summing up a whole movement, "calls for something enormous, primitive and barbaric."

If genius, according to the primitivist, is something purely expressive, a spontaneous temperamental overflow, taste, as he views it, is likewise at the opposite pole from the taste of the neoclassicist. Voltaire failed to do justice to certain writers—Shakespeare, for example—who were outside the strict neoclassical convention. According to the new doctrine, the critic should cease to be thus exclusive and become comprehensive and sympathetic. This is an important half-truth, though perhaps no half-truth since the beginning of the world has ever been so overworked. For it is not enough, as Mr. Spingarn would have us believe, that the critic should ask what the creator aimed to do and whether he has fulfilled his aim; he must also ask whether the aim is intrinsically worth while. He must, in other words, rate creation with reference to some standard set both above his own temperament and that of the creator. According to the primitivist, on the contrary, the genius has simply to let himself go both imaginatively and emotionally, and the whole business of the critic is to receive so keen an impression from the resulting expression that when passed through his temperament it issues forth as a fresh expression. By thus participating in the creative thrill of genius, the critic becomes creative in turn, and in so far genius and taste are one.

Now taste has been defined as a man's literary conscience. The transformation of the literary conscience that took place in the eighteenth century is only one aspect of the transformation that took place during that period in the conscience in general. Instead of being looked upon, as it always had been traditionally, as an inner check upon impulse and emotion, the conscience came to be regarded as itself an expansive emotion. Once discredit the veto power in human nature, once identify the spirit that says no with the devil, and the rest—for example, the tendency of genius and taste to run together in a common expansiveness, a common eagerness for expression—follows quickly. "The identity of genius and taste," says Mr. Spingarn, "is the final achievement of modern thought on the subject of art; and it means that fundamentally the creative and critical instincts are one and the same." In that case the credit of this discovery belongs to critics who antedate by at least a century Signor Croce. For example, A. W. Schlegel protests in his Berlin lectures (1803) against a "fault-finding criticism that looked upon what is truly positive in poetry—genius—as the evil principle, and wished to subordinate it to the negative principle—so-called good taste; an unreal and purely fanciful contrast. These two things (i. e., genius and taste) are indivisibly one."

II

If the creator has merely to get his own genius, i. e., his own uniqueness, expressed, it is hard to see why the critic should be more disinterested, why he should not be less concerned with the faithfulness of the impression he receives from the work of the creator than with the temperamental modifications he gives this impression, with his remolding of it into a fresh creation so that it may become expressive of *his* genius. These ultimate implications of the expression-istic-impressionistic view have been worked out by no one more consistently, perhaps, than by Oscar Wilde in his dialogue *The Critic as Artist*. "Criticism," Wilde concludes, "is the only civilized form of autobiography." Except that he falls somewhat short of this last affirmation, Mr. Spingarn runs very closely parallel to Wilde, to whom indeed he makes due acknowledgment. What underlies this whole movement from the original genius of the eighteenth century down to Wilde and Mr. Spingarn is the craving for an indeterminate vagabondage of imagination and emotion; and far more significant than the emotional emancipation is the emancipation of the imagination from any allegiance to standards, from any central control. The neoclassicists had forgotten in their devotion to what they conceived to be truth and nature, by which they meant normal human nature, the supreme rôle of the imagination, or, if one prefers, of illusion in both art and life. They hoped, as we have seen, to achieve their grandeur of generality by a merely judicious imitation. Yet Voltaire himself had declared that "illusion is the queen of the human heart." The original genius opposed to the unimaginative neoclassic notion of normality an imagination that is subject to no norm whatsoever, that is, in Young's phrase, free to wander wild in its own empire of chimeras. Wilde has the supreme effrontery to put this cult of pure illusion under the patronage of Aristotle. But this should at least serve to remind us that Aristotle, unlike the neoclassicists, recognizes the all-important rôle of illusion. The poet, he says, gives us a truth superior to that of the historian—superior because it is more representative. But in order to give us this representative truth, he goes on to say, the poet must be a master of illusion. In Goethe's phrase, the best art gives us "the illusion of a higher reality"

and this has the advantage of being strictly experimental, of
being only a statement of what one actually experiences on
reading a great poem or seeing a great picture. Imitation,
in the theory of an Aristotle and the practice of a Sophocles
or a Phidias, is not merely judicious, but creative, and creative because it is imaginative. For the Greek, genius consists not in getting one's uniqueness uttered, but in the
imaginative perception of the universal. Homer, says Aristotle, is the greatest of poets because he never entertains
us with his own person, but is the most constantly an imitator. Homer still remains the greatest of poets for this very
reason. He paints with his eye on the object, and that object
is human nature.

The opposite pole is reached when Lamartine tells us that
he wrote solely for "the relief of his heart." The fact that
the poet who overflows in this way is widely acclaimed is
no sure proof that he has attained the universal. Many
men may become abnormal at the same time and in the
same way. A whole generation saw itself reflected in *René*.
René is already more remote from us than Homer; and that
is because the quality of the imagination displayed is, from
the point of view of normal human experience, highly eccentric. It has been said, on the other hand, that Shakespeare
dwells at the very center of human nature. This is only
another way of saying that Shakespeare is one of the most
imaginative of men. His imagination, however, is not irresponsible like that of the original genius, but is disciplined
to reality. At his best he is ethical in the Greek sense. To
be ethical in the Greek sense is not to preach or to agitate
problems, but to see life with imaginative wholeness. It is
only too plain that the original genius, in his break with the
neoclassic formalist, did not rise to ethical standards—to do
this he would have needed to work out a sound view of the

imagination and of imaginative imitation—but merely fell from legalism into anarchy. One should add—and this again is a fact that every one can verify for himself—that the highest type of creator gets his general truth without any sacrifice of his peculiar personal note; he is at once unique and universal. But the original genius tends to identify— here is his underlying error—the normal with the common-place. What he sees at the center is academic routine, and he gets as far away from this center as he can by inbreeding idiosyncrasy. And then somebody finds that the eccentric position thus assumed is still too central and proceeds to fly off from it; whereupon still another comes along and secedes from this seceder from a secessionist, and so on indefinitely. The extremists in painting have got so far beyond Cézanne, who was regarded not long ago as one of the wildest of innovators, that Cézanne is in a fair way, we read, to "achieve the unhappy fate of becoming a classic."

One should indeed not forget that in the house of art are many mansions. The imagination that is more or less free to wander wild in its own empire of chimeras has its place on the recreative side of life. The question of truth and reality is not in this sort of creation primary. But it is right here that the primitivist is guilty of the gravest confusions. Mr. Spingarn holds that the would-be creator should submit to no test of truth and reality, but should simply "let himself go" emotionally and imaginatively; should get rid of "inner or outer inhibitions," and the result, one is to believe, will not be something more or less recreative; on the contrary, one will presently find Mr. Spingarn crediting the creator of this type with a "vision of reality" and "spiritual exaltation." Mr. Spingarn promises us that if we follow his prescription, we shall not only have genius—which will turn out to be identical with taste—but that we shall also go mad.

One may agree with him that the man who puts no check on his imagination, and is at the same time convinced of his "spiritual exaltation," is in a fair way to go mad, but one may disagree with him in deeming this madness a divine madness. In its mildest forms this whole theory of genius and taste encourages conceit; in its more advanced forms megalomania. Once eliminate the high impersonal standard, the ethical norm that sets bounds to the eagerness of the creator to express himself, and the eagerness of the creator to thrill to this expression, and it is hard to see what measure of a man's merit is left save his intoxication with himself; and this measure would scarcely seem to be trustworthy. Vergil, we are told, wished to burn the Æneid. The undergraduate, on the other hand, often has a considerable conceit of his own genius in writing his daily theme. "Every ass that's romantic," says Wolseley in his preface to *Valentinian* (1685), "believes he's inspired."

After all, the doctrine of imitation merely means that one needs to look up to some standard set above one's ordinary self. Any one who looked up to the standards established by the two great traditions, the classical and the Christian, tended to acquire in some measure the supreme Christian virtue, humility, and the supreme classical virtue, decorum, or, if one prefers, a sense of proportion. To repudiate the traditional Christian and classical checks and at the same time fail to work out some new and more vital control upon impulse and temperament is to be guilty of high treason to civilization.

If, on the one hand, the "spiritual exaltation" of the primitivist makes against the two virtues that sum up in a way all civilization, humility, and decorum, on the other hand it encourages the two root diseases of human nature, conceit and laziness. Mr. Spingarn's exhortation to get rid of both inner and outer inhibitions and let ourselves go amounts in effect to this: follow the line of least resistance— and be a genius. It is easy to be an unchained temperament, difficult to attain to a proportionate and disciplined view of life. By preaching sheer imaginative and emotional unrestraint in the name of expression, Mr. Spingarn is tending to discredit that very modern spirit [1] for which he professes to stand. If to be modern means anything, it means to be positive and experimental in one's attitude towards life. If such a phrase as a "vision of reality" is to have any experimental content, if it is to be anything more than a mask for egotism, the reality of which one has a vision will serve to set bounds to the expansion of one's ordinary self; will be known practically, in short, as an inner inhibition. It should be clear to any one who considers the case of those who have viewed life with some degree of centrality and wholeness that they have won their restraining ethical insight with the aid of the imagination. If a sound type of individualism is to be achieved, and this is the specifically modern problem, it is scarcely possible to stress too strongly the rôle of the ethical or generalizing imagination. Such vision of reality as is vouchsafed to finite man must ever come to him through a veil of illusion. This inseparableness of reality and illusion may embarrass the metaphysician, but not the positivist who discriminates between the sham vision and the true, not on metaphysical grounds, but by their fruits.

Now the fruits of the primitivistic theory of genius and originality have had time to become manifest. If this theory was incubated in eighteenth-century England, it received its chief developments in eighteenth-century Ger-

---

[1] For my definition of the modern spirit see *Nation*, August 2, 1917 (article on "Matthew Arnold"). For my use of the word laziness see *ibid.*, October 18, 1917 ("Interpreting India to the West").

many, where it was applied by Herder, Fichte, and others,
not merely to individuals, but to nations. When an individual becomes unduly exalted over his own "genius," there are
various ways in which he may be relieved of his excess of
conceit. But when a whole nation gets into a similar state
of exaltation and is consumed by the ardor for self-expression, when instead of submission to genuine ethical standards
there is a collective inbreeding of temperament and idiosyncrasy, then the case is well-nigh hopeless. One may then
properly raise the question that Bishop Butler is said to have
debated with himself, whether a whole nation may not go
mad. National conceit runs into national megalomania, and
the intoxication of a whole people with itself finally comes to
be felt by it as an ecstatic "idealism." A nation of this kind
may count upon having its "creative" critics, who will hope
to show their taste by simply sharing this intoxication and
their genius by giving it fresh expression.

III

This whole conception of genius and taste has about it the
flavor of a decadent æstheticism. The term creative critic,
in particular, seems destined to remain a noteworthy example of what Arnold calls the grand name without the
grand thing; and this is a pity, for there is an important sense
in which the critic should be creative, especially in an age
like the present, which has cut loose from its traditional
moorings. Before determining what this sense is, let us
consider for a moment the true relation between creator and
critic, between genius and taste. Not to speak of other and
minor differences, the creator differs above all from the
critic, not merely in having genius in general, but a mysterious and incommunicable gift. Dr. Johnson goes too far
when he defines genius as "only a mind of large general

powers accidentally determined to some particular direction."
The musical genius of a Mozart, for example, cannot be ac-
counted for in any such fashion. Dr. Johnson was nevertheless
right in condemning the whole primitivistic notion of genius
and the lazy drifting with temperament that it encouraged.
As a seventeenth-century Frenchman put it, it is not enough
to have great gifts, one must also know how to manage them.
Though a man's genius may not be in his power, the control
of this genius to some human end largely is. To determine
this end, he must look to standards, standards which, if he is
not to be a mere traditionalist, he must create with the aid
of the ethical imagination. If he does not seek to humanize
his gift, if he is content to be a mere unchained force of nature,
he may have genius, almost any amount of it, and yet remain, as Tennyson said of Hugo, only a "weird Titan."

The critic, for his part, cannot afford any more than the
creator simply to let himself go. If he is merely content to
partake of the creative thrill of genius, he may have gusto,
zest, relish, what you will, but he will not have taste. He will
begin to have taste only when he refers the creative expression
and his impression of it to some standard that is set above
both. And if this standard is to be purified of every taint of
formalism, it must not be merely traditional or rationalistic,
but must rest on an immediate perception of what is normal
and human, a perception that the critic, like the creator, can
win in its fullness only with the aid of the ethical or generalizing imagination. The best type of critic may therefore be
said to be creative in the sense that he creates standards. It
is in their common allegiance to standards that critic and
creator really come together. They ascend, and not, as in
the primitivistic theory, descend, to meet. With the elimina-
tion of the restrictive and selective principle—and the presence of standards is always felt as such a principle—what is

left is the most dangerous of all forms of anarchy—anarchy of the imagination. This is what Goethe meant when he said that "nothing is so horrible as imagination without taste."

To acquire a true literary conscience, to mediate between the restrictive and selective principle and one's vivid personal impression, to have standards and then to apply them flexibly and intuitively, is not easy. It is to be feared that Voltaire is nearer the truth when he discourses on the small number of the elect in matters of taste than Mr. Spingarn when he utters his facile assurance, so agreeable to democratic ears, that "we are all geniuses; we are all possessed of taste." Mr. Spingarn's message would seem to be the very opposite of what we need in America at the present time. For though we no doubt have "ideals"—at least we seem very certain on this point—we lack standards; and the pathway to standards would scarcely seem to lie through the glorification of impulse and unrestraint. Because certain barriers imposed by neoclassic good taste were found to be arbitrary and artificial, the primitivist assumes that all barriers are arbitrary and artificial; and the consequences of this assumption, if worked out consistently, should give us pause. Civilization, at bottom, rests on the recognition of the fact that man shows his true liberty by resisting impulse, and not by yielding to it, that he grows in the perfection proper to his own nature not by throwing off but by taking on limitations. As a matter of fact, not much is left of the values of civilized life when Mr. Spingarn has finished enumerating the things that must be thrown overboard if the creator is to express himself adequately, and the "new" or "æsthetic" critic is to partake of the creator's thrill and reëxpress it. Mr. Spingarn says that the opening night of the International Exhibition (1913) was one of the most "exciting adventures" that he had ever experienced. Many of the pictures that have been appearing in this and similar exhibitions of late years, far from being so excitingly novel, would suggest rather that our American partisans of pure expression are coming in at a late stage of a movement that from its rise in the eighteenth century was unable to distinguish between the original and the aboriginal. If Mr. Theodore Dreiser, author of *The Genius*, had set forth his views of originality in Germany about 1775 (*die Geniezeit*), they would have been wrong, but they would at least have had the semblance of novelty. As it is, it is hard for a person even moderately versed in literary history to read these views without yawning. Nothing is more tiresome than stale eccentricity. Is this country always to be the dumping ground of Europe? Americans who wish to display real virility and initiative will scarcely be content to fall in at the end of the procession, especially when the procession is moving, as in this case, towards the edge of a precipice. They will see that we must begin by creating standards, if our other attempts at creation are to have any meaning, and they will not underestimate the difficulty of the task. Primitivism leads to affirmations that are repugnant to the most elementary common sense—for example, to Mr. Spingarn's affirmation that the "art of a child is art quite as much as that of Michelangelo." But it is not enough to oppose to such aberrations mere common sense or reason or judgment. The strength of the primitivist is that he recognizes in his own way the truth proclaimed by Napoleon—that imagination governs the world. Those who believe in the need of a humanistic reaction at present should be careful not to renew the neoclassical error. Thus Dryden attributes the immortality of the Æneid to its being "a well-weighed, judicious poem. Whereas poems which are produced by the vigor of imagination only have a gloss upon them at the first which time wears off, the works of judgment are like the diamond: the more they are polished the more luster they receive." But what is preëminent in Vergil, what gives the immortalizing touch to his work, is not the judgment he displays, but the quality of his imagination. It is no doubt inevitable, in speaking and writing, to divide man up into faculties and contrast judgment with imagination. At the same time one should recollect that this division of man into more or less water-tight compartments has about it nothing positive and experimental. What is positive and experimental, let me repeat, is that in creation of the first order, creation that has high seriousness in the Aristotelian sense, the imagination does not wander aimlessly, but is at work in the service of a supersensuous truth that it is not given to man to seize directly; and that the result is "the illusion of a higher reality." Creation of this order, one may report from actual observation, is something more than the intense expression of some expansive ego, whether individual or national; it has a restrained and humanized intensity—intensity on a background of calm. Our whole modern experiment, not only in art and literature, but in life, is threatened with breakdown, because of our failure to work out new standards with the aid of this type of imagination. And this breakdown of the modern experiment is due to its not having lived up to its own program. Those who have put aside the discipline of outer authority have professed to do so because of their thirst for immediacy, of their wish to face unflinchingly the facts of nature and of human nature. Yet the veto power in human nature is nothing abstract, nothing that one needs to take on hearsay, but a matter of immediate perception. It is this fact, the weightiest of all, that the corrupters of the literary conscience and of the conscience in general have failed to face in making of the imagination the irresponsible accomplice of the unchained emotions.

PREFACE

Idealism, as it finds expression in Primitivism, is often criticized from the point of view of its moral values. The Primitivist, himself, denies that literature has moral values. He is aiming only at self-expression. If this happens to lead him into what others consider a salacious treatment of sex, he simply smiles and says he can see no harm in writing what he feels, since self-expression is literature. If there is one thing more revolting to the Primitivist than all else, it is prudery. It is possible, he says, for a prude to read immoral suggestions into the Bible or Shakespeare. Since he means no harm, he cannot understand why there is so little light and so much heat.

Professor Showerman discusses the entire subject from the point of view of common decency. He bases his criticism neither on Puritanism nor on the Ten Commandments. He allows the innate and ineradicable sense of common decency of society to direct him.

Mr. Showerman has been Professor of the Classics at the University of Wisconsin since 1910. He is widely known for his classical scholarship and for his contributions to the various literary magazines. "Art and Decency" was first published in *The Yale Review*, January, 1922.

ART AND DECENCY[1]

By Grant Showerman

Whenever, either by literal representation or by adroit indirection, an art reproduces the fleshly facts of human life, it is likely to offend the moralist. There is, however, a difference in this respect between sculpture and painting on the one hand, and letters on the other. The art of letters is by nature more prone to offend.

To be sure, we have had gusty protests against the nude in picture or statue: when Exposition decorators, for example, have made liberal use of the antique, or a young artist fresh from the Academy has plied brush or chisel with eye single to the glory of the human form, and their creations have suddenly burst upon the vision of a public hitherto ignorant of either the substance or the theory of art; but the shock has been for the time only, and due, not to anything culpable in art, but to unfamiliarity on the part of the beholder. There may be those who never recover from the shock, and who maintain a hostility because they are incapable of understanding; but they are not numerous. The quarrel between the moralist and the graphic and plastic arts is not of a really active nature. The statue and the painting remain, for the most part, in the comparative seclusion of gallery and museum, seen only by such as have the will to see because they have eyes to see.

Again, painting and sculpture are, one may say, inherently idealistic. Beauty, not fact, is their first desire; the higher truth is their aim, not mere reality; their essence is not of the

[1] From *The Yale Review*, January, 1922, by permission.

body, but of the soul. The realism of Roman sculpture is
only somewhat less idealistic than Greek idealism.   The
Dutch painter differs from the Italian more in subject than in
spirit. There have been paintings and sculpture of the grosser
type, but real obscenity has remained in the privacy of studio
or *atelier*, out of the way of offending, except as leering guide
and custodian have made use of its supposed attractions to
stimulate the good will of their prospects.

In the case of letters, we are on somewhat different ground.
Letters are not an affair of gallery and cabinet. Literature is
portable and mailable. The painting and the statue must
be sought out by the public; the public itself is sought out by
the printed page. There are few who can model or draw, but
everybody can read and talk, and everybody, after some
fashion, can write. Of all the arts, the most universal is the
art of letters.

And not only is the art of letters more universal than other
arts; it also enjoys a greater freedom than they and, consequently, a greater effectiveness. The sculptor may model the
nude surface and the languishing eye, and the painter in his
picture by employment of color may add to these something
of the warmth of passion, but both are limited as well by the
nature of their media, which confine them to momentary representation, as by the sentiment of an easily aroused public;
any painting or any statue which in the matter of certain functions or passions should descend to mere physiology or anat-
omy, would meet with immediate condemnation. Literature
is neither so hampered by technic nor so restrained by
morals. It is true, of course, that literature, unlike painting
and sculpture, cannot set before its public the tangible or
visible image of what it wishes to impress upon the imagination, and that, in so far, it is less effective; but, because its
capacity for suggestion is greater, and because suggestion is

always the complement of the object, act, or emotion set forth in the page, the art of letters is far more the mistress of its medium. The page, the paragraph, the sentence, at the same time with the distinct outlining of the image, may so employ the phrase, the word, the exclamation point, the dash, the dots of suspension, as to portray the culmination of impulse in the passion, and the consequence of passion in the act. It may do this, which amounts to the concrete and the visible, and it may still, by the use of the *Honi soit*, deny either the effect or the intention of impropriety.

To be accurate, however, it should be said that the offender of this sort does not always, or even often, plead the *Honi soit*. At least the thoroughly modern "sex novelist," who is the most frequently under discussion, is willing that the public, as it reads, should see and think and feel whatever nature prompts. Nor does he stop there; he claims the right to represent baldly and unmistakably whatever he conceives his artistic purpose to call for. Or, he will put it not only as a right but as a duty; the ground of both duty and right being the very simple one that it is the truth which he is setting forth. For him there is no limit to art but the limit of truthfulness. Not only should art say truth, but say all the truth; or at least, in the case of the novel, a very great deal more than is usually said.

The claim of literature is thus, in the mouths of the freethinking and free-spoken, that whatever is, is matter for art. This is a claim which neither sculpture nor painting has ever advanced, and which, if they should advance it, would instantly and overwhelmingly be denied.

The ground on which the claim would be denied, and the ground on which the crude realism of the "advanced" novelist is usually criticized, is the ground of morals. The too frequent sight, or the too free discussion, or the too vivid imagination of certain elemental emotions and acts makes for the hurt of our common life.

But the argument on moral grounds does not impress the sex novelist. Why single out sex? he asks. Is the representation of arson or of burglary also culpable? Is the depiction of a drunkard or a spendthrift an immorality?

We do not single out sex, replies the critic. If the act of the thief or the sot is so represented as to seem excusable, or approvable, or attractive, the result is immoral; for in such case the artist becomes the teacher, and is, in so far as his influence counts, a minister to the spirit of immorality. In other words, he is antisocial. The effect is the same when he portrays with approval the excesses of love.

But, says the artist, suppose he neither approves nor disapproves? Suppose he merely represents the facts of nature?

The supposition is hardly possible, the moralist might answer. The artist will find it difficult not to approve or to condemn what he represents. Art is in essence a matter of the emotions, and therefore in essence sympathetic. If the artist essays the depiction of carnal impulse at all, in the nature of the case it will be with approval. And besides, it takes two to make a picture or a statue or a poem or a novel. There are spectator and reader, as well as creator. The artist may be morally neutral, but his art may none the less be immoral in effect. Art is a social thing. What leaves the artist's hand is not really finished until the eye of his neighbor sees and interprets.

But the mutual attraction of man and woman, after all, is not in the same category with sottishness and theft, protests the novelist. Back of sex lies a passion as broad and as deep as humanity. It belongs to your nature and mine; it is fundamental; and it is not in itself immoral. Nature is neither moral nor immoral; it is biological fact.

Love may indeed be universal, concedes the moralist, and it may not be immoral; but back also of burglary, drunkenness, and arson are the universal passions of acquisitiveness, thirst, and revenge.

And yet these are not passions either of the same degree or of the same quality as the attraction of sex for sex, persists the artist. Love *is* different. Love is not only a passion inseparable from the life of any human being, but it is the most irresistible of all passions. Furthermore, it is unlike all others in being the social passion; and it is the only passion on which hangs the existence of the race. Any art which does not take account of it is not a reflection, but a falsification, of life. "If the novelist," says Mr. W. L. George, complaining, under the title *Publisher and Policeman,* of the compulsory lopsidedness of fiction—"if the novelist were to develop his characters evenly, the three-hundred-page novel might extend to five hundred; the additional two hundred pages would be made up entirely of the sex preoccupations of the characters, their adventures and attempts at satisfaction.

Having thus proved that the amatory emotion really is different from the passion for ownership or the craving of palatal stimulation or the impulse to destructiveness, the novelist lights his pipe and turns his back on moralist and argument. I have presented his reasoning in the usual form: a plea for artistic sincerity. It all amounts to this, that he wishes to express himself, and resents being in any way stopped. No one should be unaware, however, that there may be sincerity which has nothing to do with good art or good taste; or forget that the plea for sincerity may be advanced not only by author and critic inspired by a genuine interest in art, but by those whose interest lies in quite other things: in the success of a friend or ally, for example, in the justification of a movement, in the validation or destruction of a social condition or theory, in the stimulation of the public appetite, or in mere notoriety.

The moralist, of course, is as sure as ever that unrestrained representation is not right.

But the dispute is, after all, not one to be settled only, or even ultimately, on the ground of morality; though, by saying this, I do not wish to enroll myself with those exaggerators who will have it that morality has absolutely nothing to do with art. The artistic impulse is indeed primary and essential in art, and there may be examples of art whose origin and whose effect are alike unconnected with morals; but only those obsessed by theory will maintain that art as an energy is not implicated with morality, and that it shall not be amenable, like other energies that go to make up the complexity of human life, to moral restraint: that is, to the code of behavior which has come to serve for the convenience and the protection of civilized beings.

We shall do better to regard realism in the portrayal of sex as an offense not so much against morals as against decency. The *essence* of the sex novelist's offense lies not in the illegality or in the immorality of the matter he represents, but in its ugliness. There are things in the world which are inherently ugly and, by consequence, inherently offensive. They have always been so regarded, and, so long as men are in possession of the senses by which they are apprehended, they will be so regarded. They are in themselves neither immoral nor indecent; they are among the necessities which have been laid by nature upon man. They become indecent only, but surely, when they are obtruded upon the perceptions of other men. We have agreed not only to keep these facts out of the reach of the senses, but not to speak of them, or otherwise to represent them to the imagination. This means that they are not proper material for conversation, and that they are not proper material for art. Against some of them we have the written law, against others the unwritten.

If we transgress the written law, we are guilty not only of indecency but of misdemeanor, or of immorality in the strict and legal sense; if we transgress the unwritten law, we are still guilty of indecency, but of immorality only in the broad sense. If we resort to the plea that we have made no breach in the law of the land, we are none the less under condemnation for breach of the law of taste. We are *not* to tell *all* the truth. If this means the falsification of life, it is at worst a conventional falsification that carries no actual deceit. There may be, as Mr. George laments, no completely sincere writing; but there is likewise no completely sincere conversation, and no completely sincere dressing; nor is civilization itself, judged as an expression of nature in the ordinary sense, completely sincere. For all this let us be duly and devoutly thankful. The muzzling of art is painful to think of, but we are not left without comfort; we are not obliged to read those other two hundred pages, or to listen to those unexpressed sentiments. We already know as much of them as is either pleasurable or profitable for us to know. It may be called an outrage upon personal liberty and a crime against æsthetic sincerity when "a minority of one in a nation of fifty millions is hampered in the expression of his feelings"; but what of the forty-nine millions and odd who are asked to listen?

But the matter is not perfectly simple. We live in a world of artificialities and inconsistencies, or, at least, what seem so; we are parts of the great social machine. In civilized countries we have the institution of marriage to mark the line between indulgence which is within the law and moral, and indulgence which is without the law and immoral. To some minds it seems unjust that the law of the land should approve of those only who wed with the ring, and that the law of taste should follow.

Here again, it is not really artifice which is responsible, but nature. The experience of the race has demonstrated that, if we are to live hygienically and in peace, there must be a curb on the gratification of sex emotion; just as it has demonstrated the same principle in the domain of other passions and appetites. If we do not devise means to protect ourselves against the exaggerations of natural impulse, the result, both for individual and society, will be suffering; and it is therefore natural for us to devise the means. The artificial institution of marriage is grounded really in nature.

The legal aspect of love is thus determined ultimately by nature. The same will be true of its æsthetic aspect. Whether the work of art represent licit love or illicit love, the guiding principle will still be decency, and its ground will still be in nature. What is indecent to the sight or to the imagination in the representation of unlegalized love will also be indecent if lawful love is the theme. That the representation of illicit love will fall under double condemnation as both indecent and immoral will render it guiltier in degree, but the offense will not be different in principle or in kind.

There is one further complication. There is the less gross love without the ring which is not indecent, but only illegal, and is therefore an offense against morality without being an offense against decency in the usual sense. Is the sympathetic representation of this love to be condoned?

There is a physical indecency, and there is a spiritual indecency. We are compounded of two opposing natures; this is the essence of being human rather than brute. We exist as brutes by virtue of mere physical functions; we exist as effective members of civilized society by reason of our domination of the body. Civilized man is the only creature whose necessary state is war upon himself. It is a daily warfare whose high purpose is the welfare of his fellows, and the demand upon him for gallantry and generosity is unceasing. The man who cannot endure the test of fire, whose courage fails before the assaults of the grosser self that is his fiercest enemy, who crumbles and submits to his captor's bonds, is a craven and a traitor of the spirit. He will not dominate himself for the common good; he will not submit to discipline in the face of the foe. He is not a real soldier. He is not a free man, and slavery is degradation and ugliness in any free man's sight. The conduct of such a man is spiritually indecent. Logically, the art that bodies it forth is likewise an offender against the decency of the spirit.

The appeal against a too liberal literature of sex, then, whether it be the verse of ancient Ovid or the prose of the most recent champion of truthfulness and sincerity, is not grounded ultimately in Americanism, or in Puritanism, or even in morality, but in decency; which is to say, in nature as she is seen to operate in civilized society. The handiwork of nature is manifest with quite as much reality in civilized human institutions as in uncivilized human passions.

I have reached my conclusion. Now I should like to add a few words by way of discussion.

If in this essay I have made use of no specific examples, it has not been because I have not had them in mind. I have not failed to think of the D'Annunzios, and to remember that genius in expression is in varying degree a compensation for unworthiness of matter. This, however, does not alter my conviction that such a novel as *Il Piacere* is an ugliness, an indecency, and a treason, inexcusable whether as morals, or as art, or as mere manners. I have not failed to recall plump Jack, larding "the lean earth as he walks along," and larding with equal richness our mother tongue, and to reflect that the incongruous spectacle here presented of the spirit of man, the paragon of animals, kept in bondage by a mountain of sinful Adam's flesh, is genius's way of idealizing this old child of indecency into partial presentability. I have not forgotten Chaucer and Boccaccio, and the indulgences claimed by the fine art of story-telling, but I have also not forgotten they are indulgences. I have not forgotten Rodin and the fact that idealism may glorify the flesh, as realism may brutalize it; or that Rodin was sex realist, if at all, only in the private nooks of his *atelier*. I have been unmindful of none of these, but I have also not been blinded by examples of humorously or idealistically or otherwise artistically managed grossness to the essential sin against art in the presentation of unbecoming fact. I remark, too, for the sake of clarity, that the frankness of the art which exaggeration, humor, or idealism lifts out of the atmosphere of actual life is not the same as the frankness of the naturalistic novel and drama of to-day, which have all the effect of familiar conversation on forbidden themes.

It was not the purpose of my essay, however, to discuss individual examples or to propose definite laws, but to establish a principle. Principle is not law, but the basis for law. Principle declares the existence and the nature of the indecent and the immoral; the law prescribes what shall be its identification and treatment. If I am dealing with law at all, it is not the law of the statute-book, but the law of taste.

But is the law of taste any less uncertain than the law of the courts? Who is to say when an impression on the olfactory ceases to be a perfume and becomes a scent, ceases to be a scent and becomes an odor, ceases to be an odor and becomes rank enough to be called a smell to heaven? Who shall determine at what point the use of the beauty-box parts company with innocent impulse to self-ornamentation, or the linked-sweetness of the "movie" kiss becomes too long-drawn-out for decency? Who shall say what is the precise moment when rumoriferous mastication becomes horrible suggestion of the trough? Can decency be defined? Is there, after all, a law of taste?

There is, and there is not. If we mean exact prescription, there is not. If we mean that there is a general territory which has always been and is still recognized by the high average of cultivated people as ground that should not be trodden, there is law. You accept the judgment of these persons in the matter of sex—a judgment which is not without its debt to the general public, and which, as we have seen, is founded upon nature—and you are within the law. You refuse to accept it, and you are without the law. The dividing line is not always distinct and it sometimes shifts, but in the main it is quite visible and fairly constant.

This is, to be sure, not entirely satisfactory to those who will have everything in absolute black and white; but it is the best we have been able to do. It is what we do in other matters in which we recognize a governorship of taste; in manners, for example, or in apparel.

Of course, you may rebel. You may declare that, where so much is uncertain, all is uncertain, and that your own opinion for the moment is as valid as the opinion of cultivated men and women for all time since Adam. You may, for example, affirm that the use of facial daub by our young women is entirely proper, and in one breath defy the long line of those who have represented their times in saying it was not, beginning with the gentleman in Xenophon's *Economics* who so suavely convinced his young wife of her error, containing with Martial, who satirized it, and the Greek Anthology, which epigrammatized it, and Tertullian and the Christian Fathers, who anathematized it, and Pandolfini, the Renaissance author of *Del Governo della Famiglia*, who again condemned it, and the solicitous newspaper of 1918 which advised American girls not to use cosmetics when they visited the encampments, in order to guard against being mistaken for prostitutes, and the Aztec mother, who agreed with all the others in declaring it a mark of the evil life, and the American Indians, who expressed themselves indirectly by their use of daub on men's faces to make them horrible to their enemies. You may deny the competence of time and criticism in all other matters regarding taste as well as this, and continue to assert that whatever is true, whatever is sincere, that is, whatever a novelist feels like writing, is decent. Nobody can prevent you. But it sounds a great deal as if one should also say that whatever any human being feels like *doing*, is decent.

PREFACE

Mr. Sherman has played an active part in recent years in standing against the encroachment of mechanistic materialism. The mind of man, he believes, is something more than merely the by-product of chemical reaction down among the brain cells. He holds that the human soul relates itself to a world of eternal values, and that it is the business of literature to reveal these values. Mr. Ludwig Lewisohn accuses Mr. Sherman of being possessed with a "vision of a static universe with himself in the inner shrine determining the eternal fixities that he promulgates."

Mr. Sherman came into prominence a few years ago when he protested vigorously against the animal psychology of Dreiser's novels. Since that time he has rapidly attracted a wide audience. He has upheld the best tradition of America in an age when revolt against all tradition has been most popular. He and H. L. Mencken have engaged in many a merry duel, and no understanding of recent American criticism is complete without a rather full knowledge of the work of these two authors. Mr. Sherman's best work is to be found in *The Genius of America; Americans;* and *My Dear Cornelia*. (He is an author whose mind has shown rapid growth, so that an essay chosen from one period of his work does not represent him at another period.)

Mr. Sherman was, for a number of years, head of the English Department of the University of Illinois. He is at present the literary editor of the New York *Herald-Tribune*. The present essay was delivered first as a lecture on the William Vaughn Moody foundation at the University of Chicago, May 10, 1922.

Were you looking to be held together by lawyers?
Or by argument on paper? or by arms?
Nay, nor the world, nor any living thing, will so cohere.

WHITMAN.

The teacher of the coming age must occupy himself in the study and explanation of the moral constitution of man more than in the elucidation of difficult texts.

EMERSON.

There is that in me—I do not know what it is—but I know it is in me.
Wrench'd and sweaty—calm and cool then my body becomes;
I sleep—I sleep long.
I do not know it—it is without a name—it is a word unusual;
It is not in any dictionary, utterance, symbol.
Something it swings on more than the earth I swing on;
To it the creation is the friend whose embracing awakes me.
Perhaps I might tell more. Outlines! I plead for my brothers and sisters.
Do you see, O my brothers and sisters?
It is not chaos or death—it is form, union, plan—it is eternal life— it is Happiness.

WHITMAN.

124

THE POINT OF VIEW IN AMERICAN CRITICISM [1]

By Stuart P. Sherman

According to all the critics, domestic and foreign, who have prophesied against America during the last hundred years, the great and ever-present danger of a democratic society lies in its tendency to destroy high standards of excellence and to accept the average man as a satisfactory measure of all things. Instead of saying, like Antigone in the drama of Sophocles, "I know I please the souls I ought to please," democracy, we are told, is prone to dismiss the question whether she has any high religious obligation, and to murmur complacently, "I know I please the souls of average men." I propose to examine a little the origins of this belief, and then to inquire whether it is justified by the present condition of our civilization, as reflected in our current literature. In the course of the inquiry I shall at least raise the question whether the average man is as easy to please as he is ordinarily supposed to be.

At the very foundation of the Republic, the menace of the average man was felt by a distinguished group of our own superior men, including Washington, John Adams, Hamilton, and many other able and prosperous country gentlemen. To them the voice of the people was not the voice of God, but the clamor of a hydra-headed monster, requiring to be checked and bridled. Thus, at the outset of our civiliza-

[1] Delivered as a lecture on the William Vaughn Moody foundation at the University of Chicago, May 10, 1922. From *The Genius of America;* copyright, 1923, by Charles Scribner's Sons. By permission of the publishers.

tion, they established a point of view and they instituted a criticism, which were unfriendly to the average man and his aspirations and to all his misguided friends. They possessed, for example, certain standards of character and manners, which they applied with some austerity to what they regarded as the vulgar Jacobinism of Thomas Paine, to the disintegrating demagoguery of Jefferson, to the cosmopolitan laxity of Franklin, and to all the tendencies of French radicalism towards leveling by law the inequalities created by law and by nature.

Edmund Burke explained England's relative immunity to the equalitarian speculations of the French by this fact: "We continue," he said, "as in the last two ages, to read more generally, than, I believe, is now done on the Continent, the authors of sound antiquity. These occupy our minds. They give us another taste and turn, and will not suffer us to be more than transiently amused with paradoxical morality." Now, it is insufficiently recognized that, in the third quarter of the eighteenth century, America, like England, was at the height of her classical period—I mean the period when statesmen, poets, and painters most deliberately and successfully imitated the example of the ancients. The public characters of Washington and his friends, like those of Burke and his friends, were in the grand style, were in a style more or less consciously molded upon that of the great republicans of England, Rome, and Athens. From Cromwell and Milton, and, above all, from the heroes of Plutarch, the friends of Washington inherited the ardor and the elevation of their public spirit, and, at the same time, their lofty disdain for the vulgar herd and a conviction that the salvation of the people depended upon the perpetuation of their own superiorities.

At its best, near the source, and on its positive side,

there is something very august and inspiring in the utterances of this old Roman or aristocratic republicanism. It is not far from its best in the letters of Abigail Adams.

> Glory, my son [she writes to John Quincy Adams], in a country which has given birth to characters, both in the civil and military departments, which may vie with the wisdom and valor of antiquity. As an immediate descendant of one of these characters, may you be led to an imitation of that disinterested patriotism and that noble love of country, which will teach you to despise wealth, titles, pomp, and equipage, as mere external advantages, which cannot add to the excellence of your mind, or compensate for the want of integrity or virtue.

It is not difficult to despise "wealth, pomp, and equipage," when one is adequately supplied with them; John Quincy Adams, accordingly, found his occasion for pride in the excellence of his mind and in his integrity and virtue. And, true to his breeding, he maintained, like Coriolanus, a kind of passionate and scornful opposition to the vulgar mob. In 1795, he writes to his mother that France will remain without the means to form a Constitution till she has exploded the doctrine of submission to and veneration for public opinion. A little later, he admits to his father that "the struggle against a popular clamor is not without its charms in my mind."

There he sounds the rallying cry of our great conservative tradition. I shall not ask here whether the creative ardor of the aristocratic spirit which we observed in the mother is not already beginning to be transformed in the son to a certain ardor of repression. Nor am I concerned here to trace the evolution of this Roman-American pride from its pure high source, down through the ages, till it reappears in aris-

tocratic republicans of our own times, who still find a charm
in opposing the popular clamor. I am thinking of the railway magnate, author of the celebrated phrase, " The public
be damned"; and I am thinking of our most aggressive literary critic, a professed Federalist, who remarked the other day
in language savoring a bit, perhaps, of the Roman decadence:
"I don't care a damn what happens to the Republic after
I am dead."

We must pause here, however, long enough to recall that
the classical models of society, which the more conservative
of our forefathers kept in their minds' eye, rested upon a slave
population, and that the government which they actually
set up countenanced, in opposition to the plebeian taste of
Paine and the demagoguery of Jefferson, a slave population.
It is a question of more than academic interest to-day,
whether or not the government which they set up necessarily
implies the continued existence of an illiterate peasantry.

Those who believe that the salvation of the people depends
upon the perpetuation of their own superiorities are likely,
in the long run, to make the end subservient to the means,
to grow rather careless about the salvation of the people
and rather overcareful about the preservation of their own
superiorities. They incline, also, to a belief that these superiorities can best be perpetuated through their own offspring—a belief which, so far as I can learn, is inadequately
supported by statistics. On this assumption, however, they
endeavor to make a kind of closed corporation of their own
class, and seek to monopolize for it the administration of
government, the possession of property, the enjoyment of
higher education and culture, and the literary production of
the country.

These tendencies, as we know, appeared very early in the
history of the Republic. John Adams nearly ruined himself

in 1787 by his frank declaration that wealth and birth should be qualifications for the Senate. Hamilton, at the same time, put forth his proposals for restraining the vulgar herd by perpetuating wealth and the leadership of established families in the nearest possible American imitation of the British monarchical and aristocratic system.

The irrepressible conflict provoked by such attempts to check the rich fecundity and the unpredictable powers of our colonial "populace" is ordinarily presented to us as a contention over political principles. In its most comprehensive aspect, it may profitably be regarded as rather a conflict of religions. The short interval between the adoption of the Constitution and the end of the eighteenth century is the period of antique Republicanism triumphant, dominated by the religion of the superior man. In 1800, this religion received a blow in the election of Jefferson, the St. Paul of the religion of the populace, who preached faith, hope, and charity for the masses. In 1828, the religion of the superior man received a still more ominous blow, when the fiery, pistoling roughrider from Tennessee, Andrew Jackson, defeated John Quincy Adams. At this reverse to the sons of light, John Quincy Adams lost his faith in God, the God of superior men.

We have recently had, from the fourth eminent generation of the Adams family, Brooks, Charles Francis, and Henry, a voluminous commentary upon the effort of " the heirs of Washington " to stand against the popular clamor and uphold their great tradition. On the whole, if we may trust their testimony, it has been a tragically unavailing effort. In Boston and Cambridge and in a few tributary villages, in old New York and Washington, on a few great plantations of Virginia and the Carolinas, the civilization which the superior men contemplated obtained a struggling foothold before the

Civil War. And this civilization achieved some literary expression in the classical oratory of Webster, in the fine old English gentility of Irving's prose, and in the pale provincial flowering of our New England poetry. Sanguine observers saw in this literary renascence promise that the intrenched intelligence and culture of the settled, civilized East was to take and hold the mastery in the national life.

But for Henry Adams, at least, that hope ended with his return from England in 1868. He discovered, when he went to Washington to offer his services in carrying on the great tradition—he discovered that the great tradition was broken. There had taken place, not merely a Civil War, but a far more fundamental revolution. He and his kind, bred on the classics, and versed in law and European diplomacy, were anachronisms, survivors out of the classical eighteenth century, belated revelers in the Capitol. A multitude of unknown or ignored forces had developed in his absence, and had combined to antiquate him, to extrude him from the current of national life, and to incapacitate him for a place in the public councils. This singular new nation was no respecter of grandfathers. It took its superior men wherever it found them. It picked its chief statesman out of a log cabin in Illinois, its chief military hero out of an Ohio tannery, its most eminent poet from a carpenter's shop, and its leading man of letters from a pilot house on the Mississippi. Such standards! Henry spent a lifetime elaborating his grand principle of the degradation of energy, to explain to himself why the three grandsons of two presidents of the United States all ended miserably: one as President of the Kansas City Stock Yards; one as a member of the Massachusetts Bar; while one had sunk to the level of a Professor of History at Harvard.

From the point of view of these antique republicans, the

period from the Civil War to the end of the nineteenth century proves the truth of all the prophecies against the average man. This is the period of triumphant democracy—
meaning, of course, the triumph, not of the political party,
but of the religious principle. In this epoch, the gates of
opportunity open as never before to the populace, to the
new men. What are the results? Throughout the period,
the steadily waning influence of Eastern intelligence and culture in the national life, steadily increasing immigration from
the peasant stocks of Europe, expansion of the population
into new western territory, prosperity of industrial pioneers,
rise of the railway magnate, the ironmaster, the organizer
of large-scale production of material commodities—immense
rewards and glory for supplying the average man what the
average man, at that particular moment, wanted and had
to have.

Midway in this epoch, one of its heroes, Andrew Carnegie,
wrote a book which he called *Triumphant Democracy*—a
work which exults and rejoices in the goodness and greatness
of American life. It was an industrial captain's reply to the
foreign critics who had flitted across the country year after
year, like ravens, boding disaster. It was a reply from the
point of view of a Scotch radical, a self-made man, who could
compare the poor little Scotch town of Dunfermline, where the
revolution in machinery had ruined his father, to the boom-
ing city of Pittsburgh, Pennsylvania, where the same revolution had made him one of the masters of his generation.

Carnegie's point of view was inadequate. He offered no
effective answer to the savage criticism which Dickens had
made of our civilization forty years earlier, when he pictured
the democracy as brutal, boisterous, boastful, ignorant, and
hypocritical. He made no effective reply to Carlyle, who had
cried twenty-two years later than Dickens, " My friend, brag

not yet of our American cousins! Their quantity of cotton, dollars, industry and resources, I believe to be almost unspeakable; but I can by no means worship the like of these."

Matthew Arnold, a critical friend of ours, far more friendly to our political institutions and to our social organization than Carlyle, dropped in upon us at about the time that Carnegie published his book. "The trouble with Carnegie and his friends," said Arnold, "is that they have no conception of the chief defect of American life; namely, that it is so dreadfully uninteresting." This dullness, he explained, was due to the average man's quite inadequate conception of the good life, which did not go beyond being diligent in business and serving the Lord—making money and observing a narrow code of morality.

The particularly hopeless aspect of our case, Arnold thought, was that we, as a people, seemed quite unconscious of our deficiencies on the human side of our civilization. We displayed a self-satisfaction which is "vulgarizing and retarding." Nationally we were boasters, or, as we say nowadays, "boosters." "The worst of it is," he continues, "that this tall talk and self-glorification meets with hardly any rebuke from sane criticism over there." He cites some examples; and then he adds that, "the new West promises to beat in the game of brag even the stout champions I have been quoting."

Now, no Englishman will ever fathom the mystery of Uncle Sam's boasting. No outsider can ever know, as we all know, how often, out of the depths of self-distrust and self-contempt and cutting self-criticism, he has whistled to keep his courage up in the dark, and has smiled reassuringly while his heart was breaking. Still, if you look into the literature of the period, you find that there is much warrant for Arnold's strictures, though not always precisely where he found it. The little boasts of men like Lowell and Thomas Wentworth Higginson and Brander Matthews are only Yankee whistling, the turning of the trodden worm, a decent pride in the presence of "a certain condescension in foreigners." Lowell knew a man, he says, who thought Cambridge the best spot on the habitable globe. "Doubtless God could have made a better, but doubtless He never did." I myself am fond of declaring that the campus of the University of Illinois is finer than the meadows of Christ Church College, Oxford. But no one in America thinks anything a whit the finer for what an academic person has said in its favor. Nor, on the other hand, does anyone, outside academic circles, think anything in America a whit the worse for what a foreign critic has said against it. The Chicago journalists, for example, with true Jacksonian hilarity, ridiculed Arnold and, after his departure, stigmatized him as a "cur."

The only criticism which ever, as we say, "gets across" to the Jacksonian democracy is that which comes from one of their own number. The really significant aspects of our self-complacency in Carnegie's time were reflected in the popular literature of the period by writers sprung from the new democracy, self-made authors, who flattered the average man into satisfaction with his present state and his average achievement. I am thinking of Western writers, like Joaquin Miller and Riley and Carleton and Bret Harte and Mark Twain. I am thinking of the romantic glamour which these men contrived to spread over the hard rough life and the rougher characters of the middle-borderers, the Argonauts, and the Forty-Niners.

You recall the method. First, they admit certain facts—for picturesque effect. For example, these settlers of the Golden West, they say, included a few decent men, but they were in great part the riffraff of the world—foreign adventurers, offscourings of Eastern cities, uncouth, red-shirted illiterates from the Middle States, lawless, dirty, tobacco-spitting, blaspheming, drunken, horse-thieves, murderers, and gamblers. And then, with noble poetic vision, they cry: "But what delicacy of sentiment beneath those shaggy bosoms! What generosity and chivalry under those old red shirts! Horse-thieves, yet nature's noblemen! Gamblers and drunkards, yet kings of men!" "I say to you," chants "the poet of the Sierras," "that there is nothing in the pages of history so glorious, so entirely grand, as the lives of these noble Spartan fathers and mothers of Americans, who begot and brought forth and bred the splendid giants of the generation that is now fast following the setting sun of their unselfish and all immortal lives."

Here is the point of view of the Jacksonian democracy in its romantic mood. This, in general, was the point of view of Mark Twain, the most original force in American letters and, on the whole, the most broadly representative American writer between the close of the Civil War and the end of the century. Most of us have enough pioneer blood in our veins, or in our imaginative sympathies, to love Mark Twain nowadays. But academic people, they tell us,—and they tell us truly,—had little to do with establishing his earlier reputation. He neither flattered them nor pleased them. He pleased and flattered and liberated the emotions of that vast mass of the population which had been suppressed and inarticulate. He was the greatest booster for the average man that the country ever produced. Confident in the political and mechanical and natural superiorities conferred upon every son of these States by his mere birth under the American flag, Mark Twain laughed at the morality of France, the language of Germany, the old masters of Italy, the caste system of India, the imperialism of England, the romances of Scott, the penal laws of the sixteenth century, and at the chivalry of the court of King Arthur—he laughed at all the non-American world, from the point of view of the average American, stopping only from time to time to pat his countrymen on the back and to cry, like Jack Horner, "What a brave boy am I!" To make a climax to the bold irreverence of this Jacksonian laughter, he laughed at New England and at all her starchy immortals.

[In the *Connecticut Yankee at King Arthur's Court*, published in 1889, we hear the last full-hearted laughter of triumphant democracy. Twain himself became somber in his later years; he became cynical, and touched with misanthropy. I cannot go here, in any detail, into the causes for the darkening of his outlook. The most interesting of the causes, perhaps, was that Mark Twain had one foot over the threshold of a new age, our present era, which I shall call the era of critical and pessimistic democracy. He had begun to emerge, as I think we are all now beginning to emerge, from the great romantic illusion about the average man, namely, that liberty or equality or any kind of political recognition or literary exploitation, or even economic independence, can make him a happy or a glorious being.]

Poets and novelists, since the French Revolution, have fostered this romantic illusion in a laudable but misdirected effort to bestow dignity upon the humblest units of humanity. They liberated the emotion for a religion of democracy. They did little to give to that emotion intelligent direction.

You will recall Wordsworth's poem called "Resolution and Independence." The poet, wandering on the moor in richly gloomy thought, comes upon a poor old man, bent, broken, leaning over a pool, gathering leeches for his livelihood. The poet questions him how it goes with him. The old man replies, quietly enough, that it goes pretty hard, that it is going rather worse; but that he still perseveres and manages to get on, in one way or another. Whereupon Wordsworth falls into a kind of visionary trance. The old peasant looms for him to a gigantic stature. He becomes the heroic "man with the hoe"; a shadowy shape against the sky; man in the abstract, clothed in all the moral splendor of the poet's own imagination.

This same trick of the fancy Hardy plays with his famous dairymaid, Tess of the D'Urbervilles. She is but an ignorant, instinctive, erring piece of Eve's flesh. Yet, says Hardy, drawing upon the riches of his own poetic associations, "The impressionable peasant leads a larger, fuller, more dramatic life than the pachydermatous king." Thereupon he proceeds to invest the dairymaid with the tragic emotions and import of a heroine of Thebes or Pelops' line. He infers, by a poetic fallacy, that she is as interesting and as significant to herself as she is to him.

I will take one other case, the hero of a recently translated novel, Knut Hamsun's *Growth of the Soil.* Here we have an illiterate peasant of Norway, going into the public land almost empty-handed; gradually acquiring a pig, a cow, a woman, a horse, building a turf-shelter, a cowshed, a cabin, a mill—and so, little by little, toiling like an ox, becoming a prosperous farmer, owner of rich lands and plentiful flocks and herds. It is, in a sense, a very cheerful book, a sort of new *Robinson Crusoe.* Its moral appears to be that, so long as men stick to the soil and preserve their ignorance and their natural gusto, they may be happy. It is a glorification of the beaver, the building animal. It is an idealization of the peasant at the instinctive level.

The trick of the literary imagination in all these cases is essentially the same as that which Bret Harte played with his Argonauts, and Miller and Riley with their Indiana pioneers, and Mark Twain with his Connecticut Yankee. We are changing all that.

I chanced the other day upon an impressive new American novel, strikingly parallel in some respects to Hamsun's *Growth of the Soil*, but utterly different from it in the mood and the point of view. I refer to the story of Kansas life, called *Dust*, by Mr. and Mrs. Haldeman-Julius. Here again we have the hardy pioneer, rough, dirty, and capable, entering on the new land, with next to nothing but his expectations; acquiring a pig, a hut, cattle, and a wife; and gradually "growing up with the country" into a prosperous western farmer, with stock in the bank, and a Cadillac, and electric lights in the cowbarns, and kerosene lamps in the house. Our human beaver in America, toiling with the same ox-like fortitude as Isak in Norway, achieves the same material success. But—and this is the difference—the story is one of unrelieved gloom ending in bitter tragedy. Why this sustained note of gloom? Why has our Kansas tale none of the happy gusto of Hamsun's *Growth of the Soil?* Because the Kansas farmer is not content with the life of a peasant. Because our Kansas authors refuse to glorify man on the instinctive level, or to disguise the essential poverty and squalor of his personal life with a poetic fallacy. The book is written from a point of view at which it is apparent that our civilization has failed to solve the human problem.

Since the time of *The Connecticut Yankee* and Carnegie's *Triumphant Democracy*, our literary interpreters have been gradually shifting their ground. They are giving us now a criticism of life from a position at which it is possible to see through the poetic illusion about the average man. Making an effort now to see him as he really is, our authors are reporting that he is not satisfied with his achievements, he is not happy, he is very miserable. The most hopeful aspect of American literature to-day is its widespread pessimism. I call this symptom hopeful, because it is most fully exhibited by precisely that part of the country, and by those elements of the population, which were thought forty years ago to be most addicted to boasting and most deeply infected with the vulgarizing and retarding self-complacency of the Philistine, the red-shirted Jacksonian from Missouri. This pessimism comes out of Wisconsin, Minnesota, Illinois, Indiana, Missouri, Kansas, and California; from the sons and daughters of pioneer farmers, country doctors, small-town lawyers, and country editors; from the second generation of immigrant stock, German, Swedish, Scotch, Irish; from the hungry, nomadic semicivilization of the West.

I call this Western pessimism auspicious, because it is so sharply critical, and because the criticism is directed, not so much against the political and economic framework of society as against the kind of personalities which this society produces, and against the quantity and quality of the human satisfactions which these personalities have at their disposal. It is directed against that defect in our civilization which Arnold pointed out; it is so lacking in elevation and beauty; it is so humdrum, so dreadfully uninteresting; it so fails to appease the vague yet already acutely painful hunger of the average man for a good life. "Beguile us no longer," cry the new voices; "beguile us no longer with heroic legends and romantic idyls. The life which you celebrate is not beautiful, not healthy, not satisfying. It is ugly, obscene, devastating. It is driving us mad. And we are going to revolt from it."

The manifestation of this spirit which, at the present moment, is attracting most attention is what Mr. Van Doren, in his interesting book on *Contemporary American Novelists*, has called "the revolt from the village." I need only remind you of that long series of narratives, beginning in the early eighties with E. W. Howe's *Story of a Country Town*, and followed by Hamlin Garland's *Main Travelled Roads*, Mr. Masters's *Spoon River Anthology*, Sherwood Anderson's *Winesburg, Ohio*, Sinclair Lewis's *Main Street*, Zona Gale's *Miss Lulu Bett*, and the novel of which I have already spoken, *Dust*, by Mr. and Mrs. Haldeman-Julius.

But the interesting pessimistic and critical note in our current literature is by no means confined to representations of country life and the small town. Take Mrs. Wharton's pictures of metropolitan society, from *The House of Mirth* to *The Age of Innocence*, remembering only that Mrs. Wharton cannot be classed as a Jacksonian; then consider the dreary wide wilderness of Mr. Dreiser's picture of big business; Ben Hecht's story of a city-editor in *Erik Dorn;* Mr. Cabell's *Cream of the Jest;* Mr. Norris's broad picture of the California scene in *Brass;* Mr. Fitzgerald's account of the younger generation in *The Beautiful and Damned;* Mr. Hergesheimer's admirable new novel, *Cytherea;* and, finally, Mr. Lewis's *Babbitt*.

Here we are invited to consider a class of which the discontent cannot be explained by their struggle with the churlishness of the soil and the rigor and tragic whimsicality of the elements. Most of the characters, indeed, have reached a level at which even the economic struggle is as much a pastime as a necessity. They are business men and their womenkind, with a sprinkling of professional men, people who, as we say, know "how to live," people who live expensively, purchasing with free hand whatever gratifications are available for the senses. Nevertheless, if we may trust their interpreters, these people, too, are dreadfully uninteresting to one another, alternating between a whipped-up excitement and a stifled yawn. Their entire stratum of society is permeated by a terrible ennui. Jaded with business and card-parties, Mr. Hergesheimer's persons, for example, can conceive no relief from the boredom of the week but to meet at one another's houses at the week-ends and, in a state of half-maudlin tipsiness, kiss one another's wives on the stairs. Even when the average man is sheltered on all sides, weariness, as Pascal says, springs from the depths of his own heart and fills the soul with its poison. Our "bourgeoisie," no less than our "peasantry," are on the verge of a cultural revolt; they are quarreling with the quality of their civilization.

Now, at the time when a man quarrels with his wife, either one of two interesting things may happen. He may elope with his neighbor's wife for Cuba, fancying for the moment that she is the incarnation of all his unsatisfied desires, the divine Cytherea. Or this man and his old wife may turn over a new leaf and put their relations on a more satisfactory basis. Which course will be followed depends on the power of self-criticism which the interested persons possess.

This is a parable, with wide possibilities of social application. Our average man, in town and country, is quarreling with his wife, that is to say, with our average American civilization. If he listens to certain counselors who appeal to certain of his instincts and to his romantic imagination, his household, the material civilization which he has slowly built up out of the dust by faithfully working on certain traditional principles—this household will be in danger of disruption. If, on the other hand, his discontent with himself and his human conditions is adequately diagnosed, and if an adequate remedy is accepted, then he will look back upon this period of pessimism as preliminary to the redintegration of the national spirit and its expression in literature. Which course will be followed depends in no small measure upon our power of criticism, which, in its turn, depends upon an adequate point of view.

The elder critics in the academic tradition have in general not dealt sympathetically, or even curiously, with the phenomena. Fixed in an inveterate fidelity to the point of view established by the early classical Americans, they look with a mingling of disdain and abhorrence upon our impious younger world, as upon

> a darkling plain
> Where ignorant armies clash by night.

The critics, on the other hand, who are endeavoring to deal sympathetically and curiously with the phenomena, are utterly unorganized; are either without standards of judgment, or in a wild state of confusion with regard to their standards. They are making efforts to get together; but they have no principle of integration. I have not time to do more than mention some of their incongruous points of view.

A man whose hearty geniality touches the affections of us all, Mr. William Allen White, proposed the other day, as an integrating principle, the entire abandonment of all standards and a general adoption of the policy of live and let live. His theory of universal sympathy, which he miscalls "the democratic theory in criticism," would, if applied, destroy both criticism and democracy.

Our journalistic critics in general, conscious of the incompatibility between their private beliefs and the political and economic interests which they serve, tend at the present time, I should say, to adopt the point of view of universal cynicism.

In order precisely to escape from the troublesome clashes of political, social, and moral judgment, in order to escape, in other words, from the real problem of critical redintegration, another group has adopted the æsthetic point of view, and has made a feeble effort to revive in America, with the aid of the Crocean philosophy, the doctrine of art for art's sake.

I will mention, finally, one other point of view, to which an increasing company of the younger writers are repairing, which we may call for convenience the Freudian point of view. The champions of this point of view attempt a penetrating diagnosis of all the maladies of American civilization, with the assistance of the new psychology. To sum up their findings briefly, they hold that the trouble with American life is, at the root, due to age-long and cankering inhibitions, attributable to our traditional Puritanism. The remedy is a drop to the instinctive level; the opening of the gates to impulse; a free and spontaneous doing as one pleases in all directions.

Popular Freudianism is, perhaps, the most pestilential of all the prevailing winds of doctrine. Yet its champions have penetrated, I believe, nearer to the heart of our difficulty, they are nearer to an adequate point of view and an integrating principle, than any of the other seekers. They at least recognize that the kingdom of disorganization is within the individual breast. The fact that they approach so near to the true destination, and yet fall short of it, renders their counsels peculiarly seductive and peculiarly perilous.

They are right when they attribute the central malady of our civilization to suppressed desires. They are tragically wrong if they believe that this malady is due to the suppression by religion of any specific isolable physical instinct. They are tragically wrong if they think that this malady can be cured by the destruction of religious restraint and the release of any specific isolable physical instinct. When they prescribe, as many of them do with as much daring as they can muster, giving a new and large license, for example, to the sexual impulses; when they prescribe, as if with the countenance of fresh scientific discoveries, the restoration of the grand old liberative force of alcohol; when they flatter any of the more or less disciplined instincts of our animal nature with the promise of happiness in emancipation, they are offering us intoxicants, anodynes, opiates, every one of which has been proved, by the experience of innumerable generations, hopeless even to accomplish any permanent alleviation of the malady which they profess to cure. And when they attack the essential religious principle of Puritan-ism,—its deep human passion for perfection,—they are seek-ing to destroy the one principle which can possibly result in the integration of the national life.

Now, as I talk with the members of the beautiful younger generation which comes through my classroom year after year, I find that the Freudians are profoundly mistaken in their analysis of human nature. The deepest craving of these average young men and women is not to be unbound, and released, and to be given a license for a free and spon-taneous doing as they please in all directions. They recog-nize that nature and environment and lax educational disci-pline have made them beings of sufficiently uncoördinated desires and scattering activities.

What they deeply crave is a binding generalization of philosophy, or religion, or morals, which will give direction and purpose, which will give channel and speed, to the lan-guid diffusive drift of their lives. The suppressed desire which causes their unhappiness is a suppressed desire for a good life, for the perfection of their human possibilities. The average unreflective man does not always know that this is, in fact, his malady. And in the blind hunger and thirst of his unenlightened nature, he reaches out eagerly for opiates and anodynes, which leave him unsatisfied. But what the innermost law of his being demands, what his human nature craves, is something good and great that he can do with his heart and mind and body. He craves the active peace of surrender and devotion to something greater than himself. Surrender to anything less means the degradation and humiliation of his spirit.

This is the tragedy involved in any surrender to subordinate passions or instincts. I think that our current pessimistic literature indicates that our average man is discovering this fact about his own nature, and that, therefore, like the sinner made conscious of guilt, he is ripe for regeneration; he is ready for the reception of a higher culture than he has yet enjoyed.

Democratic civilization suffereth long, because it is always waiting for the hindmost to catch up with the middle. It is always reluctant to consign the hindmost to the devil. But, in the long run, I do not believe that the history of our civilization is going to verify the apprehensions entertained by our old Roman-Americans regarding the average man. To one whose measure of national accomplishment is not the rich flowering of a small aristocratic class, but the salvation of the people, the choices of the average man in the past do not conclusively prove the danger of giving him what he wants. In his first period, he wanted a stable government; and he got it, and whole-heartedly glorified the political and military heroes who gave it to him. In his second period, he wanted a rapid and wide diffusion of the material instruments of civilized life; he got them, and whole-heartedly glorified the industrial heroes who provided them. In his third period, the average man is growing almost as scornful of "wealth and pomp and equipage," as John Quincy Adams.

The captains of industry are no longer his heroes; they have communicated to him what they had of virtue for their hour. What the average man now wants is the large-scale production and the wide diffusion of science, art, music, literature, health, recreation, manners, human intercourse, happiness—the best to be had; and he is going to get them and to glorify whole-heartedly the heroes of culture who provide them for him.

The great civilizations of the world hitherto have been integrated in their religion. By religion I mean that which, in the depths of his heart, a man really believes desirable and praiseworthy. A great civilization begins to form when men reach an agreement as to what is desirable and praiseworthy. The leading Athenians, in their best period, reached such an agreement; and that is why, whether you meditate on their art, their poetry, or their philosophy, whether you gaze at the frieze of the Parthenon, or read a drama of Sophocles, or the prayer of Socrates, you feel yourself in the presence of one and the same formative spirit—one superb stream of energy, superbly controlled by a religious belief that moral and physical symmetry are the most desirable and praiseworthy things in the outer and the inner man.

The prospects for our American civilization depend at present upon our capacity for a similar religious integration. Our present task is, primarily, to become clear in our minds as to what is our own formative spirit. The remedy for our present discontents is indicated by the character of the malady. The remedy is, first, to help the average man to an understanding of his own nature, so that he may recognize more fully what part the things of the mind and the imagination may play in the satisfaction of his suppressed desires. It is to help him to recognize that even an intellectual and imaginative life will yield him little content unless it is organized around some central principle and animating purpose. It is to give the average man what the literature of our pessimistic democracy has at last proved that he wants, namely, an object to which he can joyfully surrender the full strength of his soul and body.

But this is not the whole of the remedy. It is necessary, at the same time, to persuade the superior men that the gods of the old Roman-American aristocrats have forsaken them, and that the time has come when even they may safely accept the purified religion of democracy. To oppose it now is to oppose the formative spirit of our national life and to doom one's self to sterility. The remedy is, in short, to effect a redintegration of the national will on the basis of a genuinely democratic humanism, recognizing as its central principle the duty of bringing the whole body of the people to the fullest and fairest human life of which they are capable.

The point of view which I advocate is not, as it has been called, moralistic. It is essentially religious. And the religion of an intelligent man is not a principle of repression, any more than it is a principle of release. Religion binds us to old morals and customs so long as they help us towards the attainment of our object; but it releases from old morals and customs as soon as they impede our progress towards that object. The object gives the standard. Confronted with heirlooms or with innovations, one's first question is, does this, or does it not, tend to assist the entire body of the people toward the best human life of which they are capable? Advance to this point of view, and you leave behind you universal sympathy, universal cynicism, universal æstheticism, and the black bats of the Freudian cave. You grasp again a power of choice which enables you to accept or reject, with something of that lost serenity which Socrates displayed when he rejected escape from prison and accepted the hemlock.   You recover something of that high elation which Emerson displayed when he said: "I am primarily engaged to myself to be a public servant of all the gods, to demonstrate to all men that there is intelligence and good-will at the heart of things, and ever higher and higher leadings."

PREFACE

American criticism has been handicapped not a little by the cleavage which has resulted from the growth of distinct sectional points of view. New England was, of course, the first to develop, and with it the Puritan point of view came to maturity. The New York School, which began with the Knickerbockers, has grown with the metropolis until its critics are the most cosmopolitan. Chicago has made rapid strides during the past decade. Harry Hansen, in his *Midwest Portraits*, has celebrated this fact. The University of Chicago has contributed its share of brilliant minds. Percy H. Boynton is among these. He is not a narrow provincial critic, but he does share the mental and emotional reactions of the Middle West. His reaction, in the present essay, to Mr. Sherman's "Point of View in American Criticism," is interesting.

Mr. Boynton has been for a number of years a Professor of English in the University of Chicago. He has also served in various capacities in the Summer Schools of the Chautauqua Institution at Chautauqua, New York. He gained his reputation as a sound critic a number of years ago through the publication of *A History of American Literature* as well as through other critical volumes. "Pessimism and the Critical Code" first appeared under the title, "Pessimism and Criticism," in *The Literary Review*, February 10, 1923. At the author's suggestion, it is here reprinted under the revised title.

PESSIMISM AND THE CRITICAL CODE [1]

By Percy H. Boynton

Cold fact is always bewildering, coming as it does into conflict with comfortable preconception; and the rising generation of critics are having an unusually hard time because the facts of to-day are unusually cold. The new arbiters of taste are passing through the experience of an average freshman with the baffling revelations of "survey" courses. When he learns in physiology that he has two hundred and odd bones in his precious body he is literally scared stiff. He tiptoes about for days in the fear of compound fracture; but gradually reassurance returns as nothing happens when whole classes descend the stairways, defying gravitation as they step from precipice to precipice without a casualty. He is saved through works. When, however, he comes to evolution and the codfish, salvation is not so easily achieved. He learns that the codfish lays two million eggs, more or less, of which only two come to maturity. It seems to him a fearful and stupid piscatorial waste—proof enough that there is no design in earthly affairs. There is no God. It does not comfort him to think that if the waste did not occur the ocean would soon be packed with cod as tight as a sardine box. They should never have been laid. No God worth respecting would ever work his will by the trial and error method. Not having any personal experience to fall back on, he throws up his hands. Works fail; he has no faith. "Two million eggs!" he says. "Well, I'll be damned!" And to that cheerful expectation he resigns himself.

[1] Reprinted by permission from *The Literary Review*.

This pessimistic resignation works itself off variously in the prevailing thought of the day. It furnishes a bond of happy union for practical statesmen, returned soldiers, red radicals, and black-browed conservatives, women who do not believe in marriage and men who do not believe in women, sophomores, anti-religionists and dyspeptics. Even Stuart Sherman in a recent article on "The Point of View in American Criticism," dwelling with his usual muscular felicity on the growth of a national consciousness, hails with satisfaction the healthy pessimism of the era. It is the usual point of arrival for any discussion of the literary self-consciousness of America, too. But on this latter aspect of American thinking there is something still to be said. So I propose to accompany the stalwart Sherman strain with an obligato on American literature's attitude towards itself, which is culminating now in an attack of pessimism *à la mode*.

The sense of manifest destiny and the irresponsible optimism to which this sense gave rise began to find voice even before the Revolution. One recalls Crevecœur's much quoted passage on the "race of men whose labors and posterity will one day cause great changes in the world," and the 1758 almanac of Nathaniel Ames, in which he looked forward to the times, after "the obscene howl" of the wild beasts should have ceased forever, when "the stones and trees will dance together at the music of Orpheus, the rocks will disclose their hidden gems and the inestimable treasures of gold and silver will be broken up."

Oh, ye unborn inhabitants of America [he addressed us], should these alphabetical letters remain legible when your eyes behold the sun after he has rolled the seasons round for two or three centuries more you will know that in *Anno Domini* 1758 we dreamed of your times.

With American independence the twin fallacy of magnificent isolation, to which some of the old guard are still forlornly clinging, became vocal in epic outbursts, particularly of the Hartford wits. But even while Dwight was adjuring mankind to

> See this glad world, remote from every foe,
> From Europe's mischief and from Europe's woe,

Freneau was confessing to the strength of a transatlantic cable more binding than any to be laid under water, in his protests at "Literary Importation":

> Can we never be thought to have learning or grace
> Unless it be brought from that horrible place
> Where tyranny reigns with her impudent face?

And Barlow, Polonius-like, was protesting too much in behalf of the model of republicanism just put on exhibition, which each land was to "imitate, each nation join."

It is an old story that this state of happy complacency could not last long; that the Old World would not permit it. Trumbull resented in behalf of his townsmen that when their ardent genius poured the bold sublime English critics carped at the style and nibbled at the rime, and Halleck was annoyed that they not only wrote from the other side, but

> paid us friendly visits to abuse
> Our country, and find food for the reviews.

Moreover, to make matters worse, as the United States were passing just then into their national adolescence, there came the bitter sense that they actually offered a fair, broad target for European shafts. With the close of the War of 1812 and the restimulation of British disfavor Americans deplored the

very characteristics which they hated to have mentioned by
foreigners. Halleck confessed to the vulgarism of urban pseudo-
culture and the Yankee shrewdness of the man on the farm.
Whittier, in retrospect, deprecated the decadence of the unco
guid,

> fearful of the Unseen Power,
> But grumbling over pulpit tax and pew rent,
> Saving, as shrewd economists, their souls
> And winter pork, with the least possible outlay
> Of salt and sanctity.

The Tory group, skeptical as to the whole theory of republican government, threw up their hands in despair at what
John Howard Payne's patron called "the desolating effects
of democracy," and the self-consciously cultured, socially
aristocratic, but politically impotent, shuddered at the new
American commoner, the irrepressible

> backwoods Charlemagne of empires new,
> Who, meeting Cæsar's self, would slap his back,
> Call him "Old Horse," and challenge to a drink.

Almost all conspired to encourage by their indignant sensitiveness the "certain condescension in foreigners" at
which later Lowell made his voluble protest, but which
will never entirely disappear until Americans learn entirely
to ignore it. And because in the years leading up to the Civil
War the Olympian gift of imperturbability was left out of
the American make-up, hypersensitiveness and self-blame
combined to pester gawky and introspective Young America,
the hypersensitiveness running all the way from Dwight's
wrath at English malicious misrepresentation (because a
certain traveler attributed chestnut trees instead of maples
to some New Hampshire mountain interval) to the fine
dignity of Irving's protest at "English Writers on America,"

and the self-blame rising from the Salmagundi and Croaker papers and Halleck's "Fanny" and "Connecticut" to the unhappy climax of Cooper's "Homeward Bound" and "Home as Found."

The lack of self-confidence to which all this palaver gave pathetic witness bore its natural fruit in literature. As a rule, the only literary solicitude in the States was that Americans should write competently and in established modes. From Freneau's graduation at Princeton in 1770 to Longfellow's at Bowdoin fifty-odd years later, commencement orators had gloried in the future of our letters. The same God who was presiding over our manifest destiny, and to whom we touchingly inscribed our trust on a debased silver dollar, was assumed to be an active patron of the arts. There was the beginning of a feeling that our writers should confine their attention to native themes. Tyler and Dunlap in dramatic prologues prided themselves on having done so, and the profiles of the plays were American, though the whole bone and sinew of them was English. Longfellow thought that the matter of indigenous material could be overstressed: "It is not necessary that the war whoop should ring in every line and every page be rife with scalps, tomahawks, and wampum. Shade of Tecumseh, forbid!" Beneath the entire half century was the assumption—sometimes tacit, sometimes expressed, but never gainsaid—that the best to be hoped for was the approximation of English models. American poets should

> bid their lays with lofty Milton vie,
> Or wake from moral themes the moral song,
> And shine with Pope, with Thompson, and with Young.
> This land her Swift and Addison shall view,
> The former honors equalled by the new;
> Here shall some Shakespeare charm the rising age,

And hold in magic chains the listening stage,
A second Watts shall strike the heavenly lyre,
And other muses other bards inspire.

The harvest of such hopes was a crop of Anglo-Americans:
Brown, the American Godwin, a Bryant for a Wordsworth,
a Cooper for a Scott, an Irving for an Addison-Goldsmith;
a generation of Byronic imitators, a transcendental school
building on what Wordsworth and Coleridge and Carlyle
had derived and transmitted from the Germans; and a
sentimental school which wrote, as Beers has so cogently
stated, of

> a needlework world, a world in which there was always
> moonlight on the lake and twilight in the vale; where
> drooped the willow and bloomed the eglantine, and jessa-
> mine embowered the cot of the village maid; where the
> lark warbled in the heaven and the nightingale chanted
> in the grove 'neath the mouldering, ivy-mantled tower
> . . . a world in which there were fairy isles, enchanted
> grottos, peris, gondolas, and gazelles.

In short, the gemmy and albuminous world of the Albums
and Gems and Gifts and Tokens and Offerings.

In the natural course of events literary criticism followed
creative writing even of this diluted sort, and with it the
expression of judgment applied to literature as a whole as
in *Representative Men;* and the censorship of American
Literature, as in *The Literati*. It was for Emerson to
protest at listening abjectly "to the courtly muses of Europe,"
and it was for Poe to mock at the domestic puffery which
betrayed "the pride of a too speedily assumed literary freedom." In this contrast lies much of what has followed in
the later generations. For though the two men spoke within
sound of each other, each was speaking very pertinently to

his own audience: Emerson to rouse the timid scholastic group to some degree of initiative and self-reliance, and Poe to persuade the bumptious pot boiling paragrapher and the public who would read him not to like stupid books simply because their stupidities were American. Between the two Lowell held the mean and packed into the *Fable for Critics* more memorable judgments on his contemporaries than any other American has ever done in equal space.

In the English writing and English reading world the tendency to "wake from moral themes the moral song" was never stronger than in these mid-century decades. In this country Poe was almost alone in apostasy. Emerson mourned that "Shakespeare led an obscure and profane life," and that Goethe was "incapable of self-surrender to the moral sentiment." Hawthorne declared that it was a mistake "relentlessly to impale a story with its moral," yet usually stuck his pin visibly through the butterfly. Melville escaped, though a little shamefacedly, on "Typee," it seems to me, and had his fling at the contemporary reviewers in what he made them say of Pierre's writings: "This writer is unquestionably a highly respectable youth"; "He is blameless in morals and harmless throughout." Thus the current of indorsement ran, finding its most substantial critical and creative expositor in Howells, who wanted to be a realist, though of the sort who would not cause the blush of shame to rise upon the maiden's cheek and who felt the presence of Mark Twain's ribald letters in his desk, as if they were a sort of ethical nitroglycerin.

Whitman's reactions to both these doctrines were perfect expressions of the democratic movement which was fulfilled in himself and Lincoln and Grant. He was out of sympathy with the old niceties and the old taboos which accompanied them. He felt no more interest in Poe's æsthetic thesis than

he felt for the actual rimes of the "jingle man." Poe's
verses to him were "poems distilled from foreign poems";
his tales had no relevance to the "divine average." He
welcomed—and capitalized—Emerson's indorsement of his
self-reliance, but bettered the instructions of his elder by
ignoring his cautions against violations of "good morals."
He was repudiated in his country because he smelled of the
barnyard rather than of the conservatory, and he was welcomed in England, as Mark Twain and Joaquin Miller were,
because the Old World was more attracted by indigenous
American growths than by provincial potted plants. In
cultural taste America was still timid and in ethical taste
still largely dominated by Cotton Mather and Jonathan
Edwards.

However, since the '90s, as every one knows, a thousand
causes have conspired to change all that, in an overturn of
critical judgment, of which we are even now feeling the full
force. As recently as 1902 Bliss Perry, in his *Study of Prose
Fiction*, declared that the American novel was free from
equivocal morality, that "people who want the sex novel and
want it prepared with any literary skill have to import it
from across the water," and that "though American fiction
may not be national and may not be great, it will have at
least the negative virtue of being clean." Then he went
on at once to prove how far he was from having the prophetic
habit of mind by showing that he failed utterly to see any
connection between this negative virtue and the interesting—
or he might have thought ominous—sign that wherever
American novelists were gathering together the talk was
certain to center about men like Tourgenieff and Tolstoi,
Flaubert and Daudet, Björnson and d'Annunzio. Yet
within a dozen years, and inevitably, the influence of the
Continentals had become so urgent that in one of their

annual meetings the National Institute of Arts and Letters, moved by the conservative element, went on record in protest against the morbid tendencies of contemporary American dramatists and novelists.

So here we are; and it is a normal, but none the less half amusing, aspect of the situation that the current anti-Puritan criticism of to-day insists on expressing itself not merely in terms of emancipation but in shrill and hysterical cries of defiance of the old régime. On the moralistic side I have nothing to say now, for the issue is clearly defined and the old ethical standards, for better or for worse, are in the hands of the Babbitts and the Mores, the Shoreys and the Shermans. But there is another side of Puritanism which is quite as momentous and on which the issue seems as yet to be quite undefined—and that is in the matter of romantic optimism.

I know of no two other words that have been so abused in recent years as Puritanism and optimism. In their fates they are the choicest illustrations of one of the most popular of modern indoor sports—that of distorting the meaning of an old and tried term and then of applying it in abusive ways to people one despises or distrusts. So Puritanism has come to connote the incarnation of a sort of universal Eighteenth Amendment and optimism a pusillanimous refusal to face the facts of life. The cry is raised against Praise-God Barebones and Pollyanna, and the would-be Delphic manger-snappers whom E. A. Robinson has so nicely characterized take it out with equal zest on sadness and gladness, on Hebraism and Hellenism. If one is to be in the latest intellectual mode he must arrogate to himself a "healthy pessimism."

As one who regards himself neither as a pessimist nor altogether as a nincompoop, I have been successively abashed, ruffled, and bewildered by the cheerful chorus of despair until a little reading and a little meditation have convinced me that the singers swelling the chorus don't know the meaning of the words of the oratorio—as though the reiterated "All we-e-e like sheep" were a hymn in praise of mutton. As I understand them—and I find almost no exceptions and none that need be taken seriously—the "healthy pessimist" is not a pessimist at all—for optimism and its antonym have to do with ultimate ends rather than with immediate conditions—but simply the type of Diogenes who thinks that he is willing to see what his lantern reveals, although he much prefers to see the things that hide in darkness and that are revealed only by artificial light.

With a good deal of stage business he glances about him and discovers what he regards as the hitherto unnoticed fact that all is not right with the world. He fails to realize that in the first two-thirds of recorded history the main social achievement, after the creation of a king and the installation of a priest, was the formulation of a myth to account for human unhappiness—as by the legends of Prometheus or of Adam and Eve—and that it was an intense conviction that all was not right with the world that made the Puritan the manner of man he was. The sudden shock of discovery that the times are out of joint fills him with disgust for childhood, laughter and sunlight, and with contempt for the cheap optimism of the mistaken souls in this vale of tears who have not left all hope behind. Dullness and stupidity become his particular aversions. He is irritated by the vast majority of unthinking people who perhaps ought to be bored to the verge of suicide by the utter tameness of their lots, but who as a matter of fact are having a very good time with life, partly because their glands are in stable equilibrium and partly because they don't know enough to be unhappy.

After all, the apostles of gloom are only part of a generation who have been like a devout and comfortable crowd assembled in a cathedral square suddenly and shockingly converted into a frightened mob and dispersed into every blind alley within easy running distance. In the meanwhile the dust of dogma has been so stirred by breezes and winds and gales, and tornadoes of fact that it is almost impossible to keep one's eyes open and see the truth. For the facts at the moment sometimes obscure it and sometimes belie it. So it is that the men who can achieve the paradox of seeing most clearly by looking within open themselves to the indictment of being blinkers, blind fools, impracticable idealists, irresponsible optimists—the vocabulary of invective is too familiar to repeat. But in the midst of the confusion one can hear the outcries of the healthy pessimists who have kept their eyes open only to get them filled with dust and who mistake their tears of irritation for spontaneous grief.

This is the most strident note in American literary criticism to-day, the latest chapter in the unfolding story of American literary self-consciousness. The insistence against both Hebraism and Hellenism—a simultaneous fight on grimness and Sunny Jimness—is an antidote against the moralism and the sentimentalism of the recent past; and the somberly realistic approach to the life of to-day is a lusty challenge to a muddled democracy in the midst of a muddled world. A lost urchin on a city street no doubt regards himself as a lost soul for the moment; but, happily, in fact, he is only a bewildered and panic-stricken pseudo-pessimist.

PREFACE

America is, in a sense, a nation of paradoxes; a strange combination of radical idealism and practical materialism; of lofty preaching and thrifty practice. We like to dream that we are making the world safe for democracy, while we are, in many ways, actually making it safe for stupidity and tight-fisted business practices. Between our high theory and our low life there seems no middle ground; no round in the ladder upon which we may rest our feet.

Mr. Brooks, in a sweeping survey of our past history, gives us, in the present essay, an insight into the causes which have produced this hiatus. He details the effects on our literature, and suggests a relief through changed emphasis upon personality.

Mr. Brooks was born in Plainfield, New Jersey, in 1886. He is a graduate of Harvard. He was a member of the faculty of Leland Stanford University from 1911 to 1913. Since this time he has been with the Century Company. Among his interesting books are *The Wine of the Puritans; America's Coming-of-Age;* and *Letters and Leadership*. "Highbrow and Lowbrow" appeared first in *The Forum* for April, 1915.

HIGHBROW AND LOWBROW [1]

By Van Wyck Brooks

I

At the time when he was trying to release humanity from the cross of gold on which, as he said, it was crucified, the Apostle of Free Silver announced that the opinion of all the professors in the United States would not affect his opinions in the least. Now that, plainly, was a very odd state of affairs. On the one hand we had a body of supposed experts in economic theory, on the other a man whose profession it was to change and reform economic practice—the one knowing, the other doing; and we found that not only was there apparently no compatibility between them, but that an openly avowed and cynical contempt of theory on the part of practice was a principal element in the popularity of a popular hero. But was Mr. Bryan to blame for it? To know anything of the sort of economic theory which is taught in American universities—in many cases compulsorily taught—is to confess that blame is not the right word. For this economic theory is at the least equally cynical. It revolves round and round in its treetop dream of the economic man; and no matter how much the wind blows political economy never comes down. Incompatibility, mutual contempt between theory and practice, is in the very nature of things.

One might extend the illustration to literature, merely substituting one professor for another and putting any typical best-selling novelist in the place of Mr. Bryan. It is a peculiar

[1] Copyrighted. Reprinted by permission from *The Forum*.

twist in the academic mind to suppose that a writer belongs to literature only when he is dead; living he is, vaguely, something else; and a habitual remoteness from the creative mood had made American professors quite peculiarly academic. "Literature," as distinguished from excellent writing, is a thing specially associated in the American universities with Westminster Abbey and the dead generally; it is a thing felt to have been done, and while for all one knows it may continue to be done, the quality in it which makes it literature only comes out, like the quality in wines, with age. Now I suppose that most of the American novelists in our day are university men; they have learned to regard literature as an august compound of Browning, Ben Jonson, and Hesiod; and consequently when they themselves begin to write it is in a spirit of real humility that they set themselves to the composition of richly-rewarded trash. I am sure of this: it is modesty that lies behind the best-seller, an extreme reluctance to set oneself up as a competitor with Ben Jonson. And there is an aspect in which the spectacle of writers regarding themselves as humble tradesfolk has a certain charm. But the conception of literature as something, so to speak, high and dry, gives to the craft of authorship in America a latitude like that of morality in Catholic countries: so long as the heavenly virtues are upheld, mundane virtues may shift as they will. In a word, writers are relieved of responsibility, and while their ethical conscience remains quite sound they absolve themselves from any artistic conscience whatever. And the worst of it is that precisely these writers of immitigable trash are often the bright, vigorous, intuitive souls who could make literature out of American life. Has it ever been considered how great a knowledge of men, what psychological gifts of the first order their incomparable achievement of popularity implies?

These two attitudes of mind have been phrased once for all in our vernacular as Highbrow and Lowbrow. I have proposed these terms to a Russian, an Englishman, and a German, asking each in turn whether in his country there was anything to correspond with the conceptions implied in them. In each case they have been returned to me as quite American, authentically our very own, and, I should add, highly suggestive.

What side of American life is not touched by this antithesis? What explanation of American life is more central or more illuminating? In everything one finds this frank acceptance of twin values which are not expected to have anything in common: on the one hand a quite unclouded, quite unhypocritical assumption of transcendent theory ("high ideals"); on the other a simultaneous acceptance of catchpenny realities. Between university ethics and business ethics, between American culture and American humor, between Good Government and Tammany, between academic pedantry and pavement slang, there is no community, no genial middle ground. The very accent of the words Highbrow and Lowbrow implies an instinctive perception that this is a very unsatisfactory state of affairs. For both are used in a derogatory sense. The Highbrow is the superior person whose virtue is admitted but felt to be an inept, unpalatable virtue which is no object for emulation; while the Lowbrow is our equivalent for the good fellow one readily cottons to, but with a certain scorn for him and all his works. And what is true of them as personal types is true of what they stand for. They are equally undesirable, they are incompatible, but they are complementary; and they divide American life between them.

II

They always have divided American life between them. And to understand them one has to go back to the very beginning of things, for without doubt the Puritan Theocracy is the all-influential fact in the history of the American mind. It was the Puritan conception of the Deity as a kind of absentee landlord, not alone all-determining, but precisely responsible for the practical affairs of the race, constituting, in fact, the State itself, which precluded in advance any central bond, any responsibility, any common feeling in American affairs and which justified the unlimited centrifugal expediency which has always marked American life. And the same instinct that made against centrality in government made against centrality in thought, against common standards of any kind. The imminent eternal issues the Puritan felt so keenly, the equally imminent practical issues they experienced so monotonously threw almost no light on one another; there was no middle ground between to mitigate, combine, or harmonize them. So that from the beginning we find two main currents in the American mind running side by side but rarely mingling —a current of overtones and a current of undertones—and both equally unsocial: on the one hand the current of Transcendentalism, originating in the piety of the Puritans, becoming a philosophy in Jonathan Edwards, passing through Emerson, producing the fastidious refinement and aloofness of the chief American writers, and, as the coherent ideals and beliefs of Transcendentalism gradually faded out, resulting in the final unreality of most contemporary American culture; and on the other hand the current of catchpenny opportunism, originating in the practical shifts of Puritan life, becoming a philosophy in Franklin, passing through the American humorists, and resulting in the atmosphere of contemporary business life.

Thus the literature of the seventeenth century in America is composed in equal parts, one may fairly say, of piety and advertisement; and the revered chronicles of New England

had the double effect of proving how many pilgrim souls
had been elected to salvation and of populating with hopeful
immigrants a land where heaven had proved so indulgent.
The Puritan fathers, it is true, were all of a piece—what indeed would have become of us all if in their eyes there had
been any rift between religion and real estate? They were
too busy for these subtle distinctions. And we may in a
sense be grateful that no unexpected turn of fortune enabled
them to be men of leisure, for who can figure the number of
witches they would then have felt themselves impelled to
burn? It was a kind destiny that never permitted Puritans
to be fancy-free and gave them only one day in the week in
which to expatiate in vacuo. But it was a costly kindness.

For three generations the prevailing American character
was compact in one type, the man of action who was also
the man of God. Not until the eighteenth century did the
rift appear and with it the essential distinction between Highbrow and Lowbrow. It appeared in the two philosophers
Jonathan Edwards and Benjamin Franklin, who share the
eighteenth century between them. In their amazing purity
of type and in the apparent incompatibility of their aims
they determined the American character as a racial fact,
and after them the Revolution became inevitable. Chan-
ning, Lincoln, Emerson, Whitman, Grant, Webster, Garrison, Edison, Rockefeller, Mrs. Eddy are all, in one way
or another, permutations and combinations of these two
grand progenitors of the American character.

The intellect of Jonathan Edwards was like the Matter-
horn, steep, icy, and pinnacled. At its base were green slopes
and singing valleys filled with all sorts of little tender wild-
flowers—for he was the most lovable of men; but as soon as
the ground began to rise in good earnest all this verdurous
life came to an abrupt end: not one green or living thing could

subsist in that frozen soil, on those pale heights. The kind
God himself was disturbed by this draft of cold air from
below; he closed his shutters, stirred the coals together in his
fireplace, and resolved to have nothing more to do with the
human race until warmer weather set in. It was this that
led Jonathan Edwards to believe that he was angry; but
it can be said quite literally that it was only the logic of
Edwards which made him so and that Edwards himself at
bottom (like the professors of political economy) was the
most reasonable and humane of men. He was even the most
romantic of men, as I thought once, and I well remember
that immense old musty book of his, covered with mildew,
with its desert of tiny print, which I carried out with me into
the fields and read, in the intervals of bird's-nesting, under the
hedgerows and along the borders of the wood. The sun fell
for the first time on those clammy old pages and the pallid
thoughts that lay in them, and the field sparrows all about
were twittering in a language which, to tell the truth, was no
more unintelligible to me. But the sentiment of romance,
like the fiat of the Pope, can make the darkest ways plain,
and in my mind's eye I used to see Jonathan Edwards in his
lonely parsonage among the Indians, looking out across the
snow. Yet it is certainly true that he spun those inept sub-
limities of his by subtracting from his mind every trace of
experience, every touch of human nature as it really was
among his innocent countryfolk, certainly true that he
exhibited for the first time the infinite inflexibility of the
upper levels of the American mind, just as Franklin exhibited for the first time the infinite flexibility of its lower
levels.

What indeed could Poor Richard have in common with an
Angry God? And what can Mr. Bryan have in common with
Political Economy?

III

But now, since a matter of this kind is at bottom a personal matter, let us imagine what may be the private history of one of our maligned economists or professors of literature. Let us imagine that he has grown up, as an American typically does grow up, in a sort of orgy of lofty examples, moralized poems, national anthems, and baccalaureate sermons; until he is charged with all manner of ideal purities, ideal honorabilities, ideal femininities, flagwavings and skyscrapings of every sort; until he comes to feel in himself the hovering presence of all manner of fine potentialities, remote, vaporous, and evanescent as a rainbow. All this time, it can fairly be said, he has not been taught to associate himself personally with ends even much lower than these, he has not been taught that life is a legitimate progress toward spiritual or intellectual ends at all, his instincts of acquisition, pleasure, enterprise, and desire have in no way been linked and connected with disinterested ends; he has had it very firmly embedded in his mind that the getting of a living is only a necessity incidental to some higher and more disinterested end, but that it is the prime and central end in things, and as a corollary to this he has been encouraged to assume that the world is a stamping ground for every untrained impulse in him which is private, empirical, and greedy—that, in short, society is fair prey for what he can get out of it.

Let us imagine that, having grown up in this way, he is sent to college. And here, in order to keep the case a typical one, we shall have to exercise a little discrimination in the choice of a university. It will not be Harvard, because the ideal of Harvard, as I shall point out, is not a typically American ideal; nor will it be one of the modern utilitarian universities, which have no ideal at all. It will be any one of the others, and when I say this I mean that each of the others is in one way or another a development of the old country American college: its ideal, its experience, its tradition spring out of and lead one back to that. Now among these old colleges Harvard might have been figured as an ever-developing, ever-liberalizing catholicism, of which they were all sectarian offshoots, established on a principle of progressive theological fragmentation, each one defending an orthodoxy its predecessors had outworn or violently setting up in defense of some private orthodoxy of its own. They founded themselves each on a remote dogma, or system of dogma, as their central and sufficient basis—they were grouped roughly about the professor of Moral Philosophy, and just as in a medieval university all the wheels turned, as it were, in relation to the central theological dynamo, so all their wheels turned in relation to him. In a sense, of course, this was true also of Harvard, but with a marked difference. The theologians who founded Harvard were men of action as well; in the seventeenth century a New England minister was also a politician and the education of ministers for which Harvard was mainly established implied also an education for public affairs, an education for society, so far as the word society can be used in connection with the early Puritans at all. Thus at the outset the founders of Harvard drove in the wedge of secularism; Harvard had from the beginning a sort of national basis, at least among New Englanders, and its dogmatic structure consequently reflected and shifted with and accommodated itself to the currents of national thought. Remaining in touch with society, it educated to a certain extent, relatively to an extraordinary extent, the social function of its students; and it is thus no accident that so large a proportion of the political, the literary, and the scientific life of America has sprung from it.

But in the eighteenth century the conditions under which Harvard had been established had ceased to exist. The minister was no longer a man of affairs—he was a stark theologian, and usually of a type which the majority of his parishioners had outgrown. Yale, Princeton, and practically all the other typically American colleges were founded by men of this type. Jonathan Edwards may figure for them all; the motive which led him to become the president of Princeton being precisely that his flock in Massachusetts could no longer see the anger of God eye to eye with him. Already in his time the fathers and mothers of Young America had submitted to the charms of Poor Richard's Almanac, they had themselves, for the most part, become inveterately Lowbrow; but they seem to have believed that an angry God might still be a good influence over Young America himself.

To return now from this long digression, let us imagine that the father and mother of our budding economist have exercised an equal care in the choice of a university. They would not, of course, being Good Americans themselves; yet if their case were typical, as we have been supposing, their choice of a university would naturally be typical also. Having arrived there would our future professor be confronted with an angry God, or any sort of direct theological dogma? By no means. But there would be intangible whispers and seductions, there would be a certain faint, rarefied, remote, but curiously pervasive and insistent influence—like the sound of an æolian harp or the thought of Plato in some uncouth slum; there would be memories and portraits of many an old metaphysician, white, unearthly, fragile. It would all seem very much as if, the significance of these remote dogmas having evaporated, only the remoteness, in a way, had remained.

One would be very insensitive who did not feel the quite

unbalancing charm of this quality—so different from its comparatively robust Oxford parallel—in the old New England colleges, as in Princeton, Yale, and the other universities which have developed out of them; but one would also, I think, feel something vaguely Circean in it. And in fact, given the preliminary method of bringing up which I have sketched for our typical student, what would be its effect upon him? Suddenly confronted during four years with just this remote influence of ideals, out of which the intellectual structure has evaporated and which never possessed a social structure, would he not find them too vague, too intangible, too unprepared for to be incorporated into his nature, would he not inevitably pass out of their presence into a manhood which would closely duplicate his childhood because the university had not enabled him to modify it? Would not the ideal have served him precisely as the water and the fruit served Tantalus? Would not ideals themselves have become permanently catalogued in his mind as wholly dreamlike, vaporous, impracticable things; would not the outward course of his life inevitably continue with an ever-increasing cynicism, covering a world of chagrins, thwarted impulses, bitterness and disillusion?

Indeed there is nothing so tragic and so ominous as the familiar saying that college is the happiest time of one's life. Yet I think the majority of college men think of their college life in this way. They deliberately put their Golden Age behind them—and, as things are, they know it is behind them. But consider what a comment this is on the American university itself,—a place, one can fairly say, where ideals are cherished precisely because they are ineffectual, because they are ineptly and mournfully beautiful, because they make one cynical, because they make life progressively uninteresting, because, practically and in effect, they are illusions and

frauds and infinitely charming lies. There surely is the last
and the most impenetrable stronghold of Puritanism, refined
to the last degree of intangibility, which persists in making
a world inevitably sordid, basely practical, and whose very
definition of the ideal consequently is that which has no
connection with the world!

Thus far our future economist is only a typical university
graduate, who has not yet decided to become an economist.
He has been consistently educated in twin values that are
incompatible. The theoretical atmosphere in which he has
lived is one that bears no relation to society, the practical
atmosphere in which he has lived bears no relation to ideals.
Theory has become for him permanently a world in itself,
a *ding an sich;* practice has become simply a world of dollars. Now supposing he has already felt the pull of economics, three courses are open to him: either he can give himself once for all to economics; or he can go the way of all
flesh, *i. e.*, into business; or he can hesitate between the two,
becoming an economist for the time being and eventually
going into business. If he is preponderantly intellectual
he will choose the first course and let society take care of
itself; if he is preponderantly a man of action he will take the
second course and let ideals take care of themselves; but
just so far as he is a normal man, with intellect and action
in equal parts, just so far he will be on the fence. The prob-
ability is that in this case he will become an economist for
as long as he can stand it and then burst into business and
become a first-rate millionaire as quickly as possible. The
sense of action in him will rebel against the sense of theory
and finding no basis of action, no relation to action, in his
theory will press him into a fresh life where the theoretical
side of his nature will at least be of some slight use in further-
ing private ends.

IV

My political economist is, of course, only typical. Any branch of human activity that is represented by professors at all—and which is not?—would serve as well. Human nature itself in America is divided on two irreconcilable planes, the plane of pure theory and the plane of stark business; and in the back of its mind is heaven knows what world of poetry, hidden away, too inaccessible, too intangible, too unreal in fact ever to be brought into the open, or to serve, as the poetry of life rightly should serve, in harnessing thought and action together, turning life into a disinterested adventure. Argue which way you will, from the individual to society or from society to the individual, it is the same. Just as the American attitude toward the State has been the attitude of an oratorical vague and self-sufficient patriotism which has not based itself on a concrete interest in public affairs; just as, in consequence of this, the "invisible government" of business has swept in and taken possession of the fields and become the actual government under which we live, overgrowing and supplanting the government we recognize: so also in the space of the individual. The cherishing of ideals that are simply unmapped regions to which nobody has the least intention of building roads, the baccalaureate sermons that are no just organic comment on the educational system that precedes them—just these themselves strengthen the forces from below; the invisible government of self-interest, built up carefully from the beginning by maxim and example, by the contact of everything that in the actual world passes as actual, takes possession of the field.

Twenty, even ten, years ago, it would have been universally assumed that the only hope for American society lay in somehow lifting the Lowbrow elements in it to the level of the

Highbrow elements. But that quickening realism which belongs to contemporary thought makes it plain on the one hand that the mere idealism of university ethics, the mere loftiness of what is called culture, the mere purity of so-called Good Government, left to themselves, not only produce a glassy inflexible priggishness on the upper levels which paralyzes life and turns its professors to dust; but that the lower levels have a certain humanity, flexibility, tangibility which are indispensable in any program: that Tammany has quite as much to teach Good Government as Good Government has to teach Tammany, that slang has quite as much in store for so-called culture as so-called culture has for slang—that the universities, while most emphatically not becoming more "practical," must base their disinterestedness on human, moral, social, artistic, and personal needs, impulses, and experience.

But society, cannot become humane of itself; and it is for this reason that the movements of Reform are so external and so superficial. The will to reform springs from a conviction ex post facto, and is strictly analogous to the "culture" of business men who retire at sixty and collect pictures. Nothing so exemplifies it as the spectacle of Mr. Carnegie spending three-quarters of his life providing steel for battleships and the last quarter of it trying to abolish war. He himself surely has not been conscious of any inward revolution; plainly with him as with others the will to create disorder and the will to reform it spring from the same inner condition of mind. The impetus of Reform springs from a hope that at least a sufficient number of reformers can be trained and brought into the fields to match the forces of business—the one group serving precisely so far as the other group has created disorder. The ideal of Reform, in short, is the attainment of zero.

The only serious approach to society is the personal approach; and what I have called the quickening realism of contemporary social thought is at bottom simply a restatement for the mass of commercialized men, and in relation to issues which directly concern the mass of men as a whole, of those personal instincts that have been the essence of art, religion, literature—the essence of personality itself—since the beginning of the world. It will remain of the least importance to patch up politics, to become infected with social consciousness, or to do any of the other easy popular contemporary things unless, in some way, personality can be made to release itself on a middle plane between vaporous idealism and self-interested practicality; unless, in short, self-fulfillment as an ideal can be substituted for self-assertion as an ideal. On the economic plane that implies socialism; on every other plane it implies something which a majority of Americans in our day certainly do not possess—an object in living.

v

It is perhaps just as well that Cervantes lived and died in Spain three hundred years ago; if he had been born an American of the twentieth century he might have found that George Ade had killed the possibility of satire. Yet his fable, which has its personal bearing in all men always, has in America a social bearing that is perhaps unique. Don Quixote is the eternal Highbrow under a polite name, just as Sancho Panza is the eternal Lowbrow; and if the adorable Dulcinea is not a vision of the night and a daily goal in the mind of our professors, then there is no money in Wall Street. One admits the charm of both extremes, the one so fantastically above, the other so fantastically below the level of right reason—to have any kind of relish for muddled humanity is necessarily to feel the charm in both extremes. But where is all that is real, where is personality and all its works, if it is not essentially somewhere, somehow, in some not very vague way, between?

PREFACE

In our present age, the layman is always associating Science with Realism. He believes that the Realist is taking a cross section of human life and placing it under the microscope where he can study it as accurately as he studies the leg of a frog or the circulatory system of an angleworm. It matters little what the realist presents; the layman is sure to say: "This is life as it actually is lived."

What the layman forgets is that the writer of realism always has his own theory of life. Sinclair Lewis, for example, believed that a small town is in no sense the idyllic place it has often been pictured. His *Main Street* gives its author's reactions toward small town life. True, Mr. Lewis bombards the reader with a ceaseless barrage of concrete observation; but, the Idealist would say, his eyes are blinded to all that does not fit into his own particular theory of village life.

In the following essay, Sherwood Anderson sketches briefly his own theory of realism, and then gives an example to illustrate his own method of achieving realism.

Mr. Anderson has succeeded in creating such original patterns for his prose writing and has been able to produce such a conviction of reality that the reader is fairly stunned by his strange effects. His mixture of Italian and Swedish parent stock gives him the fascination of a strange personality. His first novels were *Marching Men* and *Many Marriages*. His newest is *Dark Laughter*. The work which has brought him his widest and most sympathetic audience is *A Story-Teller's Story*. In this autobiographical volume, Mr. Anderson has made a distinct contribution to American literary criticism. "A Note on Realism" appeared first in *The Literary Review*, October 25, 1924.

A NOTE ON REALISM [1]

By Sherwood Anderson

There is something very confusing to both readers and writers about the notion of realism in fiction. As generally understood it is akin to what is called "representation" in painting. The fact is before you and you put it down, adding a high spot here and there to be sure. No man can quite make himself a camera. Even the most realistic worker pays some tribute to what is called "art." Where does representation end and art begin? The location of the line is often as confusing to practicing artists as it is to the public.

Recently a young writer came to talk with me about our mutual craft. He spoke with enthusiastic admiration of a certain book—very popular a year or two ago. "It is the very life. So closely observed. It is the sort of thing I would like to do. I would like to bring life itself within the pages of a book. If I could do that I would be happy."

I wondered. The book in question had only seemed to me good in spots and the spots had been far apart. There was too much dependence upon the notebook. The writer had seemed to me to have very little to give out of himself. What had happened, I thought, was that the writer of the book had confused the life of reality with the life of the fancy. Easy enough to get a thrill out of people with reality. A man struck by an automobile, a child falling out the window of a city office building. Such things stir the emotions. No one, however, confuses them with art.

[1] Reprinted by permission from *The Literary Review*.

This confusion of the life of the imagination with the life of reality is a trap into which most of our critics seem to me to fall about a dozen times every year. Do the trick over and over and in they tumble. "It is life," they say. "Another great artist has been discovered."

What never seems to come quite clear is the simple fact that art is art. It is not life.

The life of the imagination will always remain separated from the life of reality. It feeds upon the life of reality, but it is not that life—cannot be. Mr. John Marin painting Brooklyn Bridge, Henry Fielding writing *Tom Jones*, are not trying in the novel and the painting to give us reality. They are striving for a realization in art of something out of their own imaginative experiences, fed, to be sure, upon the life immediately about. A quite different matter from making an actual picture of what they see before them.

And here arises a confusion. For some reason—I myself have never exactly understood very clearly—the imagination must constantly feed upon reality or starve. Separate yourself too much from life and you may at moments still be a lyrical poet, but you are not an artist. Something within dries up, starves for the want of food. Upon the fact in nature the imagination must constantly feed in order that the imaginative life remain significant. The workman who lets his imagination drift off into some experience altogether disconnected with reality, the attempt of the American to depict life in Europe, the New Englander writing of cowboy life—all that sort of thing in ninety-nine cases out of a hundred ends in the work of such a man becoming at once full of holes and bad spots. The intelligent reader, tricked often enough by the technical skill displayed in hiding the holes, never in the end accepts it as good work. The imagination of the workman has become confused.

He has had to depend altogether upon tricks. The whole job is a fake.

The difficulty I fancy is that so few workmen, in the arts, will accept their own limitations. It is only when the limitation is fully accepted that it ceases to be a limitation. Such men scold at the life immediately about. "It is too dull and commonplace to make good material," they declare. Off they sail to the South Seas, to Africa, to China. What they cannot realize is their own dullness. Life is never dull except to the dull.

The writer who sets himself down to write a tale has undertaken something. He has undertaken to conduct his readers on a trip through the world of his fancy. If he is a novelist, his imaginative world is filled with people and events. If he has any sense of decency as a workman, he can no more tell lies about his imagined people, fake them, than he can sell out real people in real life. The thing is constantly done, but no man I have ever met, having done such a trick, has felt very clean about the matter afterward.

On the other hand, when the writer is rather intensely true to the people of his imaginative world, when he has set them down truly, when he does not fake, another confusion arises. Being square with your people in the imaginative world does not mean lifting them over into life, into reality. There is a very subtle distinction to be made, and upon the writer's ability to make this distinction will in the long run depend his standing as a workman.

Having lifted the reader out of the reality of daily life, it is entirely possible for the writer to do his job so well that the imaginative life becomes to the reader for the time real life. Little real touches are added. The people of the town—that never existed except in the fancy—eat food, live in houses, suffer, have moments of happiness and die. To the writer, as he works, they are very real. The imaginative world in which he is for the time living has become for him more alive than the world of reality ever can become. His very sincerity confuses. Being unversed in the matter of making the delicate distinction that the writer himself sometimes has such a hard time making, they call him a realist. The notion shocks him. "The deuce, I am nothing of the kind," he says. "But such a thing could not have happened in a Vermont town." "Why not? Have you not yet learned that anything can happen anywhere? If a thing can happen in my imaginative world it can of course happen in the flesh and blood world. Upon what do you fancy my imagination feeds?"

My own belief is that the writer with a notebook in his hand is always a bad writer, a man who distrusts his own imagination. Such a man describes actual scenes accurately; he puts down actual conversation.

But people do not converse in the book world as they do in life. Scenes of the imaginative life are not real scenes.

The life of reality is confused, disorderly, almost always without apparent purpose, whereas in the artist's imaginative life there is purpose. There is determination to give the tale, the song, the painting Form—to make it true and real to the theme, not to life. Often the better the job is done the greater the confusion.

I myself remember with what a shock I heard people say that one of my own books, *Winesburg, Ohio*, was an exact picture of Ohio village life. The book was written in a crowded tenement district of the city of Chicago. The hint for almost every character in the book was taken from my fellow lodgers in a large rooming house, many of whom had never lived in a village. The confusion arises out of the fact that others beside practicing artists have imaginations, but most people are afraid to trust their imaginations and the artist is not.

Would it not be better to have it understood that realism, in so far as the word means reality to life, is always bad art— although it may possibly be very good journalism?

Which is but another way of saying that all of the so-called great realists were not realists at all and never intended being. Madame Bovary did not exist in fact. She existed in the imaginative world of Flaubert and he managed to make her exist also in the imaginative life of his readers.

* * * * * * * * *

I have been writing a story. A man is walking in a street and suddenly turns out of the street to dodge into an alleyway. There he meets another man and a hurried whispered conversation takes place. In real life they may be but a pair of rather small bootleggers, but they are not that to me.

When I began writing, the physical aspects of one of the men, the one who walked in the street, were taken rather literally from life. He looked strikingly like a man I once knew, so much like him in fact that there was a confusion. A matter easy enough to correct.

A stroke of my pen saves me from realism. The man I knew in life had red hair; he was tall and thin.

With a few words I have changed him completely. Now he has black hair and a black mustache. He is short and has broad shoulders. And now he no longer lives in the world of reality. He is a denizen of my own imaginative world. He can now begin a life having nothing at all to do with the life of the red-haired man.

If I am to succeed in making him real in this new world he, like hundreds of other men and women who live only in my own fanciful world, must live and move within the scope of the story or novel into which I have cast him. If I do tricks with him in the imaginative world, sell him out, I become merely a romancer. If, however, I have the courage to let him really live he will perhaps show me the way to a fine story or novel.

But the story or novel will not be a picture of life. I will never have any intention of making it that.

PREFACE

The philosophy of life which an author holds is very sure to find expression in his work, whether he writes a fairy story, a romance, or a piece of realism. Realism, in one sense, is merely a method of expression. The author emphasizes a large number of physical details. His characters move in a world of the five senses. He bombards the reader with a constant barrage of sense images. This method naturally gives the reader the impression of actuality. The author's philosophy of life, his insight into human nature, however, are not necessarily a part of his method of writing, though recently the philosophy of naturalism has generally found expression in realism.

This truth finds an interesting expression in Mr. Lovett's present essay. The author reviews briefly the influences which have given direction to contemporary realism in France and in England.

Mr. Lovett is a graduate of Harvard. He taught English at Harvard for a year. Since that time, he has been a member of the faculty of the University of Chicago. He was editor of *The Dial* during 1919, and has been on the editorial staff of *The New Republic* since 1921. "A Note on English Realism" first appeared in *The New Republic* for March 21, 1923.

A NOTE ON ENGLISH REALISM [1]

By Robert Morss Lovett

Some years ago I received from a correspondent a vigorous protest against the distortion of the honorable philosophic term, realism, to describe the practice of a sect of mere novelists. I might have pointed out in reply that at least the English use of the word is in harmony with the philosophic doctrine in which the term originated. Realism as the Platonists used it meant the reality of ideal types of which the present world furnishes only an imperfect rendering. Its essence is belief in an unseen universe which gives significance to the actual world of our consciousness, the objects which we see and touch. Now the quality of English realism in fiction which distinguishes it from naturalism is precisely that it regards the actual world as possessing an ulterior significance, and a picture of life as being, not an end in itself, but a means to the appreciation of this significance. Hence we find English realism didactic, moralistic, reformatory, symbolistic, in general concerned not only with representation of the actual but with its interpretation in terms of a meaning or purpose beyond itself. Hence we understand the tendency of English realists to address themselves directly to their audience and to assume responsibility for a personal view of life. Naturalism, on the other hand, is realism disciplined by science to an agnosticism in regard to all that lies beyond the material world, and by artistic theory to the reproduction of that world as an end in itself. It implies not only a formal artistic creed, but also a precise æs-

[1] Copyrighted. Reprinted by permission from *The New Republic*.

thetic practice. It is by hypothesis disinterested, objective, impersonal as science itself. There are naturalists in England and realists in France, but in general the distinction corresponds to a difference in national genius. As Brunetière points out in *Le Naturalisme Anglais*, to the English realists art is made for man, while the French naturalists "conceive neither art nor literature as made for man; but on the contrary man as material delivered by nature to art."

In both England and France the rise of modern realism is closely connected with the emergence of the middle class, but very early the difference to which I have referred becomes discernible. The English middle class was Puritan; and to it the legitimate ends of literature were not beauty and pleasure, but truth and doctrine. Indeed, the demand of truth implied realism in the strict sense, an appeal to readers on the basis of actual fact; and hence we find early writers of fiction constantly claiming documentary authority for their material—Defoe, for instance, insisting that his stories, from Robinson Crusoe on, are records of actual experience, to be discriminated from "novels, romances, and such like stuff." This reliance on external rather than internal validation, on authority rather than art, is one of the flagrant habits of English realism. It becomes more insistent when the unusual and sensational elements of human experience are invoked in the effort to draw from reality the effects of romance. "I feign probabilities; I record improbabilities," wrote Charles Reade, who carried documentation as a method of realism farther than any other English writer. And Dickens, in his preface to *Bleak House*, solemnly adduces evidence to prove the possibility of death by spontaneous combustion, to which he had sentenced Mr. Krook.

Even more urgent than the demand for truth on the part of the English reading middle class, was the demand for edification. Here again Defoe is typical of English realism in the didactic purpose by which he sought to establish a significance behind his art. That purpose was in his case of two kinds, the successful conduct of life from the point of view of prosperity both in this world and the next, the compromise by which Puritanism perpetuated itself for two centuries in the form of evangelical faith and the nonconformist conscience. Richardson likewise had two lessons to inculcate, virtue and etiquette. With Fielding this curtain of moral purpose becomes so transparent that it is difficult to accuse him of hypocrisy. On the approach of the revolution the didactic and moralistic intention of fiction reasserted itself in overwhelming force; and the ethical justification of realism took on the aspect of political reform, which it held in the social novel of the nineteenth century.

The impression of timidity and hypocrisy which English realism makes by virtue of its reliance on external authority and ethical justification is strengthened by its acceptance of restrictions of subject matter and treatment imposed by ethics rather than art. We find Thackeray, while envying the full length license of Fielding, yielding to the Victorian prudery which limited him, in painting young men, to the bust. It is natural to compare with this complacence the robust defiance of naturalism in demanding the widest freedom in choice of material and, with the single object of conveying the actual impression, shrinking from no application of corroborative detail, whatever its mass or its quality. It is true, in the case of France there is a special reason for this boldness. There the battle of realism was waged largely against classicism, which subordinates the use of detail to the production of a total effect, the *couleur du fond*. Realists and romanticists were united in breaking this restriction in the interest of *couleur locale*, which became their common rallying cry. In the stress of conflict the inclusion of realities of the most sordid, grotesque or painful sort became an act of faith and a triumph of art, while the phrase "épater les bourgeois" denoted a form of reprisal justifiable in war. In England, on the other hand, where neither the representation of reality nor any other purely artistic conception was accepted as an end in itself, it was inevitable that the limits of realism should become a matter of morality. It is significant that the phrase "art for art's sake" to Anglo-Saxon ears has commonly a contemptuous reference to some indiscretion of the artist in regard to his subject matter.

But while English realism does not present an impressive front of consistent artistic method, it has maintained the quality of this defect in its matter-of-fact recognition of itself for what it is. It is almost jaunty in its refusal to take artistic conventions seriously. Fielding was imperturbably conscious of his actual relation to his characters and his readers. How to extricate his hero from the complications in which he had involved him was the actual problem confronting him in concluding his story to the satisfaction of the reader. Thackeray and Trollope likewise included themselves as novelists in the realism of their view of the world. They insisted on taking their novels literally, the former jesting at his characters as puppets of which he pulled the strings, the latter scouting the mysteries of a plot which could be resolved by a glance at the last page of the book. Now this trait, at first sight of small importance, is really significant of the entire spirit of English realism as opposed to naturalism. For while the latter aims by an artistic process to build up the effect of the actual world, the former seeks to give what Henry James calls an appreciation of experience in that world. While the naturalist holds himself in strict detachment from both the world which he reproduces and the audience to which he presents it, the English realist recognizes himself as a part of his scene and holds the fullest communication with his readers. Hence he can assure them directly of the authentic character of his fact, of his honorable intention in relating it, and of his regret that their prejudices oblige him to some curtailment. His own experience is the medium through which that of his characters appears. In the case of Thackeray it is inseparable from theirs; and, as Mr. Brownell remarks, his subjectivity contributes to the illusion by increasing the objectivity of his creations. George Eliot approached her task with a program which emphasizes the novel as a personal view of life. "My strongest effort is to give a faithful account of men and things as they have mirrored themselves in my mind," she says in Adam Bede. "The mirror is doubtless defective; the outlines will sometimes be disturbed, the reflection faint or confused; but I feel as much bound to tell you as precisely as I can what this reflection is, as if I were in the witness box, narrating my experience on oath." George Eliot is typical of English realists in the fullness of her communication with her reader and her effort through this communication to establish a significance behind her record of experience. Brunetière puts his finger on the human qualities which differentiate her from the French naturalists—her sympathy, her psychological understanding, the solidity of her metaphysic and the largeness of her morality—qualities so much in accord, it may be noted, with the didactic prepossessions of the critic.

In seeking truth of experience it is natural to find English realism making large use of the records of individual life. No other nation has so vast and impressive a literature of biography, and none has drawn its fiction so unreservedly from this source. The very birth of the English novel was due to the biographies of Newgate, which the predecessors

of Defoe wrote as a matter of journalism, and from which
they easily passed over into fiction. Defoe's own work offers
as its chief problem the tracing of the line between memoir and
novel, a problem rendered insoluble by the author's uncanny
skill in the assumption of a character and the presentation
of experience from that point of view. Defoe showed, in
this art of impersonation, the quality of the actor. He antic-
ipated Stevenson's criticism in regard to the limits of realistic art: "So far as literature imitates at all it imitates not
life but speech; not the facts of human destiny but the emphasis and the suppression with which the human actor tells
of them."

Defoe established the biographical novel as the great
tradition of English fiction. How dominant this form became is evident from the roll call—*Robinson Crusoe, Tom
Jones, Roderick Random, Tristram Shandy, Cabel Wil-
liams*, in the eighteenth century; *Pelham, Coningsby, David
Copperfield, Jane Eyre, Pendennis, Lavengro, Richard Feverel*,
in the nineteenth. The diffusion of the spirit and results of scientific inquiry opened to the novel of personal
experience a new field of significance. Heredity and environment consciously recognized as factors in evolution
give to the realism of *Jude the Obscure* and *The Way of All
Flesh* a definite intellectual content. Particularly is the
latter to be noted as the modern type of the realistic biographical novel, and the forerunner of a series of works as characteristic of the early twentieth century as the educational
novel was of the late eighteenth. Such novels as Maugham's
Of Human Bondage, Ervine's *Changing Winds*, Cannan's
Young Earnest, Beresford's *Jacob Stahl* trilogy, Bennett's
Clayhanger trilogy, Wells's *New Machiavelli*, Lawrence's
Sons and Lovers, follow the form and method of which
Butler's masterpiece set the model.

These novels testify to a change in the form of English realism, but not, I think, in its spirit. They show the breaking down of the limitation of realistic art by restrictions upon its material, and the sweeping away of moralistic conventions—a result to which Butler himself contributed in no small degree. To his thoroughly realistic habit of mind and inveterately challenging disposition the fetishes of evangelical religion and sexual asceticism, which George Eliot had treated so respectfully, went down the wind a little ahead of other ghosts of Mr. Bernard Shaw's laying. These recent novels testify to the direct influence of the French naturalistic school, faithfully reproduced in George Moore's early novels, *A Mummer's Wife* and *Esther Water*s. They illustrate recent technical inventions, the substitution of impressionism for enumeration, the investment of detail with esoteric value through symbolism, and especially the method of psychological analysis which in the work of D. H. Lawrence, May Sinclair and Dorothy Richardson justify Mr. Waugh's phrase in regard to "the new realism of the emotions." All these movements, some of them hostile to naturalism, are entirely congruous with the spirit and history of English realism, which now as in the past consists in truth of experience in the actual world brought to the test of significance afforded by the development of human character.

PREFACE

Matter-of-fact realism differs radically from philosophic realism. It is based on nature of the sort that may be observed by people in the ordinary walks of life. From the days of our American Civil War to the outbreak of the World War, our American readers were given much local color literature. Authors ransacked every nook and cranny of the United States in order to present fresh glimpses of out-of-the-way places and people. Many authentic documents, too, were studied in order that the facts might be presented accurately.

Mr. Van Doren, in the present essay, considers the interesting problem as to just how closely the author should follow his source material. John Burroughs, in considering the same problem, used to compare authorship to the process of the bee in making honey. The sweetened water which the bee gathered from the flower, Mr. Burroughs compared to the facts which the author gathered. The saliva and the acid which the bee added to the sweetened water to make it into honey, he compared to the genius of the writer in injecting his own personality into his work.

Mr. Van Doren was born in 1885. He taught English at the University of Illinois and at Columbia University. He served for a time as literary editor of *The Nation*, and at the present time holds the same position on the *Century Magazine*. Among his most interesting volumes of critical essays are *The Roving Critic; Many Minds;* and *Contemporary American Novelists*. "Document and Work of Art" first appeared in the *Century*, June, 1925.

DOCUMENT AND WORK OF ART [1]

The Next Step for the Younger Generation

BY CARL VAN DOREN

The new, if not the newest, movement in American literature has now been under way for something like a dozen
years. It was in 1913 that Randolph Bourne with his first
book proposed the league of youth which alone, as he saw it,
could rouse the age from its inertia and untangle the snarl
in which the Roosevelt generation had caught its own strenu-
ous, undirected feet. Edna St. Vincent Millay had already
sounded a vivid note which too few then heard. Eugene
O'Neill was within a few months to give himself entirely to
the theater. *Spoon River Anthology* and *Jurgen* and
Main Street were not discouragingly far in the exciting future. H. L. Mencken had nearly mastered the art of
his horrendous bludgeon. That dozen years has seen the
ground cleared for literature in the United States as no previous dozen years has ever cleared it. A poet is at present free
to write in whatever measure or rhythm he elects, without
fatal abuse, if not always with general comprehension. A
dramatist may count on a reasonable audience even when he
ventures into surprising experiment. A novelist need no
longer confine himself to any set of standard themes or
characters, or strum forever upon any set of traditional sympathies. A critic has the whole world of ideas before him if
he has the courage to travel through it. As always, it is more
profitable to agree than to disagree with the majority; but

[1] Copyrighted. Reprinted by permission from the *Century Magazine.*

the men of letters of the country have achieved victories for freedom which would put the men of theology and the men of politics to shame if those odd creatures were capable of any such respectable emotion. The question naturally arises: What is to be done with the freedom thus achieved?

II

Two rival treatments of the same material which have just appeared offer an occasion for specific comment. Both concern themselves with Paul Bunyan, that mythical hero of the lumber camps who burst with a shout into literature so lately that his voice still reverberates across the continent. Precisely where he came from, no one has decided. There are hints of a Scandinavian, of a Canadian origin. Maine claims him, and Michigan. Yet while the learned have hesitated, Paul has made his mark. For at least half a century his reputation has been carried from camp to camp. Where lumberjacks have been gathered together, particularly when there was some naïve stranger to overhear, the deeds of the supreme lumberman have been recounted. Exaggeration has been piled upon exaggeration without any limits except the limits of human language. All sorts of floating legends have been sucked into his tremendous wake. Around him are assembled a group of appropriate companions: an ox, a dog, a cook, a foreman, a timekeeper. Paul is connected by the saga with many regions, and lakes and mountains and cañons are called his monuments. A figure so striking and so amusing could not forever be left at the mercy of unwritten memories. Sooner or later Paul was bound to find himself the hero of a book. He has, indeed, almost simultaneously found himself the hero of two books, of two methods so different that the gulf between them illustrates the great current problem of American literature.

Esther Shephard's *Paul Bunyan* is essentially a document. Into it has gone a remarkable amount of investigation of the sources of the legend. Mrs. Shephard has, it is true, made a selection among her episodes, leaving out the technical and the obscene. Moreover, she has put all the stories into the mouth of one narrator instead of reporting them as tossed back and forth by contending wits. Her work has consequently a unity of tone and idiom which the originals do not have. But in the main she has preserved the materials of her theme about as they came from the woods. If ever there had been a single logger with a knowledge and a bent equal to this one, he might have told his stories in much this same way. It may be guessed that Mrs. Shephard, in whose book there are no signs of any special creative enterprise, did not see any other way. Though by threading the tales upon a single string she took a step beyond mere folklore, she took only one step. Having come upon a rich and racy vein, she was anxious to bring her ore speedily to light and exhibit it in all its native charm.

James Stevens in his *Paul Bunyan* has undertaken to go further. The task presented difficulties. To make a burlesque epic out of what was only a collection of folk tales, he had to choose among his materials with a high hand. Epics, whether heroic or burlesque, require that certain elements of their themes be enlarged to some central significance and the rest subordinated, if not neglected altogether. Moreover, selection is not all. What remains after this physical process is complete must then be passed through a chemical process, must be fused and colored into a new unity in the imagination of the artist if it is to become a work of art. Mr. Stevens was in the position that Marlowe was in when he determined to make a play out of the Faustus legends. The Elizabethan must have been embarrassed with the abundance of his matter, but he was presumably less embarrassed than the American, for the reason that Faustus had a continuous history, whereas Paul Bunyan is the hero of disjointed episodes. To have done as well as Marlowe, Mr. Stevens must have been a better artist. This he is not. He has gusto and energy, but he seems never to have quite made up his mind exactly what he wanted to do. His book lacks concentration and direction. It is written in several manners. Parts of it are magnificent, and parts are little more than a roaring in the forest.

Nevertheless, Mr. Stevens is on the right road, for he has deliberately deserted document for art. There is, of course, an art in dealing with documents, as Mrs. Shephard shows. They may be simplified and clarified; they may be rendered in a more suitable idiom than they have in the folk-mouth. Such an art is analogous to that with which folk songs are arranged by a skilled composer when he removes them from the rude circumstances of their origin, chooses among the variants which he has found, and translates them into the universal symbols of music. But the composition of a symphony is a different and larger matter. It calls for the enrichment of the bare theme with harmony and for the elaboration of a structure beyond the reach of any simple melody. The defects of Mr. Stevens's work are in part due to his own inability to leave his documents far enough behind. He is still confused by the multiplicity of his sources and by some sense of obligation to be faithful to them. In part, however, he has been handicapped by the absence of any recent tradition which, if it existed, might have furnished him with more artful models. Consequently he has allowed himself to be now satiric and now sentimental, to employ now mock-heroic and now burlesque, now to bring his narrative to bear upon actual conditions and now to send it off into the blue

sky of comic fancy. Having been schooled in an age of documents, he has not acquired that habit of scrupulous audacity
which might have led an artist with another schooling to take
merely his germ from the legend of Paul Bunyan and then
to create something independent, rounding it out with a
rigor which art demands, though fidelity to documents does
not.

III

The past age has been, indeed, an age of documents in
American literature. Ever since the Civil War, less obviously
since 1900, fiction has been engaged in making a kind of
survey of the native resources of the continent. By 1900
almost every corner had been ransacked. Village customs
had been dragged into the light of day. Rural speech had
been exhibited in all its local varieties of grammar and pro-
nunciation. Countless eccentric persons had been snatched
from their obscure nooks and given a little immortality.
Trades and callings were no longer mysteries to the un-
initiated, but had seen their special terms put into print,
their special devices used to add piquancy to stories of which
the plots might be conventional enough. For a novelist to
gain a hearing it was sufficient for him to find a new province
to expose; he need not always have anything notable to say
provided he had the knack of mimicry and a mild gift of
arrangement. No doubt the process was one through which
an expanding literature did well to go. It tried out its talents
in many directions, in preparation for greater undertakings.
The public, too, was being instructed, was learning that the
raw materials of native life were capable of being assimilated
to art. In time it came about that no reader was likely to be
startled at finding that any familiar thing had been somehow
dignified by making its appearance on a published page.

Still, the period was at best but preliminary to a period which would no longer have the duty of surveying the ground. When the materials had been collected, they were ready to be used. The use must follow, if the collection was not to have been chiefly dilettantism.

The twentieth century has proceeded so far on the road from document to art that the busy pursuit of local color has begun to seem an antique fashion. Edith Wharton in *Ethan Frome* and Willa Cather in *My Antonia*, to name no further instances of their type, have, without any sacrifice of accuracy, elevated their themes to a point where they are significant in their own right and not solely interesting as transcripts of plights or characters hitherto unencountered in fiction. Robert Frost has distilled into his few volumes of verse, with their curt dramas and honest lyrics, virtually all about New England that had come to light during a generation, and in addition has lent it, by his art, such wings that it does not have to be read with too insistent a consciousness of its special locality. Edwin Arlington Robinson, so much detached, indeed, from any particular soil that his scene is sometimes misty, has told stories which almost never call for the explanation that they are documents upon this or that prevailing circumstance in contemporary life. James Branch Cabell has left the world of outward appearances so far behind him that he seems at first glance to have strayed into a region of pure fantasy, though at second glance he will be seen to have crept back, as if after a strategic voyage around the globe, to strike at many general truths which lie beneath the outward appearances with which he does not burden his pen.

Strictly speaking, of course, the qualities by virtue of which a book may be judged a document and the qualities by virtue of which it may be judged a work of art are not altogether separable. Sinclair Lewis is a case in point. His reputation is based upon his documentary value. The little details of village existence, the little details of bourgeois careers, the little details of semiscientific professions—these he has studied with minute accuracy and revealed with all the crafts of dexterous mimicry. Moreover, he is supposed to be concerned exclusively with American manners as they now flourish among the vulgar. Nor can it be questioned that he has told his stories very largely in the mood of one who seeks to confound by the citation of evidence, of documents, which would have no great importance were this purpose lacking. But by his documents alone Mr. Lewis could not have become the national figure that he is. He is an artist of remarkable audacity. Though his interest in his documents leads him to excessive length in his novels, it does not allow him ever to be submerged. His characters may be hopelessly local in their sympathies; he is not. He gathers all his material together in a vigorous hand, beats it out according to a pattern which is his own, colors it with his temperament and salts it with his comedy, sets it moving with the racing vigor which is his greatest narrative gift. In time it must be perceived that he has done a great deal more than his documents prompted.

Further examples to the same effect might be brought forward, yet the fact would still remain that much of the best imaginative work in the United States since 1900 has consisted in the substitution of one sort of documents for another. The newer documents are bolder. They have ventured into pathless regions with a candor not hitherto displayed on this side of the Atlantic. They have made it plain that the national complacency is less secure than it was during the egregious generation which followed the Civil War. Sherwood Anderson, in particular, has drawn a whole gallery of men and women who wander eternally in a brooding suspicion that the life around them, which seems so alert, compact, clear-cut, positive, useful, and satisfying, may in reality be only a mirage. Without doubt to have done this is to have done a salutary thing, with the consequence that the edifice of national literature has a wider foundation than it had, and so has a chance to rise higher than it could formerly hope to rise. Mr. Anderson, however, is avowedly among those who inquire whether he and his fellows can be regarded as more than a second or third rank of pioneers. They have produced, he admits, many good and many clever books. Where are their masterpieces? They have produced increasingly valuable documents. Where are their works of art?

IV

His inquiries lead to the suggestion that documents bear to works of art about the relation that journalism bears to literature. The difference is not, as is sometimes held, merely a difference in finish. It lies, rather, in the processes of creation. If journalism goes in at one ear of the reader and out the other, so does it pass through the writer at the same casual speed. Trained to deal promptly with almost any subject, the journalist seizes upon some new matter, all in the day's or the week's or the month's work, turns it rapidly over in his mind, gives it such shape as he can upon such brief notice, and utters it. Supposing he is a Swift or a Voltaire or a Shaw, he may have such gifts of clarity and force that he makes literature out of those qualities alone. But ordinarily he imparts to his material no element of interest except that which lies in the material itself, and that interest is ordinarily a passing affair. Literature is produced not by transit through an orderly mind, but by secretion in an original one. Some story, some situation, some character, some mood, finds lodgment in a creative writer. It grows there, as a child in its mother. The process is obscure. Though the seed will not grow unless it has a certain vitality of its own, still it draws its substance from the peculiar constitution of the parent, and when eventually it is born, it reveals traits which it may almost be said to have inherited. The raw material has not only been neatly shaped; it has been thoroughly remade. The final product is all that counts.

Signs here and there point to a disposition among various members of the newer school to get away from raw documents. Some of them are flirting with history, some of them with a more or less bodiless pure beauty. But to this method of escape the current temper does not seem well suited. It has given itself so long to the study of documents that, when it is too far removed from them, it misses the edge and sting of reality. Another and another generation may have to pass before the symbols of romance can be generally accepted as the language of truth. Meanwhile, there is the immediate problem. Miss Cather has pointed out, and has employed, one solution, which is that of writing shorter books, and thus of avoiding the burden of detail which often overweights the artist. This is perhaps the best of all the practical devices which have been proposed. By shortening his grip, the artist can get a firmer hold. But brevity alone is not enough. It only simplifies the task by discarding documents which might otherwise prove unwieldy. What is needed is a strengthened sense that even a valuable document upon the times is not worth greatly more than a news item. Too few writers have latterly understood this. In their zeal to mirror a provoking age, they have got into the habit of thinking that a document is an end in itself. It may be that when it is frankly a document, but it should not pretend also to be a work of art. For a work of art, however grounded in documents, may properly be expected to convey its meaning or reveal its beauty to persons who do not know anything about the matters therein documented. The principal weakness of recent American literature, brilliant as it is, comes from the fact that so large a part of it is hardly more than journalism, or, at best, than autobiography beaten out into thin fiction. If that literature is to continue its development, it must cease to be contented with any modest aims whatever. It must set out to produce work which by its form and content and independence can stand alone.

It is true enough that masterpieces are not made by the sole act of taking thought, nor does one writer learn much about his own masterpiece from looking at another's. Nevertheless, changes in literary fashion are brought about by the surrender of certain prevailing ideas among writers and the acquisition of others. The present would be an excellent time to surrender the idea that the business of the new American literature is to document the new age. The age has been documented. The duty, if there was one, has been discharged. Its place has been taken by an opportunity, for any who want to grasp it, to combine materials in fresh ways, to shape them into fresh forms, to touch them with fresh colors, to lighten them with fresh moods. These may or may not call for novelties of technic, as the instinct of the particular artist may direct; but they will call for a decrease in reverence for raw material. That reverence has been a superstition. It can be overcome only when the artist learns to trust himself. If he gives sufficient thought to the matter, he will realize that his raw materials have, so far as he as artist is concerned, no rights which he is bound to respect except the right still to mean something or to be beautiful when he is done with them. He cannot even know that his materials have any existence except as he perceives them. Such being the circumstances, he is free to work his creative will upon them.   For the most part, he will want, being himself a human being, to leave them as nearly as possible in their customary human semblance; but he will not prove much of an artist unless he has the power and the courage to move among them with a hand occasionally higher than is quite human.

PREFACE

Traditional forms in American literature were firmly established by Edgar Allan Poe. In his *Philosophy of Composition*, he taught clearly how form can be made to contribute to unity of tone and to emphasis. He also illustrated his theories of form with such uncanny precision in his poems and in his short stories that his readers could not help being strongly impressed.

Foreign critics have often been mystified by the fact that our American writers have shown such perfect form in their writing, when, in their social and business life, they have proved themselves so fundamentally unconventional. Part of Whitman's early foreign vogue was due to his lack of traditional form. His "barbaric yawp" sounded exactly as foreigners thought American Literature should sound.

Since Whitman's day, many American critics have advocated the breaking away from traditional forms. The present essay by Mr. Edman discusses the relation between patterns in life and patterns in writing.

Mr. Edman is a Professor of Philosophy at Columbia University. He came into prominence very recently through his series of Richard Kane articles in the *Century*. These articles, in revised form, are being published in book form. "Patterns for the Free" first appeared in *The Bookman*, September, 1925.

PATTERNS FOR THE FREE [1]

BY IRWIN EDMAN

"A poet," says Thomas Love Peacock, "is a semi-civilized barbarian in a civilized age. The march of his intellect is like that of a crab, backwards." But even men of letters, so often the facile *ignoranti* of their generation, cannot remain long or altogether insensitive to the transformations in thought and in daily life which are making the contours of a new age. Poets breathe the common air; they cannot escape the poison of new ideas, though they may never have heard the name of the most deadly current bacillus. It was to be expected that the work of Darwin and Lyell should eventually find related imaginative utterance in a Hardy or an Anatole France. The laboratory finds its public voices among writers who have never seen a test tube. The new psychology affects novelists who could not identify an intelligence quotient or measure a reaction time.

In the same way it is inevitable that the rumble of industry should have reached even the Ivory Tower. The tumult of cities and the nervous anarchy of a jazz age must necessarily find appropriate voices and adequate patterns. Poets may yearn to move among eternities but the stream of their consciousness is colored with all the deposits of that life which most of them daily live in a mechanized, standardized and urbanized civilization.

The revolts against tradition in literature have too often been explained away as the mere exhibitionism of literary eccentrics or of writers perversely weary of beautiful classic

[1] Reprinted by permission from *The Bookman*.

205

molds. The desire for change is far more plausibly explained by the rise of mechanical science, the spread of industry and the sophistication of psychology than by any merely personal foible of an abstract littérateur.

The revolt against traditional patterns in literature has been parallel with the revolt against traditional patterns in thought and life. In comparison with the revolution of our ideas concerning God and sex (the most cosmic and the most personal of human experiences), a modification of merely literary conventions may seem altogether trivial. What is a change in a cadence compared with a change in a creed? Mechanical inventions have changed the range and the intimate detail of the lives of most denizens of the planet. A verbal device of a novelist may hope at most to touch the imaginations of thousands; a chemist deals with poison gases that may kill or synthetic foods that may nourish millions. Why, one may well ask, should changes in the patterns of literature merit the attention of those interested in the larger and more serious patterns of our lives? Why should rhetoric become more important than existence?

If changes in literary forms were simply verbal and rhetorical, they would indeed be unimportant. But the revolts in the last fifty years have been expressions of those deeper and more pervasive changes which literature is gradually learning to express. There has been, in the first place, a reaction against the genteel tradition in literature. Writers have wearied of the routine prettiness of a "literary" poetry. They have sickened of the stereotype beauties of a tepid, abstract and elegant world. Time and again in the history of literature the same phenomena have occurred. Writers who have wished to be something more than flutists in words have wanted to give expression to all the possible areas of human thought and emotion. It is precisely this concern with those larger tracts of experience that makes Shakespeare seem to most readers so immeasurably more massive than Racine's tutored rhetoric of his so beautiful, so restricted and so rhetorical a world. Now the moderns, too, wish the scope of literature to be enlarged to permit the expression of that variety of thought and that anarchy of emotion which is coming to seem so peculiarly characteristic of our age. Poets have occasionally sought new forms and devices for their own sakes, and have found in a freshness of rhythm or a strange new trick of dialogue the sheer delight of an original technical beauty. In an imperfect universe any good is a cause for gratitude; and the searchers after novel loveliness ought to be thanked rather than forgiven. But, for the most part, the novelists and poets of the last twenty-five years have been feeling for and working toward new forms for more responsible reasons. They have found the old forms inadequate to express those miscellanies of life hitherto inadmissible to the literature of the genteel tradition.

The pursuit of new forms is thus engendered as part of the interest in a newer subject matter, and a larger one. Contemporary fiction, among its more serious practitioners, is no longer content with that prescribed and gardened terrain, cultivated so exquisitely and tactfully by an Edith Wharton and with such gravity by a Henry James. Their choice and smooth human landscapes now have come to seem meaningless elegant house parties on large inclosed estates shut in by tall trim hedges from the vulgar general life. The novelists, led by Bennett in England, by Lewis in America, have been reaching out among the rich areas of dullness and poverty, of humdrum tragedy and the dull-edged comedy of the common man. They have passed from lawns in Surrey or terraces in Newport to the mean streets and mean souls of middle class life.

In the place of a poetry "warbling," as Norman Douglas

somewhere says "about buttercups," we have a Masters in America, or a Masefield or a Wilfrid Gibson in England to try to make a music out of the glare and heat and routine of our own omnipresent industrial civilization. The polite blue surfaces of social romance have been ruffled by the uprush of dark passions not hitherto recognized as decent or tolerable materials for fiction. The actual unspoken torments of sex no longer lie veiled in the urbanities of a Howells or a Henry James. The net spiritual result of the recent serious movements in fiction may be suggested by saying that fiction has been bringing into its province whole areas of human concern that the older generation would have regarded as inelegant or unliterary. Writers as different as James Joyce and Sherwood Anderson have been attempting to bring literature, as Socrates brought philosophy, from the clouds to the haunts of men.

Underlying the appearance of new forms lies thus an interest in wider materials. Literature is no longer to be regarded as the expression of a choice and pretty, but of an authentic and comprehensive cosmos. Dreiser brings the actualities of sex; Lewis brings the actualities of business; Anderson, D. H. Lawrence, James Joyce and Virginia Woolf bring the misty and turbid recesses of the spirit into the field of literary subject matter. A wider area of the social scene is uncovered, and the novelist cuts deeper into the psychological soil. The outer aspect and the inner ferment have both been more completely and more minutely studied. It has come to seem a little tepid to be interested in writing merely as a subtle working in curious and irrelevant jewels. The adult artist is beginning to recognize that to write, if one is not merely to hum, is to write about something, and that writing is ultimately rendered great by the weight and poignancy of what it says and represents. Sinclair Lewis is impressive perhaps chiefly because he renders so bitterly and unmistakably the portrait of a futile civilization; Sherwood Anderson, because he follows so sincerely the inner stream of lost and reaching souls.

The interest in the enlargement of subject matter, if it has led to the search for new forms, has been partially eclipsed in interest by these forms. There are many reasons why an artist may come to be fascinated by new forms for their own sake. One of them arises from his awareness of a wider content than the older forms have embodied. The artist may feel that the formal rhythms and the stereotyped vocabulary of the older poetry, the objective and materialistic photography of fiction are inadequate to represent those wide tracts of experience and those fine *nuances* of feeling which are the business of a responsible modern intelligence. Or the interest in new forms may be the characteristic delight of the virtuoso in experiment, the abstracted pleasure of the technician in an unprecedented handling of words.

The arguments for experiments in verse forms are by this time familiar, and the experiments by this time dull. We have ceased to hear of late of the slavery of rime and the strait-jacket of the formal meters. We have tried a little of puny imitators of Whitman's roaring freedom. But the tinkling and the controversy have left a net deposit that is all to the health of English verse. The disciples of free verse wished to remove poetry from the character of a formal ballet at a court function. They wished it to be the spontaneous song of a democratic and miscellaneous world. They have been more spontaneous than singing, and they have often widened the area of poetic materials without making that material into music. But their intention was generous and their effect salutary. Now that the heat of rebellion has died down, we know that the revolt against standard forms has

been a little silly. Milton uses a thousand forms of blank
verse in a thousand lines, and in the hands of a master, even
the jeered heroic couplet may become a singing of endless
variety; rime may become a subtle and pliable instrument
of iteration and psychological echo.

The net effect of the revolt in poetry has been to release
poets from the conventions of the poetasters and render them
free voices of whatever of passion and intelligence they are
provoked to in their life in the contemporary world. It may
be a generation yet before the atmosphere of the modern
mind becomes sufficiently pervasive to touch even poets. It
was several hundred years after naturalism started in Greece
that Lucretius appeared in Rome to translate the science of a
free spirit into music. But intelligence is becoming domestic
in modern verse. Miss Millay treats love and E. A. Robinson treats failure and success with an unremitting ironic
intelligence that is the very tincture of its time, and they sing
in forms too beautiful to date. Other poets are learning from
them that the free mind is not doomed to flee even beauty.
All forms, the sonnet included, are free, so only that they are
subdued to the articulate intention of an authentic emotion
and an honest mind. An artist will find forms to fit his moods,
and his moods may eventually be magnificent enough to
match the wide canvas of possible human settings, and the
subtilized organ of possible human passions. Only those en-
slaved to rebellion will say that free verse is the sole adequate
instrument for a free poet. It is striking that Edwin Arlington Robinson, in many ways the most emancipated in temper
and the most magnificent in reach of contemporary poets, has
found in the ancient and austere pattern of the sonnet a suitable instrument for the singing of imaginative depths and
freedom.

In the case of fiction there have been reasons far more serious than those of the virtuoso why new forms have been sought and found. James Joyce, more intelligibly and availably, Virginia Woolf, and, to some degree, May Sinclair have contrived to throw into suspicion the objective realism of Galsworthy, Bennett and Wells. Their method in fiction is indirectly—in the case of May Sinclair, fairly directly—the fruit of the new psychology and of the more recent philosophies.

From the new psychology these writers and many others have learnt the cardinal fact, known though not formulated by the common man, that people's behavior is as much determined by the things they do not think about as by the things about which they consciously do think. From philosophies new and old they have learnt that what is "really real" is what happens in, or to, a man's consciousness; that the objective world dissolves in fact and in analysis to what it is as experienced in the living stream that is a person's thought or emotion. D. H. Lawrence has tried and succeeded, despite all his turbid falterings, in making clear or at least phosphorescent what happens in the dark forest of the troubled subconscious self. James Joyce and Virginia Woolf have tried to reveal what the world is through and in the minds of those to whom it appears in broken flashes and intermingling echoes. The older method that revealed character in action and action in terms of doors and windows, tables and chairs, the meat, potatoes and furniture of our daily lives has come to seem unconvincing. It has, moreover, come to seem irrelevant to those novelists and those readers interested in the most primary of all realities, a man's soul. The new psychological method in fiction (a method, by the way, as old as Chekhov and Dostoievsky) is not a mere playful variation in form. It amounts to little short of a revolution in the fictionist's approach to life and his conception of the content of narrative literature.

The way in which, as the psychologists say, we apperceive our world is largely a matter of habit. And we are certainly habituated to the older method in fiction. Even the receptive find James Joyce as difficult as he is impressive. Our minds, as Bergson long ago suggested, are geometrized. We see life in fixities, in the routine categories of mechanism and of logic.

The sane man, it has been said, holds a lunatic in leash. And that poignant madness that lies simmering in the interior of many lives, outwardly sensible and polite, is only now being uttered in its native idiom by writers like May Sinclair, Virginia Woolf and James Joyce. That idiom of the basic hum and simmer of our lives, those glimpses of terrifying and real abysses, of haunting and ugly echoes, of thunderclaps of beauty arising suddenly in the midst of obscure reveries: these are surprising and terrible things. They fit into no usual codes and into no hitherto outspoken grammars of emotion. We are inclined to find them unintelligible or horrible or absurd. It will require many years of training to understand these new fluent languages by which novelists are trying to introduce us to the sobbing and staccato current of ourselves.

Dr. Johnson long ago pounded his walking stick testily on the pavement and thought that thus he had refused Berkeley's conviction that the world was merely our ideas and perceptions. Many critics of these newer novelists bang, too, on the pavement or on their own heads and insist that these hard things alone are realities, and that only the stiff objective language and method of the older fiction is intelligible. The newer novelists are trying to find patterns that will free us to look keenly at ourselves. These patterns in fiction are not yet found. But these writers are pointing the way toward an art that will be as lucid and succinct and intelligible as the old, and will speak more eloquently and fully to man of his own unpetrified soul.

PREFACE

The Art Imagists have propounded an interesting theory of poetry. They believe that a poem should present a hard, clear image to the eye, similar to the image presented by a painting. This theory has given rise to a considerable amount of criticism, and to no end of disagreement. Traditional critics hold that painting and poetry, art and literature, are distinct fields of expression, and hence call for distinct techniques. Literature is flexible, imaginative, more or less intentionally blurred in its imagery, while painting is hard and stiff and definite. Critics, however, who sympathize with the Spingarn-Croce point of view in believing that all forms of art are self-expression, can see no fundamental reason why art should be distinctly one sort of thing and literature another. In the present essay, Mr. Jones discusses the question in a fascinating way.

Mr. Jones is at present the Literary Editor of the *Friday Literary Review* of the Chicago *Evening Post*. "Art, Form and Expression" appeared first in *The New Republic*, November 29, 1922.

ART, FORM AND EXPRESSION [1]

By Llewellyn Jones

The quotation from the Chicago *Evening Post* with which Mr. Olive Bell begins his article is taken from a series of four editorials in the *Friday Literary Review*, which did not end, as he surmises, by saying that "literature is one thing, painting another"—which seemed rather too obvious for such an imposing place as the conclusion—but which, admitting they were different things, put forth Croce's view that they had one thing in common; they were, in so far as each was an art, methods of expressing man's intuitions. In short these articles were a very elementary and perhaps for that reason distorted restatement of the expressionist theory of art. This theory has, in common with Mr. Bell's theory of art as "significant form," enough features so that its holders will find a great deal in his book *Art* with which they will be in cordial agreement. But it seems to me that his particular notion of "significant form" as the abstract or pure forms revealed by vision when vision is free from practical motives—when, as he puts it, we see things as they are in themselves—is a mare's nest. As my original summary in the *Post* did Mr. Bell an injustice (see his parenthesis: I should have said "enables him to accept non-representative art"), I shall try to give his theory now in as much of his own language as space will permit. ꞁTo him a picture has æsthetic validity not because it portrays a beautiful object but because it portrays significant form.ꞁ Arabesque or pure ornament has validity for the same reason. The major-

[1] Copyrighted. Reprinted by permission from *The New Republic*.

ity of pictures portray natural objects or scenery simply because these are convenient approaches to pure form—the artist who tried to conjure it from the void would be trying a too difficult task. And we should not have a key to the general layout of his design. When, however, he paints a cow our æsthetic pleasure is not in the recognition of dear old Bossie, but is in the cognition of pure form, the cow's tail and horns merely serving to give us enough perspective so that we can get the lay of the land, see how the planes are arranged.

And Mr. Bell explains that we recognize pure form only by the æsthetic emotion it induces. But although he recognizes it only by a subjective emotion he is sure that it carries an objective reference: "Now to see objects as pure forms is to see them as ends in themselves. . . . What is the significance of anything as an end in itself? What is that which is left when we strip a thing of all associations. . . . What is left to provoke our emotion? What but that which the philosophers used to call 'the thing in itself' and now call 'ultimate reality'? Shall I be altogether fantastic in suggesting, what some of the profoundest thinkers have believed, that the significance of the thing in itself is the significance of reality?"

Perhaps Mr. Bell would not be fantastic in suggesting it if he did so in some more inescapable way than he has chosen. Before saying that certain forms give him such an emotional reaction that he is sure they represent ultimate reality—an idea which suggests that philosophers should be barred from university chairs if it be found that they are astigmatic or shortsighted—he should check his emotions by those of others. And it happens that other people just as sensitively endowed as Mr. Bell, perhaps, have had æsthetic emotions —pure ones, unconnected with mere literary associations

—before pictures, and with the aid of experimental psychologists they have analyzed these and have come to the conclusion that the emotion is due to the picture inducing in the gazer a certain motor set, a "feeling into" the picture. This is of course the well-known Introjection or Empathy theory of Lipps and Groos, which I shall not discuss, but merely adduce as an obvious alternative to Mr. Bell's very ambitious theory, and one which he ought to have disposed of before setting up his own.

And his theory does make him more unfair to the other arts then he is willing to admit in his present article. Here he says: "The fact is, subject and the overtones emanating from it, wit, irony, pathos, drama, criticism, didacticism even— qualities which in painting count for little or nothing—do seem to be of the essence of literature. . . . So, when a writer tries to confine himself to territory which he can cultivate in common with painting and music, when he reduces content and its overtones to a minimum, when he sets himself to create form which shall be abstractly beautiful, he invariably comes short of greatness: what is worse, he is apt to be a bore."

But in his *Art*, Mr. Bell took a different tack. There he told us that the significance of great poetry—"its intellectual and factual content"—had very little to do with its greatness. He quoted two songs from Shakespeare, "Come away . . . death," and "Hark hark, the watchdogs bark," and instead of saying that they were short of great or boring, he said that they were, in common with Shakespeare's other songs, "the purest poetry in English" and that nevertheless they were "nursery rhymes or drawing-room ditties," that the first he quoted was utterly commonplace and the second nonsense, but that, like the poetry of the second greatest poet, Milton, these songs derived their value from their formal music: "The poet expresses in verbal form an emotion but distantly related to the words set down. But it is related; it is not a purely artistic emotion. In poetry, form and its significance are not everything; the form and the content are not one."

Well, that is what comes of making "form" into an ontological bogy man. Surely no theory that makes a nonsense rime—as Mr. Bell calls it—like "Hark, hark, the watchdogs bark," the purest poetry we have, leaving King Lear to be branded, like a food going into interstate commerce, as "Artificially colored and flavored," need be taken too seriously. It is only too evident that Mr. Bell uses the word æsthetic in a restricted and semimathematical sense—except when he uses it to include appreciation of cheroots and draws a scolding from Mr. Bernard Shaw. Why should one sense, the visual, be the particular vehicle of ultimate truth, with the ear for formal rhythm perhaps as a secondary witness? That the forms in a picture or a landscape do mediate a purely æsthetic emotion, I grant, but it is also a human emotion rather than a cosmic one.

And Mr. Bell is surely wrong in saying that in literature content is more than form and different from it. Even in Leslie Stephen the form and content are one—although as he is a thinker rather than an artist I do not see why he is dragged in. But when Alice Meynell puts a landscape into words, as she does at the end of her *The Lady Poverty* who is found not among modern men,

> But in the stony fields, where clear
>   Through the thin trees the skies appear,
> In delicate, spare soil and fen,
>   And slender Landscape and austere.

the æsthetic emotion is not caused by a formal music which has no connection with life, and then hindered by the fact that the words not only sing in the void but describe a land-scape which has a connection with life—as Mr. Bell would have to say on his theory—but it is caused by the fact that a certain beautiful austere sort of landscape is not only de-scribed but presented to us—as opposed to represented—by means of a rhythm and verbal music which is itself as austere as its subject. That the content is invariably molded by the form is nicely shown by A. C. Bradley in his *Oxford Lectures on Poetry*. He quotes Byron's lines:

"Bring forth the horse! " The horse was brought.
  In truth he was a noble steed.

Now we could change the form and leave the content intact by reading "steed" to begin with, the "horse" in the last line. Try it and see what happens. Is the content the same?

Of course, poems and novels have form, in so far as they are æsthetic documents and not mere chronicles—which too may be interesting, even as Balzac is interesting to Mr. Bell, though his form may not be apparent to him. But it is not form in the sense of pattern, as the critic seemed to think who compared a novel of George Moore's to a sym-phony. And I shall devote my remaining space to giving, as opposed to Mr. Bell's theory of form, the expressionist theory of form. What I shall really do is to summarize very briefly the best statement of the matter that I have so far seen, in *Toward a Theory of Art* by Lascelles Abercrombie. Mr. Abercrombie's æsthetic is based in part on Croce, but is developed quite independently and he does not raise the issue of idealism so acutely—to say nothing of the fact that he is easier reading than Croce. He agrees with him, however, in saying that experience enjoyed for its own sake, knowledge by intuition of the particular thing, before we start to gen-eralize about that thing and try to bend it to practical uses, is æsthetic experience. But in life we never stay on the level of æsthetic experience: we break it up, pass judgment upon it, use it for practical ends. The artist is one who not only enjoys æsthetic experience but seeks to fix it, so that it may be enjoyed again. To do this he isolates it from all practical and contingent consideration. He wishes to get it pure and the fact that it can be put in pure form is what makes it so exciting or satisfying. For a pure experience is one in which every element hangs together.

Nothing in it is meaningless. We know that in the universe everything does hang together, that all things are mutually dependent: but we can seldom see the fact; there are too many contingencies. The artist's expression of the æsthetic experience—that is his use of any method, empirically proven, that will induce in us the emotions which were his reaction to that experience—is successful in so far as it puts over the experience and not any of the accidentals that accompanied it or that might be suggested by it. What we all wish, above all things, is for a universe that shall be all significance and no mere brute contingency. In artistic experience that is just what we get. And it is through form in the work of art that we get it. For as the æsthetic experience had to hang together to be taken in as one experience, so the work of art must have a formal unity that expresses that hanging together—that coherence:

For it is by form that the matter, whatever it may be, is accepted as a unity; and form is not, as we have seen, a boundary imposed on matter from without, not even a final fastening together of matter already tolerably shaped, as a tire binds the felloes of a wheel; form as the expression of ultimate unity is inherent through all the matter of a work of art, and is constantly working through every detail of expression towards its completion: artistic expression, indeed, merely has to complete itself in order to achieve its most important aspect, Form.

In the fact that in one activity the spirit of man can find a realm where there is no contingency, no sudden irruption of the alien, the out-of-the-picture, lies the significance of art. And to confine the æsthetic experience to the eye, to say that only in visual form is there æsthetic experience, and to say it, as Mr. Bell does, with an assurance that does not feel even called upon to take into account any other æsthetician from Aristotle to Croce—some of whom at least must have gone on as personal æsthetic experience as Mr. Bell himself—to say it in that manner is perhaps to exhibit that much discussed form of artistic vision, the sublime, or else it is to take the step beyond that.

PREFACE

The theory of free verse is simple. It is argued that a definite verse pattern imposes restrictions; that it is impossible to attain natural, unhampered expression in meter. The regular recurrence of accented and unaccented beats is artificial. What is needed is a verse form which allows absolute freedom as far as the expression of thought and feeling is concerned. Free verse is, then, merely the flexible form in which the pattern changes at will to accommodate the change in thought.

Those who do not favor the use of free verse believe that a poet of distinction can attain perfect freedom within the regular forms of meter and stanza. They believe, also, that free verse, in the hands of any but a first-rate poet, is void of distinction. At its best, free verse is not essentially different from the purple passages of the great literary prose writers.

For a justification of free verse, the reader should become familiar with *A Rational Explanation of Vers Libre* by John Gould Fletcher as published in the *Dial*, January 11, 1919, and also with the discussion of Amy Lowell in *Tendencies in Modern American Poetry*, Macmillan, 1917.

Theodore Maynard was born of American Missionary parents in India. While studying for the Congregational ministry in America, he preached a sermon on "Fools" that led ultimately to his resignation. Later he became a Professor of English Literature. He is the author of a number of volumes of poetry and of criticism. In 1916 he won the Malory Prize, London, for the best volume of poetry. *Our Best Poets*, Holt, 1822, is of interest to all students. "The Fallacy of Free Verse" first appeared in *The Yale Review*, January, 1922.

THE FALLACY OF FREE VERSE [1]

By Theodore Maynard

In view of the fact that Miss Harriet Monroe (who seems to be not only editor of *Poetry* but of poetry) has announced that the discussion of free verse is now closed, I feel a little diffident about forcibly reopening it. My apology is that most attacks upon free verse, like most defenses, have been unintelligent; and that mine, I venture with all due modesty to believe, will be intelligent.

The whole controversy, intelligent or not, has become so confused in its issues, so much entangled with personal ambitions and prejudices, that it is difficult as well as dangerous to make any attempt to reduce the matter to orderly arrangement. It can only be done by painfully clearing, at each step, the ground of its cumbering misconceptions.

To be fair to the *vers librists* we should not take the wild eccentricities of the notoriety-seekers among them as typical of the movement. It would, I think, be just to draw unfavorable conclusions from the prevalence of eccentricity among even the staider innovators who, like Miss Amy Lowell, have protested against the "nefarious persons who endeavor to keep themselves before the public by means of a more or less clever charlatanism." But it would not be just to hold Miss Lowell and her co-workers guilty of crimes that, in intention at least, they do not commit. This is an easy, often-used, and discreditable method for bringing free verse into contempt. I disdain to employ it.

[1] From *The Yale Review*. Republished in *Our Best Poets* by Theodore Maynard (Henry Holt and Company). Reprinted, after slight revision by Professor Maynard, with permission.

Moreover, there is much to be said for the widely diffused notion that free verse is a better mode for expressing the emotions of our age than traditional metrical forms. I think it quite probable myself: so much the worse for the age!

A paradoxical circumstance about modernism, however, is that it is never modernism: it is invariably futurism. And the central doctrine of futurism is that we are all poor fools—which also is a highly tenable proposition. For the modernist is continually making violent efforts to be revolutionary, although he carries in his breast the exasperating knowledge that he must in due course appear a reactionary to his children. He is obliged, in short, to begin as a young freak merely to end up as an old fogy.

Any philosophy behind futurism is a philosophy of negation which doubts, without daring to deny, the validity of reason and the existence of all absolutes. Truth has fallen into the hands of the pragmatists; goodness into the hands of the psychoanalysts; and beauty—well, the natural result of the age's deliquescence is free verse. The one thing certain is that nothing is certain. We have fallen into the abyss of hopeless skepticism. The very title of the most characteristic of Miss Lowell's books *Pictures of the Floating World*, is significant and appropriate.

Mr. Santayana's genius for profound criticism has noted this state of affairs and has drawn from it the correct conclusions. "The interest abroad," he says, to summarize him, "in the condition of flux, in the process of becoming rather than in what has or will result, is the unmistakable mark of the barbarian." In saying so he touches the root of modern æsthetic experimentalism.

The artist is no longer concerned with the impossible but happy task of capturing absolute beauty: he does not believe in an absolute beauty. Consequently, he is thrown back upon himself, and must use as the material of his art not reality but his personal reactions to the unsubstantial phenomena of appearances. He gives up in despair the ancient ambitions of his craft and confines himself to the narrowing circle of his own ego. It is a terrible fate; but one that has, at present, the delusive attraction of novelty. The poet is spurred on by the craving to be "original"; and as he has nothing to reflect in the distorted mirrors of his fantastic art but his reactions, he is compelled to be as idiosyncratic as possible in order to justify himself.

It is frequently asserted that free verse is lacking in form. That is an ignorant contention and one easily demolished by the exponents of modernism. The point at issue is not whether free verse has form but whether it has poetic form; whether it is a satisfactory medium for poetry. Its advocates maintain that they are able to get out of it effects of which other literary modes are incapable. They say, with a great show of reasonableness:

> Stick to your traditional forms, if they are adapted to what you are trying to do. Free verse is adapted to what *we* are trying to do. We have not only the right to use it, but—since an artist must work in his medium —no right to use anything else.

It may be so. It would be partially proved to be so if the *vers librists* were able to produce any example of pure poetry that could not have been written in any other way. But one does not feel the inevitability in even *Out of the Cradle Endlessly Rocking* as one feels it in the case of the *Ode to a Nightingale*. For free verse is always more or less of a *tour de force*. It has form, but unnatural form.

The mere technic of free verse is a feat. "H. D." achieves it within a small compass; few others do. Most of the so-called free verse poets write either dithyrambic prose, whose cadences they emphasize by a typographical device, or else meters mingled and broken in such a way as to be unrecognized as meters.

Far from traditional poetry concentrating on form, it is free verse that does so. The one mode accepts a convention (not perhaps, as a rule, realizing that it is more than a convention) and is in consequence at liberty to forget form. But not for an instant is free verse able to possess the carelessness of freedom. Its refusal of limitation binds it, of necessity, in the strictest of limits.

Indeed, in the latest developments of technic we have what is equivalent to an abandonment of the earlier free verse position. Imagism removes the discussion outside of the question of form to that of method; and "polyphonic prose" is nothing more than a synthesis of every conceivable method, ranging from bald statement to frank doggerel—a haggis pie into which innumerable ingredients are thrown at hazard.

Imagism brings together, with an indulgent catholicism, those who use meter with a brilliant exactness, those who use only cadence, and those who use both. But they are to a man sticklers for form. And in the tenets agreed upon among them and published in their first anthology, free verse is fought for merely as a principle of liberty. The sole rule that distinguishes them from other schools is that of the presentation of images. As Miss Lowell, their spokesman, puts it, throwing Aristotle overboard, "Imagism is presentation not representation."

No other of their six rules can be caviled at by the most conservative. Poets have never abandoned the principle of using always the exact and not the nearly exact word, though they have not always been successful in finding it. (Neither are the Imagists.) Poetic diction has practically disappeared as good usage. Every poet of consequence has invented some new rhythms. Most poets have felt free in the choice of subject. Concentration is no new poetic ambition. And poetry that is "clear and hard, never blurred nor indefinite," existed before the Imagist manifesto appeared.

Nevertheless, a restatement of these hoary precepts is to be welcomed. Like all precepts they are frequently forgotten in practice; and to do the Imagists justice they have made an attempt to carry out their rules with meticulous conscientiousness.

Moreover, their central idea—that of rendering particulars exactly without vague generalities—is valuable when not pushed too far. But the Imagists *have* pushed their doctrine too far. They are like that group of painters whose fad it was to paint sand with real sand; hair with real hair. Like them this group of poets is out for "presentation not representation." They will describe sand with words that are as sandy as possible; hair with words that are as hairy as possible. It is onomatopœia ceasing to be a casual trick and stiffening into a habit with the likelihood of freezing into a ritual.

One must, nevertheless, recognize that at the bottom of Imagism lies a hunger for actuality, for close contact. This, like the other fine elements in the movement, is not novel. "It is an odd jealousy," said Emerson, "but the poet finds himself not near enough to his object. The pine-tree, the river, the bank of flowers before him, does not seem to be nature. Nature is still elsewhere." The Imagists would accept the first but not the second part of the dictum. Their hands must touch the wood of chairs, the skin of flowers— and reproduce in words the sensations of their curious fingers. So far so good. But their eyes must be pressed against the

object of their love—and they will be too close to it to see it.
They forget that "Nature is still elsewhere," that beyond the
material substance is a mysterious essence—the beauty
which should be the object of their search—and the closest
scrutiny fails to yield the results that they had expected.

Along with this, as a corollary, goes a desire to strip life to
the bare bones, which now and then achieves an austere
economy of speech that is, in itself, wholly admirable. But
while the Imagists are refining down their material from all
alloy, making it ready for use, they generally do not remember that they have to go on and use it. The process is
doubtless one that is necessary to poetry. But it is a preliminary process. And the Imagists usually stop there. As
Miss Lowell herself states—

> We will scatter little words
> Upon the paper,
> Like seeds about to be planted.

Unfortunately the Imagists omit to plant them.

Wakefulness, for example, is full of the material of poetry
carefully prepared for use. The preliminary process is
complete. (As a matter of fact all the process should be put
into operation simultaneously, and the poet refine, design,
and build with the same hand at the same moment. Still,
one may be glad of an embryo for purposes of biological
data.) A poem and a good poem is ready to be made—but
where is the poem?

> Jolt of market carts;
> Steady drip of horses' hoofs on hard pavement;
> A black sky lacquered over with blueness
>
> And the lights of Battersea Bridge
> Pricking pale in the dawn.

> The beautiful hours are passing
> And still you sleep!
> Tired heart of my joy,
> Incurved upon your dreams,
> Will the day come before you have opened to me?

If anyone doubts my assertion that this is not a poem, let him read another suggested by it, Wordsworth's sonnet on Westminster Bridge. I am sure that my point will then be clear, and will be accepted by the reader.

The majority of free verse poets, however, do not follow the Imagist example in this matter. I wish they did. Much more common faults are vast prolixity and an utterly unselective dealing with life in raw slabs.

We could not take three more representative examples of the various brands of free verse than that written by Edgar Lee Masters, Carl Sandburg, and Amy Lowell, who among them cover nearly the whole field and will provide more than enough illustrations for our purpose. Their methods differ widely, as do the subject matter and the temperament of each. To classify them roughly, let us say that Masters is a free verse poet by accident; Sandburg by fate; Amy Lowell by choice; Sandburg by natural bent; Amy Lowell by cleverness; Masters by shrewdness helped out by luck.

Edgar Lee Masters, who, oddly, is one of the most famous free verse poets, once told me that he did not call himself a free verse poet at all. It is quite true that the larger part of his work is composed in formal meters. He has an ambition to be known as a poet pure and simple; and he plods along writing bad blank verse and feeble lyrics which would never attract attention were it not for the *éclat* of the *Spoon River Anthology*. Apart from the fine *Silence* (in free verse as it happens) included in *Song and Satires*, none of the other poems in this volume is worth a straw.

The *Domesday Book*, despite its glaring faults, has power.
It is in many ways a remarkable performance. But out of
its twelve thousand lines hardly twelve possess any distinction.

> An inquisition taken for the people
> Of the State of Illinois here in Le Roy,
> County aforesaid, on the 7th of August,
> Anno Domini, nineteen hundred nineteen,
> Before me, William Merival, coroner.

That passage has no more and no less reason for being written
in blank verse than the rest of a volume which may be magnificent but which is not poetry.

Even the *Spoon River Anthology* has no technical subtlety.
Mr. Masters, with rare candor, has explained that he picked
up his hint from the Greek Anthology. He does not hesitate
to go to the length of turning one of Meleager's epigrams into
verse before our eyes as an object lesson to explain his own
literary method. This is certainly a striking illustration of
what typographical arrangement will do:

The holy night and thou, O Lamp, we took as witness of
our vows; and before thee we swore, he that he would love
me always and I that I would never leave him. We swore,
and thou wert witness of our double promise. But now he
says that our vows were written on the running waters.
And thou, O Lamp, thou seest him in the arms of another.

This becomes:

> The holy night and thou,
> O Lamp,
> We took as witness of our vows;
> And before thee we swore,
> He that he would love me always
> And I that I would never leave him.

We swore,
And thou wert witness of our double promise.
But now he says that our vows were written on the running
  waters.
And thou, O Lamp,
Thou seest him in the arms of another.

Reading this Miss Harriet Monroe declares, with a toss
of her head, that Mr. Masters has more of the authentic
classic note than Tennyson, Browning, and Arnold combined!
But the indication of where we are to breathe cannot make
anything except prose out of a prose passage. This is still
truer of the *Spoon River Anthology*, for which it served as a
model but to which it did not impart its beauty. We may
grant, however, that, though Mr. Masters defaced his book
with a morbid preoccupation with satyriasis and nympho-
mania, he produced a highly interesting collection of thumb-
nail sketches and deserved his triumph.

To an English reader, and I suppose to many American
readers as well, Mr. Carl Sandburg's three volumes, on first
acquaintance, must appear to be a chaos of cacophony. The
poet is at no trouble to placate his audience. He throws
words as he might throw bricks at your head.

And yet, amid all this welter of verbiage, a beauty is to be
discerned—a beauty often smothered by ugly jargon, but
still beauty. To cite Whitman's superb phrase, one hears
"a horn sounding through the tangle of the forest and the
dying echoes."

A great deal of Sandburg's success is, I suspect, due to the
fact that he is supposed to write "American." He does, but
not nearly so often as is generally supposed. He does get,
however, a considerable amount of publicity because of a
tendency current in some quarters to connect free verse
with "hundred-per-cent Americanism"—a tendency that

can do no good either to free verse or Americanism. For metrical experiments are by no means peculiar to America. And Robert Frost and Edwin Arlington Robinson are, to say the least, as rooted in the national soil and as informed with the national spirit as Carl Sandburg. Chicago is not the world. It is not even the whole of the United States. And when Mr. Sandburg defends Chicago by bellowing: "Come and show me another city with head lifted singing so proud to be alive and coarse and strong and cunning!" I feel like saying, with cold contempt, that if Chicago is what he says it is—which I have reason to doubt—then he ought not to be proud of Chicago. He speaks with the brutal violence of the barbarian.

Now, the barbarian, I hasten to add, may possess many splendid qualities which civilized men are inclined, during periods of decay, to neglect. But to exalt the barbarian at the expense of the civilized man is cosmic treason. And Mr. Sandburg, I regret to say, is guilty of that crime. He has many finer elements in him—tenderness, humor, gayety; but to me he is the barbarian.

There are signs, nevertheless, that Mr. Sandburg is mellowing. The crudity of his adolescence is gradually wearing off; and as a consequence his verse is growing more delicate and nearer to the Imagist ideal. In *Smoke and Steel* he is under the disadvantage of being less sure of himself than he was in *Chicago Poems;* but, on the other hand, he was a little too sure of himself in the earlier book. He will acquire poise in time.

Probably the best way of illustrating Carl Sandburg is to set out his poem *Good Night*, and let it make its own vivid contrast with a poem bearing a similar title by Walter de la Mare, recently published in the anthology *The Enchanted Years*:

Many ways to spell good night.
Fireworks at a pier on the Fourth of July spell it with
    red wheels and yellow spokes.
They fizz in the air, touch the water and quit.
Rockets make a trajectory of gold and blue and then go
    out.
Railroad trains at night spell with a smokestack mush-
    rooming a white pillar.
Steamboats turn a curve in the Mississippi crying in a
    baritone that crosses lowland cottonfields to a razor-
    back hill.
It is easy to spell good night.
    Many ways to spell good night.

Now for Mr. de la Mare's poem, *Goodbye:*

The last of last words spoken is, Goodbye—
The last dismantled flower in the weed-grown hedge,
The last thin rumor of a feeble bell far ringing,
The last blind rat to spurn the mildewed rye;

A hardening darkness glasses the haunted eye,
Shines into nothing the Watchman's burnt-out candle,
Wreathes into scentless nothing the wasting incense,
The last of last words spoken is, Goodbye.

Love of its muted music breathes no sign,
Thought in her ivory tower gropes in her spinning,
Toss on in vain the whispering trees of Eden,
Last, of all last words spoken, is, Goodbye.

This is one of those few cases in which two poems can be
fairly compared. They are equal in theme, in length, and in
mood—but how unlike each other they are! Mr. Sandburg
has all the originality of detail and of manner; Mr. de la
Mare has all the originality of effect.

Good Night, though characteristic, is not the best of Sandburg's poems. There are other pieces which would supply more vivid examples of single points, and one poem (which, though I cannot quote it here, I must in justice mention), *Flash Crimson* from *Smoke and Steel*, where all of Carl Sandburg's admirable qualities are gathered together, and the ultimate word he has to say—courage.

Miss Amy Lowell is much the most completely equipped and, therefore, the most satisfactory example of a *vers librist* to be found. For Masters writes free verse without finesse, and Sandburg without any clear understanding of his own purpose. Amy Lowell possesses both: she is dexterous and doctrinaire. Moreover, though "H. D." excels all the members of her group in exquisite restraint, Amy Lowell excels "H. D." in power and the width of her sweep. And though no one could accuse of mystical humility the author of a book on American poetry written in order to justify her private poetics, Miss Lowell is at least free of the fantastic egotism of Ezra Pound and the callow pedantry of John Gould Fletcher. In addition there is no "hundred-per-cent Americanism" nonsense about her—a Lowell does not need it. She is cosmopolitan, complicated, clever, and self-conscious. All her books have prefatory explanations; and all the poems in them are obviously written to sustain a thesis.

If Miss Lowell were unable to indicate successful instances of regular verse in her later volumes, the early work of *A Dome of Many-Colored Glass* would incline the critic to conclude that she went in for revolution because she was a failure as a conservative.

When, however, *Men, Women and Ghosts* appeared, it became demonstrated beyond question that Miss Lowell is not merely an important free verse poet, but an important poet. Indeed, the finest things in the second book are cast

in a strict mold—*Patterns* and *Pickthorne Manor* being
written in odic form, the latter actually in elaborately con-
structed stanzas; and *The Cremona Violin* in the Chaucerian
style affected by Mr. Masefield.

The Cremona Violin becomes a literary curiosity by being
broken by brief interludes of *vers libre*. They are intended
to represent—perhaps I should say "present"—the notes
of a violin. If they are read critically they will look more like
the notes the poet put down, meaning but omitting to polish
in stanzas. This is a thing we come upon frequently, not
only in Miss Lowell but in the other poets of her school:
the jottings for incomplete poetry or the jottings for incomplete
prose allowed to appear before the public as finished articles.
How admirably this might have been worked into a descriptive essay:

> Leaves fall,
> Brown leaves,
> Yellow leaves streaked with brown.
> They fall,
> Flutter,
> Fall again.
> The brown leaves,
> And the streaked yellow leaves,
> Loosen on their branches
> And drift slowly downwards.
> One,
> One, two, three,
> One, two, five.
> All Venice is a falling of Autumn leaves —
> Brown,
> And yellow streaked with brown.

Almost invariably the free verse poem that is successful in
making its desired effect is very short and suggestive of a

translation. Miss Lowell, for her part, has studied to acquire the tang of *hokku*. She will be as delicate, as deliberate, and as limited as the art of Japan—but it is an art remote from us, one alien to the texture of our souls. Whether the *vers librist* translates from the Japanese, like Miss Lowell; or from the Chinese, like Mr. Pound; or from the Greek, like Mr. Aldington, he betrays a natural bent towards translation. And this, I think, is because his original work suggests a flower plucked from the grave of a dead language.

This tendency has made Miss Lowell grow more and more metallic. Whole pages in *Legends* are covered with plates of foil. All her prints might be called, as she calls some of them, *Lacquer Prints*. Her handling of lifeless substances is significant. Where Shakespeare heard the lark singing at heaven's gate, she sees that

> A golden weather-cock flashes smartly,
> His open beak "Cock-a-doodle-dooing"
> Straight at the ear of Heaven.

In the final analysis it will be discovered that what is wrong with the *vers librists* is not so much their technic as their conception of poetry. It would not matter even that they rebelled against one kind of vicious virtuosity to bring in another kind equally vicious, if their fundamental understanding of art were sound.

The Imagist itch to "present" instead of represent, and the "advanced" attitude towards the limitations of meter reveal a false view of the nature of poetry. I have already tried to show that meter is much more than a convention; that though it is not the soul of verse there can be no verse without it— for it is the body which contains the soul. And hence to speak of bad poetry (as I, in this essay, for convenience have done) is a contradiction in terms. Bad poetry is an impossibility: it is either poetry, and therefore good, or nonexistent. Poetry is nothing less than perfect speech—and how rare that is! It is unique among the arts in that it cannot be tolerated unless it attains excellence.

The poet accordingly lays upon himself the most heart-breaking of labors—and the happiest. He is on fire with desire. He is tormented with frustration. Beauty is a constant lure—and forever eludes him. Thrice blest is he who once in a lifetime is able to consummate in himself the marriage of the genius of mortal language with the divine Logos!

The *vers librists*, so far from being daring innovators, are really shirkers of the vocation. They take the safe middle course, in which they will neither fail so badly as those who aspire to the highest nor succeed so well as those who attain the highest. They renounce the hope of perfection.

And yet they have performed an exceedingly useful service to literature—one for which we should be grateful: they have carried out the dead. The vogue of the loose and the sentimental and the decorative is over. The world may learn from the *vers librists'* fantasticality, sometimes, and from their frigidity, always, salutary lessons in technic. They are the schoolmasters—should I not add "and schoolmarms"?—to bring us back to poetry.

PREFACE

Much has been written concerning the dominance of the commercial spirit in America. Emerson's "Things are in the saddle, and ride mankind," has never ceased to echo. More recently Professor Fred N. Scott has brilliantly discussed the situation in *Poetry in a Commercial Age*. In a country and in an age when values are based largely on the length of wheel base of a man's automobile rather than on any spiritual rating, it seems to many that literature is struggling in its enemy's day.

From another point of view, the commercial spirit is being used in an attempt to produce literature and also to advertise it to prospective readers. This again, instead of working to the advantage of literature, works largely to the advantage of cheap journalism. The exploiter of easy methods of writing and the blurb artist are not at all interested in the truth; they are paid to produce results in terms of dollars and cents. Mr. McFee, in the present essay, gives a spirited discussion of the whole situation.

Mr. McFee was born and educated in England, though now he is an American citizen. Formerly he was a seagoing engineer. He is the author of *Casuals of the Sea*, *Command*, and other interesting tales of the sailor's life. At present his home is at Westport, Connecticut. "The Cheer-Leader in Literature" was first read at the annual meeting of the Modern Language Association in Chicago, in December, 1925. It was first published in *Harper's Magazine*, March, 1926.

THE CHEER–LEADER IN LITERATURE [1]

BY WILLIAM McFEE

Pausing in the midst of the morning mail, when an invitation to speak at a book-fair, letters from publishers in praise of their new novels, and a note from a young lady seeking counsel in the business of authorship are to be found with more urgent communications, the transplanted Englishman finds himself reflecting once again upon the peculiar problem of the expatriate. He is aware of a special duty towards the land of his adoption. He has to cultivate a reasonably agreeable attitude towards American institutions without losing, any more than he can help, that first sharp freshness of observation which gives value to the criticisms of the newcomer and the transient.

Unfortunately such a combination of virtues is not easy, and they seem often to be mutually exclusive. The process of acclimating the mind dulls it to the essential peculiarities of the new surroundings. This may account for the failure of the philosophers of our day to comment upon one very remarkable characteristic of modern American life. I allude to the practice of training large bodies of students in schools, colleges, and by mail, in the profession of novel and story writing.

This, however, is only the visible result of a fundamental and exclusively American attitude towards the young idea in Literature. Readers of Kipling's *Stalky and Co.* will remember the schoolboy author who was good-humoredly

[1] Copyrighted. Reprinted by special permission from *Harper's Magazine*.

239

cuffed and derided by all the schoolmasters except the Head, who showed his wisdom merely by exposing the boy to good literature in his private study. Kipling was describing his own youthful experience, and we are justified in doubting whether he would have benefited by the modern courses in short-story and verse writing.

To quote Kipling's case is legitimate. It is typical of the English attitude towards literary aspirants. Not only in schools, but in the home, in factories, offices, and in ships at sea, I have encountered that harsh inclement state of mind which discouraged the weaklings, so that their ambitions died away and they became reconciled to some modest and useful function in our industrial system.

In America the opposite seems to be the rule. The general sentiment is one of eager welcome for the faintest sign, real or fancied, of the literary and artistic faculties. We have reached a point where the manufacture of authors on a quantity-production basis is in full force all over the country. It is accepted as a logical development of university work, and so it may strike many Americans as highly unreasonable to suggest that the propagation of authorship, especially of fiction, is no part of a university's responsibilities. Nevertheless, this proposition is herewith seriously advanced, and it is especially contended that the ultimate achievement of schools for fiction is the establishment of mediocrity as the controlling influence in American literature.

The general atmosphere of warm, humid and profitable benevolence towards authorship, however, is not confined to our great institutions of learning. It parades the market place, and scores of gentlemen teach novel-writing and short-story writing by mail. It permeates the home, and parents whose children have revealed the shocking precocity of a poem or essay forthwith begin to plan a literary career for the little monster, instead of giving the child a good spanking and sending it out to play.

This may be thought an uncharitable view. I have no hesitation in asserting that it strikes anyone raised in England as remarkable—this lack of a sense of proportion in dealing with the adolescent beginnings of literature. I speak from experience. I wrote from the age of eight. I am convinced that the fairly happy life I have led since, and also any success in the business of writing I have achieved, is largely due to the bracing animosity of schoolmasters, fellow-scholars, and the home circle. Success in any of the arts, I imagine, derives fundamentally from a profound and usually unconscious conviction, situated in the very center of the child's being, that there is some mystical connection between itself and writing or drawing or music. It is, to speak fancifully, a sort of burning incandescent point in the child's inmost soul, which is the promise of greatness. To imagine that family antagonism and derision will quench this conviction of the child is to ignore the almost universal lesson of biography.

This strongly expressed opinion is not an attack upon the teaching of English, or upon education, but upon the present-day infatuation for "courses" in the practice of fiction-writing. And if teachers of literature, who understand how such aids to students are straitly confined to the mere outlines of the subject, imagine the general public so regard them, I may mention an adventure of my own when I lived in New Orleans.

The lady with whom I boarded for a while had a son, a youth in his teens, and when I came home at night he was to be found in the parlor, studying from a series of severely practical-looking textbooks. He was about sixteen, and my own conjecture was that he was learning algebra and trigonometry, or possibly French and Latin. One evening I took up the open book and I was dumfounded to find that he was learning how to write short stories. Another little book was devoted to electrical engineering. Sheaves of papers, received by mail from a college in Western America, were spread over the table. He was a quiet respectable lad, and I was moved to lead him into conversation. Yes, he was going in for short-story writing. No, he didn't find it very difficult. He was "studying the structure," he said. I bashfully remarked that some years previously I had had a small book published. "Of course," said this remarkable young man, "that comes later."

Now the extraordinary thing about this boy and his little textbooks was that he possessed not the remotest conception of what he was trying to do. He had no curiosity, and the writer who has no curiosity is condemned for all eternity. Here was I, a foreigner, a stranger within his gates, sitting there telling him I had not only written a book but had got it published in London—the Mecca of the Western World in the Nineteenth Century—and he never even glanced in my direction! When I was his age, anyone who had written even a magazine article was enveloped in a golden glamour. If it be asked what that has to do with the subject, I can only say that literature is glamour and nothing else. If you cannot master the evocation of that, all your writing is no more than a sorrowful waste of time. If your music, your painting has no glamour, you were better employed in a garage or a carpenter's shop. Indeed, I would go further and say that a man can achieve that magic in the garage and joinery if he is a true craftsman. And there are many, many young men and women in this country to-day industriously fagging through courses in fiction and playwriting and short-story writing who are destined to the most tragic disillusionment in the future, and who might have had true happiness in making engines or clocks, or tables and cabinets.

II

Now this nation-wide illusion that all arts and professions can be taught by mail and works of art produced by the methods successful in commerce has engendered a correspondingly artificial state of mind in everybody connected with literature. It has brought forth a crowd of ladies and gentlemen who bear a remarkable resemblance to the white-jerseyed squad at a big football game. They are, in fact, the cheer-leaders of literature. They work upon the principle that if you only *believe* in your side and yell loud enough you can overturn the laws of God and of nature and score a goal.

This argument is sound if literature is merely a struggle between publishers, each with his team of star authors who are being trained to bear down all opposition. It is justified if literature is to be classed with motor cars and steel-billet manufacture or the stockyard industry. But if, as we are assuming here, literature is one of the fine arts, then the cheer-leaders, the bally-hoo barkers, the artful dodgers of the advertising department and the deep-breathing press agents, the producers of the spurious exfoliations of rococo English so dear to the blurb-writer's heart, are arrogating to themselves a position out of all proportion to their real significance.

Literature as a fine art is to-day in the position of a parasitic growth. It is the poor relation of the standardized trade goods which keep the presses rumbling. The publisher who finds the capital involved in producing the works of original thinkers and creative artists derives that capital from the production by hundreds of thousands of copies of what I call trade-goods. He probably derives it also from the sale of magazines which, in their turn, are supported by advertising of merchandise. The fact that a work of outstanding original beauty occasionally runs into six figures and makes money is no rebuttal of the main truth of my statement. The change in our lives during the last fifty years, the materialization of pleasure through machinery, has thrust literature as a fine art into the discard. It is in the position of a gentleman of breeding who has fallen on evil days and whose stately residence has been bought by a lusty full-blooded young barbarian who has installed a gasoline station and a delicatessen store.

I am prepared to hear vigorous protests against such a view, but an honest survey of modern life will prove the essential truth of this statement, even though it be unpalatable to idealists, that literature exists on sufferance in the midst of an immense army of mechanical devices for the production of pleasure. I can explain what I mean by this new aspect of the standing of literature by a comparison and a story.

I live in a small town and, like every other small town in America, we have a motion-picture theater. We are pretty well served in the matter of pictures; but what I call trade-goods, that is to say, goods useful for trading with the natives of these regions, predominate. In the movies such goods consist of pictures which are the descendants of the Nick Carter dime novel. It may surprise the motion-picture people, but it is a fact that the public which supports such pictures is not really seeking pictures at all, but stories. What they want is the dime novel without the fatigue of reading it. Here they get it. About forty per cent of the footage of such pictures is titles, and if you look round you can see your neighbors forming the words of those titles with their lips, if not actually reading aloud. It was a picture of this kind one evening not long ago which drew us in, and the heroic

cowboy with the three-gallon hat was having a hot time with
the bad men of those parts. The action consisted of an in-
terminable series of sudden mountings, gallopings, and shoot-
ings. The theater was well patronized by small boys who
applauded vigorously. But seated next to me was an elderly
woman who had just run out from her home to seek a little
change from her life of drudgery. She had no hat, and her
toil-worn hands were ungloved. And how she clapped! It
was almost painful to watch the desperate fascination that
foolish cheap picture had for her. When the hero leaped into
the saddle and tore away down the street her emotion became almost ungovernable. Her lips quivered. Her eyes
were full of tears. Her frame was shaken by gusts of genuine
feeling. She raised a clenched fist to her lips.

And it suddenly struck me that for such as she that shabby
little theater is a church. It gives her a window looking out
upon the golden country of romance. It offers in the one form
which she is able to comprehend an escape from the deadening effects of our much-vaunted age of mechanism.

The position of literature to-day is something like the position of religion in the mind of that poor woman. It is very
fine, no doubt, and worthy of respect, but she does not understand what it is all about. When she wants to forget her
troubles she goes, not to the church, not to the library, but
to the movies when there is a good "western." It is there
she is taken out of herself, and by ways impossible to you and
me finds some of that glamour of which I have spoken, which
justifies many despised forms of art, and which leads us back,
by a reasonable transition, to my main argument.

It is this, that the systematized exploitation of courses in
writing assumes two major fallacies: First, that there is
any real need for developing a large population of writers;
second, that the methods adopted are of any use for stimulat-

ing the creation of literature. It is to be understood, of course, that I am now expressing solely my own views. It is possible that there is not a single other person in the United States who holds these views.

As I see it, a wholesome neutrality on the part of public educational bodies would be a sound position to take with regard to the creative urge in young people. I have a suspicion that educators and their colleges have ample work before them in providing a good grounding in what used to be called the humanities. If the eager young people who want to get a story accepted by the popular magazines insist that they don't want to bother with *Beowulf* and *Piers Plowman* and Molière and De Musset, that they want to be taught "how to do it," it is proper to tell them that there is nothing in the world, from the beginnings of history down to the present day, from Aristotle to Santayana, from Genesis to a tour through a tire factory, which will not be of some sort of use to them in showing them how to do it. The chief duty of those who teach English should be to show how the poem, the story, the novel grows out of the writer's own personality. If there is anything in it at all of value, it is because virtue has gone out of him into that piece of writing. I fancy it is the same with music and painting. I fancy that it is because so many young men and women are devoting their lives to literature before they have any life in their minds to devote that we discover nothing of any value in what they write. They lack something which I have mentioned more than once in writing on this subject, something which La Farge calls "the acquired memories of the artist." No college, no university, no institution in itself can offer as part of its curricula these acquired memories. Compared with these, the study of rules and fetishes in order to make your product marketable is of microscopic importance. Every age has its market conditions, and if you go back, say thirty years, you will find men in America, who are utterly forgotten to-day, who understood those conditions and became wealthy by writing for the magazines, although they had no courses in "the structure of the short story" to aid them.

Someone may insist, at this juncture, that if literature is to lay claim to the title of a fine art, it must be taught to those seeking to practice it as are the arts of painting, sculpture, dancing, drama and music. It is an interesting contention and deserves some consideration.

As regards the plastic arts, the analogy is defective because practically the whole of the vast paraphernalia of tuition is devoted to the teaching of an unfamiliar medium. The majority of people go through life ignorant of drawing, but they nearly all have a reasonable acquaintance with the arts of reading and writing. They arrive at the age of intelligence equipped with what we may call the rough elements of literature. They read and write, in some crude fashion, every day. Their daily life is carried on in a medium of which literature is merely the art-form. Painting, sculpture, and music have no such advantage in daily life. The very tools and materials of such vocations are unfamiliar to all save their practitioners. They have, in the true meaning of the word, a technic. Painters and musicians have the same road to travel as the woodcarver, the jeweler, the etcher, and lithographer. They have a world of technical difficulties to master, and the only way to master them is by practical instruction.

The same thing applies to the art of the playwright and the scenario-writer, who is only a playwright after all. It is said that Pirandello writes his plays at a table on the stage, just as the Hollywood scenarist works out the intricate details of his script on the studio set. This art of providing the raw materials of a stage-play or a motion picture is so far

removed from both literature and life that there is no real
analogy between it and the art of the novel and short story.
These latter are presented directly to the reader and depend
for their success upon an appeal to his imagination in the
medium most familiar to him. The script of a play depends
for its success upon the actor, the manager, and the scenic
artist. It is as hot in the dark. The technical difficulties are
so numerous and so elusive that after years of distinguished
practice, combined with imagination and genius, the result
is often flat failure and heavy financial loss.

Nothing of all this applies to the art of fiction, long
or short. Our problem is something utterly different.
We have to compete not only with all the other arts, not
only with love and business and the intercourse of daily life,
but with the inevitable indifference engendered by familiarity with our medium. Four out of five bankers, lawyers,
doctors, and bond salesmen, to say nothing of newspapermen,
have the plot of a story in their systems, which they are going
to work out when they get the time. We who write are only
doing what they simply cannot find time to do. This is
bound to have an influence upon their attitude towards what
they read, even though to be an unconscious influence. It
is so easy to read! The work upon which we toil for weeks and
months, upon which we ruminate for years before we come
to the dreadful moment of beginning to write, is scanned and
scorned in a few minutes of boredom when there is nothing
else to do.

Moreover, the majority of authors are far from dependable
witnesses as to their own methods. They attribute to technical processes the glamour deriving from their own unique
and inimitable quality as literary artists. The result is that
about the only book of first-hand value on this subject is
a savage satire. If you wish to know how to write short

stories, read *How to Write Short Stories*. I commend it in place of the dreary volumes of research so exquisitely derided in Leonard Bacon's *Ph.D.s*. The lesson Mr. Lardner's remarkable book teaches is one I have not seen mentioned in the comments upon it. It is that the quality in a story, the art, the glamour is utterly unteachable, either in class or by mail.

III

My own feeling in this matter is that "research," as it is called, is scarcely applicable to the business of writing. The secret of an author eludes you if you begin to analyze. How can you analyze glamour? How can you "teach" writing short stories and novels to young people who know nothing of the world, the flesh, or the devil? Literature comes out of our lives. It is not embedded in textbooks. The impulse to write springs from within, the sense of form can be derived only from the acquired memories of endless reading. As for the rules about "structure," if I were to offer advice based on my own experience I would say that the best way to sell a story is to break every rule in every textbook ever published. Conrad, Sherwood Anderson, Katherine Mansfield, and A. E. Coppard, all of whom know something of short-story writing, go through the conventional rules like a bull through a fence. Who taught them what they know? I was once told that John Bentley, the architect of the great Byzantine cathedral in London, designed it almost on his knees. Some of our great writers give you that impression. You can perceive, wrought into their style, the years of conflict with life and its illusions. Most of them, you will find, are humble. They do not talk big about themselves and slightingly of those who have gone before. That, you will discover, is one of the prerogatives of the present-day fashionable short-story writer. He not only feels that he is superior to John Milton because that author received forty-five dollars for "Paradise Lost" while he himself gets perhaps a couple of thousand dollars for ten thousand words, but he feels his story is superior to Milton's. Perhaps it is. Perhaps we are now in the upward surge of a vast renaissance of literature. We are assured by what I call the cheer-leaders of letters that such is the case. They leap into the air before us and go through astonishing contortions of speech and gesture to evoke a burst of cheering from us for their side. Whether we are really renascent or not, we must wait a few decades to discover; but we are certainly complacent. One of the most remarkable teams of cheer-leaders we have with us to-day is composed of the new-style reviewers. I am not blaming them, because the writers of jacket-blurbs have stolen their thunder. They have been forced by penury and the increase in the amateur literary population to adopt strange antics in order to attract attention. To be quoted you must use strong language. You must do handsprings and bellow through the megaphone at the same time. In the course of a single week recently I learned from reviews that John Galsworthy is the worst short-story writer who ever lived; that most of Conrad, Stevenson, and Walter Pater is sheer bad writing; that Jack London has come back from Hell and has written a new novel under another man's name; that Molière is an overrated bore, and Congreve so insignificant that a single story by Ring Lardner overwhelms all he ever wrote. One of the above reviewers complains that reviews are ignored by the public when buying books. Is it any wonder? Not one of those statements is believed by the person who made it. They are simply frantic bids for the attention of a willing mob of people who care very little for literature anyway, who amuse themselves with radio, motoring, golf, bridge, phonographs, vaudeville, newspapers, and movies, and to whom books are furniture. Reading books are to be had from the library, while works of reference, bought during the cross-word puzzle epidemic, are now tolerated because they make a good base for the loud-speaker.

These reviewers are a symptom of what I have mentioned, that literature is now a parasitic growth, and the sooner we realize it the sooner we shall come to our senses. Making incantations over it, gnashing our teeth, clenching our fists, and leaping into the air with a blood-curdling yell is of no avail in competition with modern mechanical diversions. The *rah-rah* spirit in the literary world will inevitably react against the exploited books. People read what they will. Sooner or later they drift back to what they like. I am beginning to wonder, now that I am middle-aged and acquiring a sense of proportion, whether that particular quality which we recognize as genius has any bearing at all upon an author's acceptance. I think it is more a "divine accident," to borrow a phrase from Arnold Bennett. To take a concrete instance, the extraordinary vogue of Dickens was and is in no way dependent upon those qualities we value most in him as a master of English and an unsurpassed delineator of character. As we say, people read a book for the story.

This fact, however, is often used nowadays to pooh-pooh the existence of any quality in a book except the popular story. Popular authors point to the fact that authors whom nobody would ever accuse of genius have exceeded Dickens as a seller. They state bluntly that their own duty is to their readers who demand pep and punch and zip and zoom, and art can go hang. The inference we are asked to draw is that if they chose they could produce great art, but they don't choose to do it. They deceive themselves. They can do only what they are doing. They are the product of their century as much as are the makers of radio sets and motor cars and movies. They are very useful and estimable members of society. They are—as I have found by personal correspondence, and an industrious perusal of interviews—very anxious not to be regarded as artists. They have no need to worry. A few years, and they will have had their day and ceased to be.

I said they deceive themselves; but what is their error compared with those leaders of literary thought who embrace the deception and endeavor to win the favor of the illiterate public by enthroning the writers of tedious potboilers in the halls of light? Are they not described with disturbing veracity in Kipling's poem of "The American Spirit," who

> ". . . dubs his dreary brethren Kings"?

It is possible these cheer-leaders of mediocrity are sincere, but they have no right to the positions they hold if literature is one of the fine arts. I suspect that in the back of their minds they have a confused notion that, if three or four million people buy the books of a certain author, we are to concede him or her a prominent position in literature. At the risk of being regarded as conceited and highbrow, I assert that we have no right to do anything of the kind. Literature is not a democracy where numbers rule. It is an aristocracy where brains and originality are paramount. It is a fond foolishness on the part of many apologists for popular mediocrity, that to be sincere, to reach the great heart of the common people, is all that we know or ever need to know. That is very fine, but it has nothing to do with literature. Democracy is very fine, no doubt, but its principles are fundamentally opposed to the principles of literature and of art. It may be said indignantly, and the cheer-leaders will support it with a crescendo of yells, that if we must choose between democracy and literature we will abandon literature. I can only retort, in the vigorous jargon of the day, that that is all right with me. It is more than likely that we shall all have to make that choice sooner or later in the coming years. The doctrine that those who have the money and the numbers should dictate the nature of religion and science, has already become established in the Republic. What more probable than that the quality of a work of art should be referred to the same omniscient tribunal? In that day, "when the windows of the house shall be darkened and the mourners go about the streets," we shall have no more of the "excellent beauty that hath a strangeness in its proportion." We shall all be thoroughly grounded in the rumble-bumble of psychoanalysis; we shall all have graduated in the structure of the novel, and the short story, and we shall all have hearts pounding with sincerity and moral felicities.

Well, it may be asked, and what then? Is there any objection to literature being organized? Will not the product be better than now, with no supervision? It is quite possible. Let that pass. When that day comes I am going to read, not books, but advertisements. It is my guess that American originality will seek this escape from an intolerable régime. The change will be imperceptible, of course, but inevitable. Those who want fine art in what they read will turn the pages of the magazines and read the publicity. Already in many organs it transcends the text. They will buy books like Mr. Shaw's plays—with a small thin slice of authorship in the middle between fifty or sixty pages of clever and readable blurb. Advertising corporations will hire standardized authors to write stories to fit their new volumes of appreciations. Perhaps we shall not be so badly off after all. When the news of the day comes into every room over the radio, the newspapers will consist entirely of brilliant comments on the season's merchandise. When the scenarists of the movies adapt their titles to normal intelligences, the need of novels will vanish. The time may come when the very existence of literature as a fine art will depend on the advertisement. The contemplation of such a possibility leads one to conjecture whether literature, in the sense of being a manifestation of that incandescent point in the soul of man, in the sense of being the expression of an original personality rather than the common denominator of a many-headed mediocrity, is destined to endure throughout the ages. There was a time when it did not exist and that time may come again. "The literary art," says Havelock Ellis, "lies in the arrangement of life." It implies "the transforming of the facts of life into expressive and beautiful words." For several hundred years men have been doing that in the English language, and some of us have felt that the achievements of the masters have been worthy of our admiration. So far from believing that their success can be duplicated by everybody who takes a course in the art of writing, we have nursed a foolish undemocratic conviction that what they did was inimitable. In this matter of art, the rules governing commerce and industry are not to be invoked. It is dangerous, in art, to do as others do, says a French writer whose name I have forgotten. He meant that it ought to be dangerous. His statement implies an attitude towards art which I suggest is worthy of our attention. It implies that the evocation of works of art by means of words and phrases is not a trade to be learned by every earnest young person who can read an advertisement, but a holy mystery, demanding a special equipment of heredity and experience.

Then what is the conclusion of the whole matter? What

can we teach of English? My own impression is that we can teach very little, but we can inspire. Our first need is to be at ease among the masterpieces. Reference books and books of familiar quotations tend to be over plentiful in these days of card indexes and specialists. More than in any other calling, has the teacher of English need of a colossal general knowledge. He should be a master of allusion. He must take all knowledge for his province. And he must maintain an indomitable faith that somewhere among those unpromising young people before him there is one at least with a spark of the divine fire.

PREFACE

The game of the critic is not generally understood. The layman often thinks that critics are as judicious and as fair-minded as a Saint Peter, in their judgments of the just and the unjust. He does not rightfully understand the up-to-the-minute methods of practical journalism.

In a different way, the layman thinks that critics are decidedly influential in determining the books that shall be read and those that shall be sent direct to oblivion. Despite the present commercial methods in vogue to stimulate the interest and to intrigue the curiosity of the public, critics, themselves, are at times skeptical of their influence. Most books get into wide circulation, they believe, because those who read the book recommend it to their friends. Questions of this sort find an enjoyable discussion in Mr. Macy's present essay.

Mr. Macy gained the approval of many shrewd, penetrating readers when he published *The Spirit of American Literature* in 1913. Mr. Macy was born in Detroit in 1871. He is a graduate of Harvard University. Later he did editorial service on *The Youth's Companion*, *The Boston Herald*, and *The Nation*. He has published many interesting essays. "The Critical Game" appeared first in *The Literary Review*, January 7, 1922.

THE CRITICAL GAME[1]

By John Macy

Criticism is one form of the game of writing. It differs from other forms only as whist differs from poker and as tennis differs from golf. The motives are the same, the exercise of the player's brain and muscles and the entertainment of the spectators, from whom, if the player be successful, he derives profit, livelihood, applause, and fame. The function of criticism at the present time, and at all times, is the function of all literature, to be wise, witty, eloquent, instructive, humorous, original, graceful, beautiful, provocative, irritating, persuasive. That is, it must possess some of the many merits that can be found in any type of literature; it must in some way be good writing. There is no other sound principle to be discovered in the treatises on the art of criticism or in fine examples of the art. Whether Charles Lamb writes about Shakespeare or Christ's Hospital or ears is of relatively slight importance compared with the question whether in one essay or another Lamb is at one of his incomparable best moments of inspiration.

Remy de Gourmont says, apropos Brunetière's views of Renan:

> Contre l'opinion commune, la critique est peut-être le plus subjectif de tous les genres littéraires; c'est une confession perpétuelle; en croyant analyser les œuvres d'autrui, c'est soi-même que l'on dévoile et que l'on expose au public . . . voulant expliquer et contredire Renan, M. Brunetière s'est une fois de plus confessé publiquement.

[1] Reprinted by permission from *The Literary Review*.

That is true, except that it may be doubted whether one type of literature is more subjective than another, since all types are subjective. Even a work that belongs, according to De Quincey's definition, to the literature of information as distinguished from the literature of power, even an article in an encyclopædia, an article, say, on Patagonia, has a man behind it; it cannot be quite objective and impersonal.

Criticism should not be set off too sharply from other forms of literary expression. It has no special rights, privileges, and authority; and at the same time it has no special disabilities that consign it to a secondary place in the divisions of literature. In any unit of art, a sonnet or an epic, a short story or a novel, a little review or a history of æsthetics, a man is trying to say something. And the value of what he says must, of course, depend partly on the essential interest of his subject; but it depends to a greater extent on the skill with which he puts words together, creates interest in himself. Arnold's essay on Keats is less Keats than Arnold. It could not have been if Keats had not existed. But the beauty of that sequence of words, that essay in criticism, is due to the genius of Arnold. Francis Thompson on Shelley adds no cubit to the stature of Shelley, but his interpretation is a marvelous piece of poetic prose which cannot be deducted without enormous loss from the works of Thompson, from English criticism. We read Pater on Coleridge, not for Coleridge but for Pater, and we read Coleridge for Coleridge, not for Shakespeare. Thackeray's lecture on Swift, which is full of animosity and miscomprehension, is a well-written revelation of Thackeray. Trollope's book on Thackeray, which is full of friendship and admiration, is an ill-written revelation of Trollope.

Some men of great ability, like Trollope, who have written good books themselves, lack the faculty, whatever it may be, of writing in an entertaining fashion about the books of other men. Swinburne is a striking example. His knowledge of literature was immense, and he had the enthusiasms and contempts that make the critical impulse; but except when the poet in him seized the pen and made a passage of lyrical prose, his excursions into criticism are bewildering and difficult to read. His sonnets on Dickens, Lamb, and the Elizabethans are worth more than all his prose. On the other hand, Lamb, who wrote like an angel about the Elizabethan dramatists, failed completely as a dramatist.

Every man who plays with literature at all must be ambitious to succeed in some form of art that may be called "creative," as distinct from critical—a distinction which, since Arnold taught us our lesson, we know does not exist. The reason for this ambition is plain enough. A novel or a play reaches a wider audience than a volume of essays, however admirable; it has a more obvious claim to originality, and it brings the author a greater degree of practical satisfaction. A few doubly or trebly gifted men, Dryden, Coleridge, Poe, Arnold, Pater, Henley, Stevenson, Henry James, can do first-rate work in more than one *genre*, including criticism. And a good case could be made out to prove that a man who knows how to handle words in many ways is on the whole the best qualified to comment on the art of handling words. However that may be, it is certain that in English literature a critic who is only a critic seldom wins a conspicuous position. Even Johnson was something more than a critic, and he was, with all due respect, somewhat less than a good one. And Hazlitt, who was a good one, wrote on many subjects besides books and art.

Because so many little people went into the business of reviewing and presumed to sit in judgment on their betters, criticism early got a bad name in English literature, and not all the dignified work of Arnold and others has yet succeeded in restoring the reputation of the word or the art. Criticism came to mean censure, a connotation which persists in current speech. The degeneration had already taken place in Dryden's time, and he protested that "they wholly mistake the nature of criticism who think that its business is principally to find fault." Authors of imaginative works became resentful and felt that the critic was an enemy, a nasty and incompetent enemy, as indeed he often was. An interesting compilation could be made—and probably Saintsbury or somebody else has done it—of the retorts and counter-attacks made by writers of other things than criticism against the whole critical crew. Here are a few examples:

Gentle Jane Austen in *Northanger Abbey* amusingly defends her heroine's habits of reading novels:

> I will not adopt that ungenerous and impolitic custom, so common with novel writers, of degrading, by their contemptuous censure, the very performances to the number of which they are themselves adding . . . if the heroine of one novel be not patronized by the heroine of another, from whom can she expect protection and regard? . . . Let us leave it to the Reviewers to abuse such effusions of fancy at their leisure, and over every new novel to talk in threadbare strains of the trash with which the press now groans.

That sounds as if Miss Austen's pride in her craft had been wounded. I know of no record that anybody ever spoke ill of her until Mark Twain went wild.

Scott, whose generous soul was hurt by the harsh squabbles of the Scottish reviewers, took a shot at the tribe in the letter which appears in the introductory note to *The Lay of the Last Minstrel* in the Cambridge edition:

As to the herd of critics, it is impossible for me to pay much attention to them, for, as they do not understand what I call poetry, we talk in a foreign language to each other. Indeed, many of these gentlemen appear to me to be a sort of tinkers, who, unable to *make* pots and pans, set up for *menders* of them, and, God knows, often make two holes in patching one.

The idea that the critic is a secondary fellow who cannot make first-hand literature goes back to Dryden, the champion and exemplar of sound criticism, who wrote in *The Conquest of Granada:*

They who write ill and they who ne'er durst write
Turn critics out of mere revenge and spite.

Landor repeats the idea in a "Conversation" between Southey and Porson, in which Porson says: "Those who have failed as writers turn reviewers."

Writers and other artists are usually sensitive and often vain. Some have taken critics too seriously, given them too much importance while pretending to despise them, and have allowed themselves to be stung instead of brushing the flies off. Thanks to Shelley, the idea became current that the "viperous murderer," the critic, killed Keats. It was not so. Keats died of tuberculosis. Though he was, like all poets, delicately organized, he was an unusually sane and self-reliant man, quite sure of the value of his work. Moreover, in a day when rough criticism was the fashion, the critics were, though stupid, not especially rough on Keats. Shelley's "*J'accuse*" is flaming poetry, but—it is not good criticism. Byron had the right idea. With his superior wit and vigor he gave the reviewers ten blows for one and used his opponents as the occasion of a delightful exhibition of boxing. The reviewers were knocked out in the second round. *Eng-*

lish Bards and Scottish Reviewers is still in the ring, as I have just now pleasantly discovered by rereading it.

The notion that the critic will, or can, do damage to the artist persisted long after Shelley and is perhaps still believed. In 1876 Sidney Lanier, a man of good sense and great bravery, whom the flies, or the "vipers," had but lightly nipped, wrote, in a letter to his father:

> What possible claim can contemporary criticism set up to respect—that criticism which crucified Jesus, stoned Stephen, hooted Paul for a madman, tried Luther for a criminal, tortured Galileo, bound Columbus in chains, drove Dante into a hell of exile, made Shakespeare write the sonnet "When in disgrace of fortune and men's eyes," gave Milton £5 for "Paradise Lost," kept Samuel Johnson cooling his heels on Lord Chesterfield's doorstep, reviled Shelley as an unclean dog, killed Keats, cracked jokes on Gluck, Schubert, Beethoven, Berlioz, and Wagner, and committed so many other impious follies and stupidities?

Lanier's charges are not all quite true. He has mixed up the sins of criticism with the sins of politics, economics, and other dreadful affairs. But his outburst is a good illustration of the quarrel between the "author" and the "critic." Especially when the author has for the moment lost his sense of humor.

The best treatment of the critic by the author, as also, perhaps, of the author by the critic, is humorous. In *One of Our Conquerors* Meredith lays out the art critics:

> He had relied and reposed on the dicta of newspaper critics; who are sometimes unanimous, and are then taken for guides, and are fatal.

Washington Irving in a delightful little paper called *Desultory Thoughts on Criticism* quietly places the reviewer in the low seat where he belongs. I shall not quote from the essay, but merely refer the reader to it and especially to the introductory quotation from Buckingham's *Rehearsal*, in which the critic is set in a still lower seat.

Finally—for these quotations—Dr. Holmes, who lived all his life surrounded by praise and comfort, puts his finger gently on the parasitism of the critic. The passage is in *The Poet at the Breakfast Table:*

> Our *epizoic* literature is becoming so extensive that nobody is safe from its *ad infinitum* progeny. A man writes a book of criticisms. A *Quarterly Review* criticises the critic. A *Monthly Magazine* takes up the critic's critic. A *Weekly Journal* criticizes the critic of the critic's critic, and a daily paper favors us with some critical remarks on the performance of the writer in the *Weekly*, who has criticized the critical notice in the *Monthly* of the critical essay in the *Quarterly* on the critical work we started with. And thus we see that as each flea "has smaller fleas that on him prey," even the critic himself cannot escape the common lot of being bitten.

To what extent is the critic parasitic? To this extent: he is dealing with ideas already expressed, with cooked and predigested food. It is easier for any mind to think of something to say about an idea that has already gone through cerebral processes than it is to take the raw material of life and make something. You may sit on a bench in the park and watch the people and never, for the life of you, conceive a good story. Then O. Henry comes along and makes twenty stories. After he has done it, you can write something very brilliant about what O. Henry saw from the same bench that you sat on. And you can make neat remarks about the resemblances and differences between O. Henry, Boccaccio, and H. C. Bunner. That may be worth doing, if your remarks are really neat. For then you may be readable.

And that is the function of the critic, to be readable, to make literature of a sort. The critic is always playing his own game, selfish, egotistical, expressive of his own will, and no more disinterested than was Arnold himself when he took his pen in hand to slay a Philistine or to sign a contract with his manager for a lecture tour in America. In playing his own game the critic may help the game of another author by crying him up and advertising him. But a hundred critics, clamoring in the fatal unanimity at which Meredith pokes fun, cannot make the fortunes of a book or influence at the creative source the work of a man sufficiently strong and original to be worth reading. And the same hundred critics with lofty hatred of bad writings cannot prevent bad books from being written and read. George Eliot made it a rule not to read criticisms of her work because she found it necessary to be preserved "from that discouragement as an artist which ill-judged praise no less than ill-judged blame tends to produce in me." The implication that criticism, favorable or unfavorable, is ill-judged gives us an addition to our notes on what authors think of critics. I doubt whether, if that strong-minded woman had read everything that was written about her before and after her death, she would have altered a single sentence. Did Hardy stop writing novels because of the ignorant attacks on *Jude?* I would not accept without question Hardy's own word for it. I suspect that it was his own inward impulse, not determined by the opinions of other people, that turned his energy to that stupendous epic, *The Dynasts*.

To what extent can the critic play the game of the reader,

be guide and teacher, maintain standards, elevate taste, make the best ideas prevail? Not to a very great extent. Criticism, good or bad, is read only by the sophisticated, by people whose tastes are formed and who can take care of themselves in matters literary and intellectual. Who that had not already looked into Shakespeare and Plato ever heard of Pater? The journals that print intelligent articles about literature and art have a small circulation; they are missionaries to the converted; their controversial discussions of general principles or of the merits of an individual are only family feuds. Critics play with each other in a professional game. The few amateurs who sit as spectators are a select minority who have seen the game before and who, though not in the professional class, are instructed, cultivated, have some knowledge of the plays. The critical game is enjoyed by those who are themselves critical and least in need of enlightenment.

Nevertheless, it is a great game—when it is played well.

PREFACE

Book reviewing is held in general disrepute by many intelligent people. Its faults are all too well understood. Books are reviewed by professional blurb writers purely for commercial considerations. They are reviewed hastily, after an ill-digested skimming of the chapter headings, by opinionated individuals who like to air their own ideas. They are reviewed favorably to attract advertising from the publisher. They are reviewed purely from a point of view sympathetic to the editorial policy of the particular journal. Seldom are they reviewed from a point of view sympathetic to the purpose of the author.

There is possible, however, an entirely different point of attack. Given the present opportunity of the book review, how can conditions be improved to make it contribute to the production of sound literature? Mr. Canby, in the present essay, suggests what has been done to dignify the book review, and discusses further improvement.

Mr. Canby became popular as the writer of such interesting essays as "Back to Nature" in the days when he was an assistant editor of *The Yale Review*. He attained a wide esteem as editor of *The Literary Review*. His volume, *Definitions*, is helpful in that it deals with contemporary values in literature. He is now carrying on the best traditions of his past success as editor of *The Saturday Review of Literature*. "A Prospectus for Criticism" first appeared in *The Literary Review*, December 31, 1921, under the title, "An Apologia."

A PROSPECTUS FOR CRITICISM [1]

By Henry Seidel Canby

Criticism, in one respect, is like science: there is pure science, so-called, and applied science; there is pure criticism and applied criticism, which latter is reviewing. In applied science, principles established elsewhere are put to work; in reviewing, critical principles are, or should be, put to work in the analysis of books, but the books, if they are really important, often make it necessary to erect new critical principles. In fact, it is impossible to set a line where criticism ceases and reviewing begins. Good criticism is generally applicable to all literature; good reviewing is good criticism applied to a new book. I see no other valid distinction.

Reviewing in America has had a career by no means glorious. In the early nineteenth century, at the time of our first considerable productivity in literature, it was sporadic. The great guns—Lowell, Emerson—fired critical broadsides into the past; only occasionally (as in "A Fable for Critics") were they drawn into discussions of their contemporaries, and then, as in the Emerson-Whitman affair, they sometimes regretted it. Reviewing was carried on in small type, in the backs of certain magazines. Most of it was verbose and much of it was worthless as criticism. The belated recognition of the critical genius of Poe was due to the company he kept. He was a sadly erratic reviewer, as often wrong, I suppose, as right, but the most durable literary criticism of the age

[1] Copyrighted. Reprinted by permission from *Definitions*. Harcourt, Brace and Company.

came from his pen, and is to be found in a review, a review of Hawthorne's short stories.

After the Civil War the situation did not immediately improve. We had perhaps better reviewing, certainly much better mediums of criticism, such, for example, as *The Nation*, and, later, *The Critic*, but not more really excellent criticism. The magazines and newspapers improved; the weekly, as a medium of reviewing, established itself, though it functioned imperfectly; the individuals of force and insight who broke through current comment into criticism were more plentiful, but not more eminent.

The new era in reviewing, our era, began with two phenomena, of which the first had obscure beginnings and the second can be exactly dated.

The first was modern journalism. Just when journalism became personal, racy, and inclusive of all the interests of modern life, I cannot say. Kipling exhibits its early effects upon literature, but Kipling was an effect, not a cause. No matter when it began, we have seen, in the decade or two behind us, reviewing made journalistic, an item of news, but still more a means of entertainment.

The journalistic reviewer, who is still the commonest variety, had one great merit. He was usually interesting. Naturally so, since he wrote not to criticize the book that had been given him, but to interest his readers. Yet by the very nature of the case he labored under a disadvantage which forever barred him from calling himself critic as well as reviewer. He was a specialist in reporting, in making a story from the most unpromising material, and also in the use of his mother tongue, but a specialist, usually, in no other field whatsoever. Fiction, poetry, biography, science, history, politics, theology—whatever came to his mill was grist for the paper, and the less he knew of the subject and the less he had read and thought, the more emphatic were his opinions.

The club and saber work of Pope's day and Christopher North's has gone—advertising has made it an expensive luxury, and here at least commercialism has been of service to literature. It was wholesale and emphatic praise that became a trade-mark of journalistic reviewing. First novels, or obscure novels, were sometimes handled roughly by a reviewer whose duty was to prepare a smart piece of copy. But when books by the well known came to his desk it was safer to praise than to damn, because in damning one had to give reasons, whereas indiscriminate praise needed neither knowledge nor excuse. Furthermore, since the chief object was to have one's review read, excessive praise had every advantage over measured approval. Who would hesitate between two articles, one headed "The Best Book of the Year," and the other, "A New Novel Critically Considered"!

Thus, journalism *per se* has done little for the cause of American reviewing, and directly or indirectly it has done much harm, if only by encouraging publishers who found no competent discussions of their wares to set up their own critics, who poured out through the columns of an easy press commendations of the new books which were often most intelligent, but never unbiased.

The newspapers, however, have rendered one great service to criticism. In spite of their attempts to make even the most serious books newsy news, they, and they alone, have kept pace with the growing swarm of published books. The literary supplement, which proposed to review all books not strictly technical or transient, was a newspaper creation. And the literary supplement, which grew from the old book page, contained much reviewing which was in no bad sense journalistic. Without it the public would have had only the advertisements and the publishers' announcements to classify, analyze, and in some measure describe the regiment of books that marches in advance of our civilization.

We were not to be dependent, however, upon the budding supplements and the clever, ignorant reviewing, which, in spite of notable exceptions, characterized the newspaper view of books. The technical critic of technical books had long been practicing, and his ability increased with the advance in scholarship that marked the end of the nineteenth century. The problem was how to make him write for the general intelligent reader. For years the old *Nation*, under the editorship of Garrison and of Godkin, carried on this struggle almost single-handed. For a generation it was the only American source from which an author might expect a competent review of a serious, non-technical book. But then weight of the endeavor was too much for it. Fiction it largely evaded, as the London *Times Literary Supplement* does to-day. And with all the serious books in English awaiting attention in a few pages of a single weekly, it is no wonder that the shelves of its editorial office held one of the best modern libraries in New York! Or that Christmas, 1887, was the time chosen to review a gift edition of 1886! The old *Dial* had a like struggle, and a resembling difficulty.

It was in 1914 that *The New Republic* applied a new solution to the problem, and from its pages and from the other "intellectual weeklies" which have joined it, has come not merely some of the best reviewing that we have had, but also a distinct lift upwards in the standard of our discussion of contemporary books of general interest. After 1914 one could expect to find American reviews of certain kinds of books which were as excellent as any criticisms from England or from France.

But the solution applied was of such a character as to limit definitely its application. *The New Republic*, the present *Nation*, *The Freeman*, *The Weekly Review*, and, in a little different sense, *The Dial*, were founded by groups held together, with the exception of *The Dial* coterie, not by any common attitude towards literature, or by any specific interest in literature itself, but rather by a common social philosophy. These journals, again with the one exception, were devoted primarily to the application of their respective social philosophies. Even when in reviews or articles there was no direct social application, there was a clear irradiation from within. When *The New Republic* is humorous, it is a social-liberal humor. When *The Freeman* is ironic there is usually an indirect reference to the Single Tax. And *The Dial* will be modern or perish.

As a result of all this the space given to books at large in the social-political journals was small. And in that space one could prophesy with some exactness the reviewing to be expected. Books of social philosophy, novels with a thesis, poetry of radical emotion, documented history, and the criticism of politics or economic theory have had such expert reviewing as America has never before provided in such quantity. But there was a certain monotony in the conclusions reached. "Advanced" books had "advanced" reviewers who approved of the author's ideas even if they did not like his book. Conservative books were sure to be attacked in one paragraph even if they were praised in another. What was much more deplorable, good, old-fashioned books, that were neither conservative nor radical, but just human, had an excellent chance of interesting no one of these philosophical editors and so of never being reviewed at all. Irving, Cooper of the Leatherstocking Series, possibly Hawthorne, and quite certainly the author of *Huckleberry Finn* would have turned over pages for many a day without seeing their names at all.

Thus the intellectual weekly gave us an upstanding, competent criticism of books with ideas in them—when the ideas seemed important to the editors; a useful service, but not a comprehensive one; the criticism of a trend rather than a literature; of the products of a social group rather than the outspeaking of a nation. Something more was needed.

Something more was needed; and specifically literary mediums that should be catholic in criticism, comprehensive in scope, sound, stimulating, and accurate.

To be catholic in criticism does not mean to be weak and opinionless. A determination to discuss literature honestly and with insight, letting conclusions be what they must, may be regarded as a sufficient editorial stock in trade. It is fundamental, but it is not sufficient. Just as there is personality behind every government, so there should be a definite set of personal convictions behind literary criticism, which is not a science, though science may aid it. Sterilized, dehumanized criticism is almost a contradiction in terms, except in those rare cases where the weighing of evidential facts is all that is required. But these cases are most rare. Even a study of the text of Beowulf, or a history of Norman law, will be influenced by the personal emotions of the investigator, and must be so criticized. Men choose their philosophy according to their temperament; so do writers write; and so must critics criticize. Which is by no means to say that criticism is merely an affair of temperament, but rather to assert that temperament must not be left out of account in conducting or interpreting criticism.

Ideally, then, the editors of a catholic review should have definite convictions, if flexible minds, established principles, if a wide latitude of application. But although a review may thus be made catholic, it cannot thus attain comprehensiveness. There are too many books; too many branches upon the luxuriant tree of modern knowledge. No editorial group, no editorial staff, can survey the field competently unless they strictly delimit it by selection, and that means not to be comprehensive. Yet if the experts are to be called in, the good critics, the good scholars, the good scientists, until every book is reviewed by the writer best qualified to review it, then we must hope to attain truth by averages as the scientists do, rather than by dogmatic edict. For if it is difficult to guarantee in a few that sympathy with all earnest books which does not preclude rigid honesty in the application of firmly held principles, it is more difficult with the many. And if it is hard to exclude bias, inaccuracy, overstatement, and inadequacy from the work even of a small and chosen group, it is still harder to be certain of complete competence if the net is thrown more widely.

In fact, there is no absolute insurance against bad criticism except the intelligence of the reader. He must discount where discount is necessary, he must weigh the authority of the reviewer, he must listen to the critic as the protestant to his minister, willing to be instructed, but aware of the fallibility of man.

Hence, a journal of comprehensive criticism must first select its reviewers with the greatest care and then print vouchers for their opinions, which will be the names of the reviewers. Hence it must open its columns to rebuttals or qualifications, so that the reader may form his own conclusions as to the validity of the criticism, and, after he has read the book, judge its critics.

All this is a world away from the anonymous, dogmatic reviewing of a century ago. But who shall say that in this respect our practice is retrograde?

It is a great and sprawling country, this America, with all manner of men of all manners in it, and the days of patent medicines have passed, when one bottle was supposed to contain a universal cure. But in this matter of reading, which must be the chief concern of those who support a critical journal, there is one disease common to most of us that can be diagnosed with certainty, and one sure, though slow-working, remedy, that can be applied. We are uncritical readers. We like too readily, which is an amiable fault; we dislike too readily, which is a misfortune. We accept the cheap when we might have the costly book. We dislike the new, the true, the accurate, and the beautiful, because we will not seek, or cannot grasp, them. We are afflicted with that complex of democracy—a distrust of the best. Nine out of ten magazines, nine out of ten libraries, nine out of ten intelligent American minds prove this accusation.

And the cure is more civilization, more intellectuality, a finer and stronger emotion? One might as well say that the cure for being sick is to get well! This indeed, is the cure; but the remedy is a vigorous criticism. Call in the experts, let them name themselves and their qualifications like ancient champions, and then proceed to lay about with a will. Sometimes the maiden literature, queen of the tournament, will be slain instead of the Knight of Error, and often the spectators will be scratched by the whir of a sword. Nevertheless, the fight is in the open, we know the adversaries, and the final judgment, whether to salute a victor or condemn an impostor, is ours.

Thus, figuratively, one might describe the proper function in criticism of a liberal journal of catholic criticism to-day. One thing I have omitted, that its duty is not limited to criticism, for if it is to be comprehensive, it must present also vast quantities of accurate and indispensable facts, the news

of literature. And one prerequisite I have felt it unnecessary
to dwell upon. Unless its intent is honest, and its editors
independent of influence from any self-interested source,
the literary tournament of criticism becomes either a parade
of the virtues with banners for the favorites, or a mêlée
where rivals seek revenge. Venal criticism is the drug and
dishonest criticism the poison of literature.

PREFACE

The present movement in American poetry is so recent that it seems, at first thought, that the time is not yet ripe to give it any sort of appraisal. Beginning scarcely more than a dozen years ago, it came to flower almost immediately. Already the movement is becoming decadent.

Miss Lowell contrasts the contemporary generation of poets with the generation immediately preceding it. She writes with the warm enthusiasm of a defender of her own day.

Miss Lowell is renowned for her eager inquisitiveness and for her amazing versatility. She was both a propagandist and a poet. She early joined the insurgent movement. She introduced Imagist poetry to America, experimented with Polyphonic Prose, and defended *vers libre* against all its enemies. She abhorred *clichés* and reveled in chinoiseries. In her personality is found an eternally sensitive, artistic femininity blended with a masculine vigor. She has been frequently dubbed the female Roosevelt, and it was partly because of her powers of controversy that the modernist movement secured a favorable hearing in America. She reached the height of her career with the publication of her last critical work, *John Keats*. Her other critical works are: *Six French Poets; Studies in Contemporary Literature;* and *Tendencies in Modern American Poetry*. She is also the author of half a dozen volumes of poetry. The present essay, "Two Generations in American Poetry," first appeared in *The New Republic*, May 25, 1923.

TWO GENERATIONS IN AMERICAN POETRY [1]

By Amy Lowell

Some fifty years ago, more or less, a handful of unrelated men and women took to being born up and down these United States. What impulse was responsible for them, what submerged law of change and contradiction settled upon them as its tools, it is a little hard to say—at least, to say in any sort of reasonable compass. They appear to have been sporadic efforts of some force or other, operating over a period of nearly twenty years; but so disconnected were they geographically, socially, and atavistically, that one thing is certain: however they may have derived from a central urge, they did not derive in the least from one another. This little handful of disconnected souls, all unobtrusively born into that America which sighed with Richard Watson Gilder, wept with Ella Wheeler Wilcox, permitted itself to dance delicately with Celia Thaxter, and occasionally to blow a graceful blast on the beribboned trumpet of Louise Imogen Guiney, was destined to startle its progenitors. This was a world of sweet appreciation, a devotee of caged warblers, which species of gentle music-makers solaced it monthly from the pages of the *Century* or the *Atlantic Monthly*. How pleasant to turn away for a moment from the rattle of drays and horse cars and listen to a woodland strain repeated in a familiar and well-loved cadence! That these robins of ours were best to imitate the notes of English blackbirds and nightingales, only made their efforts the more precious; and, to be sure, their imitations were done with a modesty

[1] Copyrighted. Republished by permission from *The New Republic*,

worthy of all admiration. They knew their place in the
world's harmony and saw to it that they did not overstep it.
This was expected and loyally adhered to. What if America
had time for these not too exciting titivations of the emotions,
harkened and was pleased; the busy rest of the populace
heeded not all at and missed very little.

Now how it was that a handful of young persons, growing
up in the seventies and eighties (for the widely spaced ar-
rivals lasted thus long), found themselves, one and all, so
out of sympathy with the chaste and saccharine music
wandering through the ambient air of current periodicals,
is one of the wonders of psychological phenomena. It is a
fact, nevertheless, that with no one to talk to or compare
notes with, each as separate as conditions could well make
him, one and all they revolted against the taste of their
acquaintances and launched, the whole flotilla of them, out
into the turbulent sea of experiment and personal expression.

Upheavals make for art, as is well known. The debacle
of the Franco-Prussian war gave France the galaxy of poets
and musicians which made the last two decades of the nineteenth century so rich a period in her annals. But here, in
America, there had been no war sufficiently recent to cause
an effect of leaf turning. The Civil War was too long gone
by. No, the change in poetry seems to have sprung from
something far more prosaic. From the great tide of commerce and manufacture, indeed. Prosperity is the mother
of art, no matter how odd such an idea may seem. Look at
the Elizabethan age in England. It followed immediately
upon an expansion of the world's markets, did it not? But
this expansion was all bound up with the romance of daring
adventure and exploration. Quite so, and was not ours?
A continent crossed and settled at infinite peril; rivers run
into clacking factories; electricity caught and chained to

wires, forcing the very air to obedient echo—are not such things as these romantic and adventurous? Whether people had the wit to see them in this light or not, the little devils who rule the psychological currents which man ignores and invariably obeys found them so. Nemesis is extraordinarily ironical. While the men of the race were making fortunes, and the women were going to concerts and puzzling their heads over a Browning whom, having invented themselves, they could not in the least understand, so different was he from dear Mr. Gilder—while all this was going on, in New England, the Middle West, in Pennsylvania and Arkansas, by one, and one, and one, like beads before they are strung upon a string, the makers of this poetic renaissance of ours were obscurely working all toward one end and that as various as the strands in a piece of rope.

Who the pioneers of this movement were, I am not going to say. They are perfectly well known to every one interested in present-day literature. Besides, we are still too near to them to render absolute statement possible. Were a suffrage taken, some names would appear in all lists, others would differ. Time alone can make the actual personnel of the movement secure. My intention here is to analyze a movement, not criticize individual talents. When I mention such, I do so as illustration merely.

With all their diversity, there was a central aim which bound the group together. Conscious with some, unconscious with others, their aim was to voice America. Now you cannot voice one country in the accents of another. Therefore the immediate object of these poets was to drop the perpetual imitation of England. It is interesting, if painful, to realize what a desperately hard time these young poets had. When they could get themselves printed, which was seldom, they were either completely ignored or furiously lampooned. And still they were alone, none knew the others; but they were a courageous little band, and on they went, writing, and putting their poems in their writing-table drawers.

Suddenly, explosively, the movement came to a head in 1912 and the years immediately succeeding. In October, 1912, Harriet Monroe brought out her magazine *Poetry*, but, splendid work though that magazine has done, I cannot subscribe to its often expressed opinion that it is largely responsible for the recognition the group began to achieve. Instead I should say that it was another manifestation of the fulminating spirit which produced the poets themselves. Every one of these poets had been writing for years, some of them for many years, others were already the authors of neglected volumes, before *Poetry* arrived on the scene. It seems to me rather that the ferment had reached a point when it was bound to burst. For burst it did and bore down on the American consciousness with an indomitable violence not to be resisted. Horrified professors shuddered and took to umbrellas and arctics, newspaper fulminators tried all the weapons in their armories from snubs to guffaws. It was no use; what must come, comes. The caged warblers were swept out of court. Those people who hated the new poetry were forced back on the classical old which antedated the warbler era. And that alone was a good thing.

But this movement which we speak of so glibly, do we really know what it was? Let us observe it a little. In the first place, it was an effort to free the individual from the expression of the herd; in the second, it had for its object the breaking down of mere temperamental barriers. This looks like paradox, but it is not. The poetry of the two preceding decades had been almost entirely concerned with recording personal emotions, but recording them in a perfectly stereotyped way. The new poetry found that emotions were not confined to the conjugation of the verb to love, and whether it said "I love" or "Behold the earth and all that is thereon," if it followed its natural inclination, it would say it quite differently from the way its father had said it. The truth is that this new poetry whether written by men or women, was in essence masculine, virile, very much alive. Where the nineties had warbled, it was prone to shout. When it concerned itself with love, its speech was natural and unrestrained; when not concerned with love, it found interests as manifold as the humanity crowding on its eyes from every street corner. It had so much to say that it simply could not say it, and so huge a country to speak for that no one poet could do more than present a little by-lane of it. It took the whole handful of poets which made up the group to give any adequate expression of the movement or the age which produced it; but, taking the work by and large, book after book, here was a volume of energy, a canvas so wide and sparkling, that something very like the dazzling tapestry of American life, thought, and activities, was obtained.

As the poets were, so was their work. One gave simple facts; another approached the central truth obliquely; a third abandoned America as far as direct allusion went, and presented it the more clearly in reactions on distant countries and periods viewed through American eyes. For instance, take Frost and Sandburg and juxtapose them with "H. D." Not one of these three could have sprung from any country but America, and yet where Frost and Sandburg portray their special countrysides, town and open, "H. D." occupies herself with an ancient loveliness alive again through the eager vision of a young race to which nothing is stale. Wherever posterity may place the group in the rôle of American poets, one thing it cannot deny them: the endeavor after a major utterance. They may have failed; they dared the stars. They hitched their wagons to the tails of comets. There was nothing the matter with their aim; success is another thing, and not for us to gauge.

The world learned to like them pretty well, although they were not very much understood. It is not the way of our modern world to accord greatness its due, even when it slyly supposes that it may exist. The very feeble educations which are all most of us can boast tend to caution rather than to acclaim. It is safer to doubt, for then the odds are with you. No, the world was interested, but took refuge in the old cry: "These men are precursors, we await the great poet for whom they are clearing the way." And what happened? Rather a curious thing. At first the pioneers rolled up their tallies of disciples. Incipient "Spoon Rivers" rippled on every side; bits of here, there, and everywhere à la Frost appeared; red-blooded followers travestied Sandburg's least successful pictures, stupidly unaware that it was his tenderness and insight which made him the man he was; the Imagists almost despaired of ever freeing themselves from the milk and water imitations with which young hopefuls flooded the nonpaying magazines. Still the great poet who was to go all of them one better did not make his appearance. Instead came a volte face, Reaction, by Jove! Or so it appeared. Reaction after ten years! But things move swiftly nowadays.

The bewildered elders rubbed their eyes. Had all their work been in vain? By no means, for the reaction owed more to them than it has ever been willing to acknowledge. Without them, the younger poets could not have existed. Now constant reaction is a law of art. When one impulse is exhausted, the artistic undercurrents turn to another. Finding it impossible to outdistance the pioneers on their own ground, the next generation veered off at a tangent and sought other grounds of its own. But a reaction, to be effective, must produce poets of something like the caliber of the poets reacted from. Without attempting to answer this question one way or the other, we can, at least, peer a little more closely at the type of poetry coming on the stage to-day.

The younger group appears to be composed of two entirely distinct companies. Unlike the pioneers, who had among them the tie of a concerted effort, these two sections are completely at variance with one another. To name them, one calls itself the Secessionists; the other we may christen, for purposes of differentiation, the Lyrists. It is not a very good name, for all poets write lyrics, but as these poets write practically nothing else, it will serve. Of these two groups, the Lyrists are unquestionably doing the better work. They proclaim no tenets, but confine themselves to writing poetry, and doing it uncommonly well. Their expertness is really amazing. They have profited by the larger movement in finding an audience ready-made to their hands, a number of magazines eager to welcome them, and a considerable body of critical writing bearing on the poetical problems of the moment—aids to achievement which the older group entirely lacked. Through the practice of the elders, the younger group has learned to slough off the worst faults of the nineties, and, in the matter of versification, there is scarcely a fault to be found with their work. I refer, of course, to that of the leaders. The strange thing here, however, the crux of the reactionary situation, is its aim. For where the older generation aimed at a major expression, these younger poets are directly forcing themselves to adhere to a minor one. The terms major and minor in poetry have nothing to do with good and bad; a minor poet is often meticulously careful and exceedingly fine. Major and minor refer to outlook, and it is a fact that this younger group deliberately seeks the narrow, personal note. It is a symptom, I suppose, a weariness of far horizons, a breath-taking before a final leap.

Where emotion is the chief stock in trade, we should not expect a high degree of intellectual content, yet in one member of the group we find it—in Elinor Wylie, who unlike Edna St. Vincent Millay, that delightfully clever exponent of the perennial theme of love, is one of the most intellectual and well equipped of American poets. These two are the acknowledged chiefs of the company. For, while the older movement was innately masculine, the new one is all feminine. It is, indeed, a feminine movement, and remains such even in the work of its men.

The Secessionists are quite apart. Their object is science rather than art; or perhaps it is fairer to say that to them art is akin to mathematics. They are much intrigued by structure, in a sense quite other than that in which it is usually employed in poetry. They have a host of theories, and are most interesting when stating them, but the doubt arises whether a movement which concerns itself more with statements about poetry than with the making of poetry itself is ever going to produce works of art of a quality to justify the space taken up by pronunciamentos.

The outcome of all this is somewhat hazy. It is a fact that, side by side with the youths, the elders are still writing. Whether the younger group will sweep aside the older, it is too soon to see. That the far easier poetry of the Lyrists will be, and is, immensely popular, is only natural. The question is how long can it maintain itself in the face of its wilfully restricted limits. Whether the future will bring a period of silence preceding another vigorous dash forward, or whether the present feminine mood will lead directly into the next advance, who shall say? Not I, at any rate. Both possibilities are in order, and for the present I think we may be satisfied. The time has been short, and considerable has been done in a variety of ways by the two generations at the moment writing. As Whitman said, here is "a lapful of seed, and this is a fine country."

PREFACE

The present essay takes up, more in detail, the movement sketched in the previous essay by Miss Lowell. Mr. Aiken here gives a vivid summary of our present-day American poetry. Being a poet himself, the author voices his own individual theories of art somewhat, in his criticism of his contemporaries.

Mr. Aiken is the author of eight different volumes of poetry. His second work, *Turns and Movies*, 1916, contains, perhaps, his best work. His Discordants: *Music I Heard* and *Dead Cleopatra* are likely to live long after most of his other poetry has been blurred by time. Mr. Aiken has also published an interesting volume of criticism, *Scepticisms*.

Mr. Aiken was born in Savannah, Georgia, in 1889. He is a graduate of Harvard. He has lived abroad at various times, in London, Rome, and Windermere. "The New American Poetry" appeared first as a chapter in *Civilization in the United States*, Harcourt, Brace, 1922.

THE NEW AMERICAN POETRY [1]

By Conrad Aiken

There are many fashions, among contemporary critics, of regarding American poetry, each of them perhaps of equal helpfulness, since each is one facet of an imaginable whole. There is the view of Mr. John Middleton Murry, an English critic, that it depends perhaps a shade too much on narrative or dramatic interest, on *bizarrerie* (if I may very freely elaborate his notion), or, in general, on a kind of sensationalism, a use of superficially intriguing elements which are not specifically the right—or at all events the best—elements of poetry. There is the view of Mr. Louis Untermeyer, one of the ablest of our own critics and also one of the most versatile of our parodists and poets, that our contemporary poetry is good in measure as it comes in the direct line from Whitman: good, that is to say, when it is the voice of the poet who accepts, accepts joyously and largely, even loosely, this new world environment, these new customs, social and industrial, above all, it may be, the new sense of freedom which he might, if pressed, trace back to Karl Marx on one hand and Sigmund Freud on the other. There is again the view of Miss Amy Lowell that our poetry is good, or tends to be, precisely in proportion as it represents an outgrowing, by the poet, of his acute awareness of a social or ethical "here and now," and the attainment of a relatively pure preoccupation with beauty—the sense of freedom here exercising itself principally, if not altogether, with regard to literary tradi-

[1] From *Civilization in the United States*, 1922, by permission of Harcourt, Brace and Co.

tion, especially the English: once more, I dilate the view to make it the more broadly representative. And there is, finally, the view of the conservative, by no means silent even in this era, that what is good in contemporary American poetry is what is for the moment least conspicuous—the traditional, seen as it appears inevitably in America to be seen, as something graceful, sentimental, rightly ethical, gently idealistic.

What will be fairly obvious is that if we follow a little way any particular one of these critics, we shall find him attempting to urge our poetry in a particular direction, a direction which he prefers to any other direction, and analyzing its origins in such a way, if he analyzes at all, as to make plausible its (postulated) growth in that direction. This is the natural, even perhaps the best thing, for a participant critic to do—it contributes, certainly, an interest and an energy. But if in some freak of disinterestedness, we wish if for only a moment to see American poetry with no concern save that of inordinate and intelligent curiosity, then it is to all of these views that we must turn, rather than to any one, and to the obverse of each, as well as to the face. For if one thing is apparent to-day in a study of American letters, it is that we must heroically resist any temptation to simplify, to look in only one direction for origins or in only one direction for growth. Despite our national motto, American civilization is not so much one in many as many in one. We have not, as England has and as France has, a single literary heart; our literary capitals and countries are many, each with its own vigorous people, its own self-interest, its own virtues and provincialisms. We may attribute this to the mere matter of our size, and the consequent geographical sequestration of this or that group—that is no doubt a factor, but of equal importance is the fact that in a new country, of rapid and chaotic material growth, we must inevitably have, according to the locality, marked variations in the rapidity of growth of the vague thing we call civilization. Chicago is younger than Boston, older than San Francisco. And what applies to the large unit applies also to the small—if the country in general has not yet reached anything remotely like a cultural homogeneity (as far, that is, as we ever in viewing a great nation expect such a thing) neither has any section of it, nor any city of it. It is no longer possible, if indeed it ever was, to regard a section like New England, for example, as a definite environmental factor, say "y," and to conclude, as some critics are so fond of doing, that any poet who matures there will inevitably be representable as "yp." This is among the commonest and falsest of false simplifications. Our critics, frantically determined to find an American poetry that is autochthonous, will see rocky pastures, mountains, and birches in the poetry of a New Englander, or skyscrapers in the poetry of a New Yorker, or stockyards in the poetry of a Chicagoan, as easily as a conjurer takes a rabbit from a hat.

What refuge we have from a critical basis so naïve is in assuming from the outset, toward contemporary American poetry, an attitude guardedly pluralistic—we begin by observing merely that American poetry is certainly, at the moment, if quantitative production and public interest are any measure, extraordinarily healthy and vigorous. We are accustomed to hearing it called a renaissance. The term is admissible if we carefully exclude, in using it, any implication of a revival of classicism. What we mean by it is simply that the moment is one of quite remarkable energy, productiveness, range, color, and anarchy. What we do not mean by it is that we can trace with accuracy where this outburst comes from. The origins of the thing are obscure. It was audible in 1914—Mr. Edwin Arlington Robinson and Mr.

Ezra Pound were audible before that; it burst into full chorus
in 1915; and ever since there has been, with an occasional
dying fall, a lusty corybantic cacophony. Just where this
amazing procession started nobody clearly knows. Mr.
Untermeyer would have us believe that Walt Whitman was,
as it were, the organizer of it, Miss Monroe tries to persuade
us that it was *Poetry: a Magazine of Verse.* But the facts,
I think, waive aside either postulate. If one thing is remarkable it is that in this spate of poetry the influence of Walt
Whitman—an influence, one would suppose, as toxic for
the young as Swinburne—is so inconsiderable: if another is
even more remarkable, it is that in all this chorus one so
seldom hears a voice of which any previous American voice
was the clear prototype. We have had, of course, our voices—
of the sort, I mean, rich enough in character to make imitation an easy and tempting thing. Longfellow, Lowell,
Bryant, Sill, Lanier, are not in this regard considerable,—
but what of Poe, whose influence we have seen in French
poetry on Baudelaire, and in contemporary English poetry
on Mr. Walter de la Mare? No trace of him is discoverable,
unless perhaps we find the ghostliest of his shadows now and
then across the work of Mr. John Gould Fletcher, or Mr.
Maxwell Bodenheim, or Mr. Wallace Stevens, a shadow cast,
in all these cases, amid much else, from a technical and
coloristic standpoint, which would have filled Poe with
alarm. And there is another American poet, perhaps as
great as Poe, perhaps greater (as he in turn is perhaps greater
than Whitman—as poet, though not as personality)—Emily
Dickinson. Of that quietist and mystic, who walked with
tranquillity midway between Blake and Emerson, making of
her willful imperfections a kind of perfectionism, why do we
hear so little? Do we catch now and again the fleetingest
glimpse of her in the early work of Mr. Robert Frost? If

so, it is certainly nowhere else. Yet it would be hard to prove that she has no right to a place with Poe and Whitman, or indeed among the best poets in the language.

But nowhere in America can we find, for contemporary poetry, any clear precursive signal. Little as it may comfort our fuglemen of the autochthonous, we must, I think, look to Europe for its origins. This is not, as some imagine, a disgrace—it would be a melancholy thing, of course, if we merely imitated the European, without alteration. But Browning would hardly recognize himself, even if he cared to, in the *Domesday Book* of Mr. Edgar Lee Masters, Mallarmé and Rimbaud would find Mr. Fletcher a mirror with an odd trick of distortion, Laforgue would have to look twice at Mr. T. S. Eliot's *Prufrock* (for all its Hamletism), M. Paul Fort would scarcely feel at home in Miss Amy Lowell's *Can Grande's Castle*, Mr. Thomas Hardy and the ghost of Tennyson would not quarrel much for the possession of Mr. Robinson's work, nor Mr. Chesterton and the author of *The Ingoldsby Legends* for the lively sonorities of Mr. Vachel Lindsay. In such cases we have not so much "influence" as fertilization. It is something of Mr. Masters that *The Ring and the Book* reveals to Mr. Masters: something of Miss Lowell to which M. Paul Fort offers her the key. Was it a calamity for Baudelaire that he lived only by a transfusion of blood from an American? Is Becquer the less Becquer or Spanish for having fed upon the *Buch der Lieder?* . . . Culture is bartered, nowadays, at open frontiers, and if to-day a new theme, chord, or color-scheme is French, German, or American, to-morrow it is international.

If we differ in this respect from any other country it is only that we are freer to exploit, really exhaust, the new, because we hold, less than any other, to any classical traditions: for traditions our poets seldom look back further than the 19th century. We have the courage, often indistinguishable from folly, of our lack of convictions. Thus it comes about that as America is the melting-pot for races, so she is in a fair way to become a melting-pot for cultures: we have the energy, the curiosity, the intelligence, above all the lack of affiliations with the past, which admirably adapt us to a task—so precisely demanding complete self-surrender —of æsthetic experiment. Ignorance has some compensations—I mean, of course, a partial ignorance. If Mr. Lindsay had been brought up exclusively on Aristotle, Plato, Æschylus, and Euripides, and had been taken out of the shadow of the church by Voltaire and Darwin, perhaps he would not have been so "free" to experiment with the "higher vaudeville." It will be observed that this is an odd kind of "freedom," for it amounts in some ways to little more than the "freedom" of the prison. For if too severe a training in the classics unfits one somewhat for bold experiment, too little of it is as likely, on the other hand, to leave one with an æsthetic perceptiveness, a sensibility, in short, relatively rudimentary.

This, then, is something of the cultural *mise en scène* for our contemporary poetry. We have repeated waves of European suggestion breaking Westward over our continent, foaming rather more in Chicago than in New York; and we have our lusty young company of swimmers, confident that they are strong enough to ride these waves farther than any one in Europe rode them and with a more native grace. What is most conspicuously American in most of these swimmers is the fact that they rely not so much on skill and long training as on sheer energy, vitality, and confidence. They rely, indeed, in most cases, on a kind of exuberance or superabundance. Do we not feel this in the work of Mr. Edgar Lee Masters—does he not try, in these

many full books of his, where the good is so inextricably
enmeshed with the bad, simply to beat us down as under a
cataract? *Domesday Book* is, rather, an avalanche. He never
knows what to exclude, where to stop. Miss Lowell, Mr.
Fletcher, Mr. Carl Sandburg, and Mr. Lindsay are not far
behind him, either—they are all copious. I do not mean to
imply that this is a bad thing, at the moment—at the moment
I am not sure that this sheer exuberance is not, for us, the
very *best* thing. Energy is the first requisite of a "renaissance," and supplies its material, or, in another light, its
richness of color. Not the beginning, but the end, of a renaissance is in refinement; and I think we are certainly within
bounds in postulating that the last five years have given us
at the least a superb beginning, and enough more than that,
perhaps, to make one wonder whether we have not already
cast Poe and Whitman, Sidney Lanier, and Emily Dickinson,
our strange little quartette, into a shadow.

All that our wonder can hope for is at best a very speculative answer. If parallels were not so dangerous, we might
look with encouragement at that spangled rhetorical torrent
which we call Elizabethan literature. Ben Jonson did not
consider Shakespeare much of an artist, nor did Milton, and
classicists ever since have followed them in that opinion.
If one can be the greatest of poets and yet not much of an
artist, we may here keep clear of the quarrel: what we get
at is the fact that Shakespeare and the other Elizabethans
participated in a literary movement which, like ours, began
in energy, violence, and extravagance, was at its best ex-
cessively rhetorical and given to unpruned copiousness,
and perished as it refined. Will a future generation see us in
a somewhat similar light—will it like us for our vitality, for
the reckless adventurousness of our literature, our extrava-
gances, and forgive us, if it does not precisely enjoy as some-

thing with a foreign flavor, our artistic innocence? That is conceivable, certainly. Yet the view *is* speculative and we dare not take it too seriously. For if we have kept hopefully and intelligently abreast of the contemporary we have kept none the less, our own very sufficient aloofness, our own tactilism and awareness, in the light of which we are bound to have our own skepticisms and self-distrust. I do not mean that we would perhaps prefer something more classical or severe that *Spoon River Anthology* or *The Congo* or the color symphonies of Mr. Fletcher, merely on the ground that it is the intrinsically classical and severe which we most desire. What we seem to see in contemporary American poetry is a transition from the more to the less exuberant, from the less to the more severe; and what we most *desire* to see is the attainment of *that point,* in this transition, which will give us our parallel to the Shakesperean, if we may hope for anything even approximately so high; a point of equipoise.

This hope gives us a convenient vantage from which to survey the situation, if we also keep in mind our perception of American cultural heterogeneity and the rashness of any attempt to generalize about it. The most exact but least diverting method would be the merely enumerative, the mere roll-call which would put before us Mr. Edwin Arlington Robinson and Mr. Ezra Pound as the two of our poets whose public literary activities extend farthest back, and after them the group who made themselves known in the interval between 1914 and 1920: Mr. Robert Frost, Mr. Fletcher, Mr. Masters, Mr. Sandburg, Miss Lowell, Mr. Lindsay, Mr. Alfred Kreymborg, Mr. Maxwell Bodenheim, Mr. Wallace Stevens, "H. D.," [1] Mr. T. S. Eliot and Miss Sara Teasdale. These

---

[1] The signature of Hilda Doolittle. She was born September 10, 1886, at Bethlehem, Pennsylvania, and in 1913 married Richard Aldington, an Englishman. They are among the best poets of the imagist school.

poets, with few exceptions, have little enough in common
—nothing, perhaps, save the fact that they were all a good
deal actuated at the outset by a disgust with the dead level
of sentimentality and prettiness and moralism to which
American poetry had fallen between 1890 and 1910. From
that point they diverge like so many radii. One cannot say,
as Miss Lowell has tried to persuade us, that they have all
followed one radius, and that the differences between them
are occasioned by the fact that some have gone farther than
others. We may, for convenience, classify them, if we do
not attach too much importance to the bounds of our classes.
We may say that Mr. Robinson, Mr. Frost, and Mr. Masters
bring back to our poetry a strong sense of reality; that Mr.
Fletcher, Mr. Pound, Miss Lowell, "H. D.," and Mr. Bodenheim bring to it a sharpened consciousness of color; that Mr.
Eliot, Mr. Kreymborg, and Mr. Stevens bring to it a refinement of psychological subtlety; Mr. Sandburg, a grim sense of
social responsibility; Mr. Lindsay, a rhythmic abandon mixed
with evangelism; Miss Teasdale, a grace. The range here
indicated is extraordinary. The existence side by side in
one generation and in one country of such poets as Mr. Masters and Mr. Fletcher, or Mr. Eliot and Miss Lowell, is
anomalous. Clearly we are past that time when a nation
will have at a given moment a single direct literary current.
There is as yet no sign that to any one of these groups will
fall anything like undivided sway. Mr. Frost's *North of
Boston* and Mr. Fletcher's *Irradiations* came out in the same
year; *Spoon River Anthology* and the first *Imagist Anthology;*
Mr. Robinson's *Lancelot* and Mr. Bodenheim's *Advice*. And
what gulfs even between members of any one of our arbitrary
"classes"! Mr. Frost's actualism is seldom far from the
dramatic or lyric, that of Mr. Masters seldom far from the
physiological. Mr. Masters is bitter-minded, tediously ex-

planatory, and his passionate inquiries fall upon life like so many heavy blows; his delvings appear morbid as well as searching. Mr. Frost is gentle, whether in irony, humor, or sense of pain: if it is the pathos of decay which most moves him, he sees it, none the less, at dewfall and moonrise, in a dark tree, a birdsong. The inflections of the human voice, as he hears them, are as tender as in the hearing of Mr. Masters they are harsh. And can Mr. Robinson be thought a commensal of either? His again is a prolonged inquiry into the way of human behavior, but how bared of color, how muffled with reserves and dimmed with reticence! Here, indeed, is a step toward romanticism. For Mr. Robinson, though a realist in the sense that his preoccupation is with motive, turns down the light in the presence of his protagonist that in the gloom he may take on the air of something larger and more mysterious than the garishly actual. Gleams convey the dimensions—hints suggest a depth. We are not always too precisely aware of what is going on in this twilight of uncertainties, but Mr. Robinson seems to whisper that the implications are tremendous. Not least, moreover, of these implications are the moral—the mirror that Mr. Robinson holds up to nature gives us back the true, no doubt, but increasingly in his later work (as in *Merlin* and *Lancelot*, particularly the latter) with a slight trick of refraction that makes of the true the exemplary.

We cross a chasm, from these somber psycho-realists, to the colorists. To these, one finds, what is human in behavior or motive is of importance only in so far as it affords color or offers possibilities of pattern. Mr. Fletcher is the most brilliant of this group, and the most "uncontrolled": his colorism, at its best, is a pure, an astonishingly absolute thing. The "human" element he wisely leaves alone—it baffles and escapes him. One is aware that this kaleidoscopic whirl of color is "wrung out" of Mr. Fletcher, that it conveys what is for him an intense personal drama, but this does not make his work "human." The note of "personal drama" is more complete in the poetry of "H. D.," but this too is, in the last analysis, a nearly pure colorism, as static and fragmentary, however, as Mr. Fletcher's is dynamic. Mr. Bodenheim is more detached, cooler, has a more conscious eye for correspondences between color and mood: perhaps we should call him a symbolist. Even here, however, the "human," the whim of tenderness, the psychological gleam, are swerved so that they may fall into a fantastic design. Miss Lowell, finally, more conscious, deliberate, and energetic than any of these, brilliantly versatile, utterly detached, while she "sees" more of the objective world (and has farther-ranging interests), sees it more completely than any of them simply as raw color or incipient pattern. If the literary pulse is here often feverishly high, the emphatic and sympathetic temperature is as often absolute zero.

Mr. Pound shares with Miss Lowell this immersion in the "literary"—he is intensely aware of the literary past, rifles it for odds and ends of color, atmosphere, and attitude, is perpetually adding bright new bits, from such sources, to his Joseph's coat: but if a traditionalist in this, a curio-hunter, he is an experimentalist in prosody; he has come far from the sentimental literary affectedness of his early work and at his best has written lyrics of a singular beauty and transparent clarity. The psychological factor has from time to time intrigued him, moreover, and we see him as a kind of link between the colorists and such poets as Mr. T. S. Eliot, Mr. Alfred Kreymborg, and Mr. Wallace Stevens. These poets are alike in achieving, by a kind of alchemy, the lyric in terms of the analytic: introspection is made to shine, to the subtly seen is given a delicate air of false simplicity.

Mr. Stevens is closest to the colorists. His drift has been away from the analytic and towards the mere capture of a "tone." Mr. Kreymborg is a melodist and a mathematician. He takes a pleasure in making of his poems and plays charming diagrams of the emotions. Mr. Eliot has more of an eye for the sharp dramatic gesture, more of an ear for the trenchant dramatic phrase—he looks now at Laforgue, now at John Webster. His technical skill is remarkable, his perception of effect is precise, his range narrow, perhaps increasingly narrow.

Even so rapid and superficial a survey cannot but impress us with the essential anarchy of this poetic community. Lawlessness has seemed at times to be the prevailing note; no poetic principle has remained unchallenged, and we have only to look in the less prosperous suburbs and corners of this city to see to what lengths the bolder rebels, whether of the "Others" group or elsewhere, have gone. Ugliness and shapelessness have had their adherents among those whom æsthetic fatigue had rendered momentarily insensitive to the well-shaped; the fragmentary has had its adherents among those whom cynicism had rendered incapable of any service, too prolonged, to one idea. But the fetishists of the ugly and the fragmentary have exerted, none the less, a wholesome and fructifying influence. Whatever we feel about the ephemerality of the specifically ugly or fragmentary, we cannot escape a feeling that these, almost as importantly as the new realism or the new colorism, have enlarged what we might term the general "poetic consciousness" of the time. If there was a moment when the vogue of the disordered seemed to threaten, or predict, a widespread rapid poetic decadence, that moment is safely past. The tendency is now in the other direction, and not the least interesting sign is the fact that many of the former apostles of the disordered are to-day experimenting with the things they yesterday despised—rime, meter, and the architecture of theme.

We have our affections, in all this, for the fragmentary and ugly as for the abrupt small hideousness—oddly akin to virility—of gargoyles. We have our affections, too, for the rawest of our very raw realisms—for the maddest of our colorisms, the most idiosyncratic subtleties of our first introspectionists. Do we hesitate a little to ask something more of any of the poets whom we thus designate? What we fear is that in attempting to give us our something more, they will give us something less. What we want more of, what we see our contemporary poets as for the most part sadly deficient in, is "art." What we are afraid they will lose, if we urge them in this direction, is their young sharp brilliance. Urge them, however, we must. What our poets need most to learn is that poetry is not merely a matter of outpouring, of confession. It must be serious: it must be, if simple in appearance, none the less highly wrought: it must be packed. It must be beautifully elaborate rather than elaborately beautiful. It must be detached from dogma —we must keep it away from the all too prevalent lecture platform.

What we should like to see, in short, is a fusion, of the extraordinary range of poetic virtues with which our contemporary poets confront us, into one poetic consciousness. Do we cavil too much in assuming that no one of our poets offers us quite enough? Should we rather take comfort in the hope that many of their individual "personalities" are vivid enough to offset their one-sidedness, and in that way to have a considerable guarantee of survival? We have mentioned that possibility before, and certainly it cannot be flatly dismissed. But I think it cannot be contested that many of these poets already feel, themselves, a sharper responsibility, a need for a greater comprehensiveness, for a finer and richer tactile equipment, a steadier view of what it is that constitutes beauty of form. They are immeasurably distant from any dry, cold perfectionism, however; and if we cheer them in taking the path that leads thither, it is in the hope of seeing them reach the halfway house rather than the summit. For to go all the way is to arrive exhausted; to go halfway is to arrive with vigor. . . . That, however, is to interpose our own view and to lose our detachment. We return to a reiteration of our conclusion that American poetry is at the moment extraordinarily healthy. Its virtues are the virtues of all good poetry, and they are sufficient to persuade us that the future of English poetry lies as much in America as in England. Its faults are the faults of a culture that is immature. But again, we reiterate that we have here many cultures, and if some are immature, some are not. Let those who are too prone to diagnose us culturally from *Spoon River Anthology* or *Smoke and Steel* keep in mind also Mr. Robinson's *Merlin* and Mr. Frost's *North of Boston;* Mr. Fletcher's *Goblins and Pagodas* and Miss Lowell's *Can Grande's Castle.*

PREFACE

It is perfectly natural for Americans to believe in what they possess. Ask the first three men you meet to name the best make of automobile on the market, and invariably they will tell you, in all seriousness, that the machines they own are the best machines in the world. The same trait is found among writers. Authors who deal in realism recommend this as the only style; those who are at heart romanticists, will have nothing but romance.

In the present essay, Mr. Pattee gets the theme for his discussion of the comparative importance of various types of writing from Vergil. He discusses his subject from the Humanist point of view. The essay possesses the warm brilliance born of personal conviction.

Mr. Pattee has been a professor of English at the Pennsylvania State College for a number of years. He first attracted wide attention in 1915 through the publication of *A History of American Literature since 1870*. He later collected a number of his essays and addresses under the title, *Sidelights on American Literature*. The first two essays in this volume, "A Critic in C Major" and "The Age of O. Henry," are among the most interesting essays that he has written. His latest volume of critical essays is *Tradition and Jazz*. "The Shot of Acestes" first appeared in *The Literary Review*, December 1, 1923.

It is perfectly natural for Americans to believe in what they possess. Ask the first three men you meet to name the best make of automobile on the market, and invariably they will tell you, in all seriousness, that the machines they own are the best machines in the world. The same trait is found among writers. Authors who deal in realism recommend this as the only style; those who are at heart romanticists, will have nothing but romance.

In the present essay, Mr. Pattee gets the theme for his discussion of the comparative importance of various types of writing from Vergil. He discusses his subject from the Humanist point of view. The essay possesses the warm brilliance born of personal conviction.

Mr. Pattee has been a professor of English at the Pennsylvania State College for a number of years. He first attracted wide attention in 1915 through the publication of *A History of American Literature since 1870*. He later collected a number of his essays and addresses under the title, *Sidelights on American Literature*. The first two essays in this volume, "A Critic in C Major," and "The Age of O. Henry," are among the most interesting essays that he has written. His latest volume of critical essays is *Tradition and Jazz*. "The Shot of Accoster," first appeared in *The Literary Review*, December 1, 1923.

THE SHOT OF ACESTES [1]

By Fred Lewis Pattee

I refer, of course, to the fifth book of the *Æneid* and the famous games at the tomb of Anchises. The races had been run off, the boxing bout was over, and the archery event was on. There were four entries: Hyrtacus, Mnestheus, Eurytion, and Acestes—I will use only their sweater numbers. The target was a mast from one of the defeated racing boats or a fluttering dove tied to the masthead; the shooters could take their choice. The distance was not mentioned, but it was deemed ample. Admiral Æneas was sole judge and referee and distributor of prizes.

The shooting that followed was sensational. It was more; it was unique, for each of the contestants established a new record. No. 1, selecting the mast for his target, clove to a hair the very heart of it and instantly *ingenti sonuerunt omnia plausu*, or, in current United States, "the Teucri bleachers arose as one man and gave him the yell." A bull's-eye through the dead center—even the Sicilian townies could feel that. According to Vergil's record, No. 1 alone of all the four that day captured the crowd to the extent of a yell. No. 2 chose perforce the dove, but he would not kill the bird; he would not do a thing so ordinary as to shoot a tied dove. He aimed at the all but invisible string that bound the bird, and he cut it clean, freeing the captive, which instantly bounded into the sky. The bleachers sat in silence and watched the joyous creature. Then No. 3, holding his arrow on the taut string while he followed the bird in the air, at

[1] Reprinted by permission from *The Literary Review*.

303

last let drive and pierced her among the very clouds. Her life she left among the deathless stars, but her lifeless form restored the arrow to its owner's hand. Acestes's turn to shoot and no mark. All hope of prize-winning gone, he felt free to cut loose and shoot not for the crowd, but for the gods who ruled his soul. Lifting his eyes from the solid mast and from the mast top, even from the low-lying cloud where had perished the dove, he drew his arrow to the head and did a thing no archer had ever dreamed of before: he launched the shaft with mighty arm straight into the Olympian blue where dwell the gods. And then—I'll leave the rich Latin, which no generation before mine would have insulted its readers by translating—the arrow, speeding swift among the thin clouds, burst into flame and, like a star unloosed from heaven, left behind it a long train of light.

The Trojan crowd, unable to fathom an unprecedented thing like that, sat in stolid silence awaiting the verdict of Æneas. They had not long to wait. To Acestes instantly he awarded the first prize. As it runs in the swift Latin hexameters, he loaded the man with great gifts and bound his temples with the laurel sacred alone to victors. To No. 3 he awarded second prize, for had he not brought down the loosened dove from the lofty sky? To No. 2 went third honors, for by his skill had he not cut the bonds that held the wingéd one to earth? But to No. 1, the darling of the bleachers, the one of them all who had felt most certain of the rich prize, to him he gave no award at all; only bare mention that he also had shot, for what had he done but make a mere bull's-eye on the earth-rooted target?

Whether Vergil intended it or not, the thing is a parable. It rings true; it actually happened; it is happening every day. It clears one's thinking; it sets up standards of measurement: Among men four attitudes towards life; in every contest four types of shooters; for critics four rules for determining values. Let us apply them to the modern novel, the worst tangle in modern literature.

Hyrtacus shoots always first; eternally he stands for the younger generation; eternally he opens the tournament, the new literary period—for "literary period" is always synonymous with "generation." He is the loudest of all the shooters; he is young, he is confident: cocksureness sits on him like a chip on a shoulder. Eternally he cries that the old is outgrown, rule-bound, moribund; that manner and manners have obscured the Truth; that he stands for Nature, NATURE! Young Alexander Pope cried aloud for "Nature" before Wordsworth was born. Hyrtacus stands on the solid earth and shoots at the solid mast—*Main Street, Winesburg, Ohio, Sister Carrie.* He looks not up into the heavens: his business is with Life, the solid earth, the main-mast.

His slogan varies in form with every generation, with every decade even, but it never changes its substance. In the eighteen-eighties it was "realism," the realism of James and Howells—parlor realism; in the nineties it was "veritism," then "naturalism." There was young Frank Norris: "By God, I told them the Truth!" I hit the solid mast; I pierced the very heart of it. There was young Hamlin Garland: "I believe in the mighty pivotal present. I believe in the living and not the dead. Veritism deals with life face to face." And there was Eugène Véron, whom he quoted: "We care no longer for gods or heroes: we care for men." And behind them all Zola. Skip three decades: Dreiser, Lawrence, Sherwood Anderson—realism, starknakedism. Pick one at random to voice this new school of archery—Walter B. Pitkin, short-story coach, revamper of handbooks for correspondence courses, assembler of "As We Are," 1923. Read his entire preface; this is a fragment:

It is partly a matter of scientific progress and partly one of intelligence level. Men read and write realism with a steadily growing passion as a consequence of the swiftly widening and deepening culture of this century. . . . The man who has been touched with the spirit of science puts little trust in his so-called "intuitions." He suspects those moods which the poet calls "deep spiritual insights." . . . In a word, he is a realist as every scientist must be, whether he knows it or not. Ours is the first generation in which there has lived more than a handful of realistically minded men and women. . . . Our popular magazines are responding to a firm demand for realism by printing stories which tell the truth and shame the devil as well as horrify the herd. . . . Our better magazines furnish realism in proportion to the numerical power of highly intelligent readers among their *clientèle*. So much for the general trend.

Thereupon he exemplifies "realism" by a series of tales so deadly faithful to the immediate contacts of life that some he declares are not fiction at all, but genuine biography, actually studies in actual back alleys, true to the minutest detail. He has held a clinic; he has made a dissection. You do not like such ghastly revelations? "Then we must debate this with you on the spot." You are belated in the march of evolution towards civilization; you are confessing your "lowbrowness"; the race evolves upwards into realism. "If you want the proof of this look at the history of our great literary successes."

I pick up a more recent book, *Midwest Portraits*, studies in recent Chicago archery, "literature" as up to date as a city reporter's notebook. Everywhere life viewed objectively and microscopically. Every author of them a tireless worker in contemporaneousness; every one of them self-hypnotized in umbilical contemplation, obsessed with the immediate contacts of life—shooters at the mast. To a man they have been trained in the school of metropolitan journalism—superficiality, headlong impressionism. No perspective, no poise, no serenity of soul, no skylights, no silences. In the words of the author himself: "In nearly all of them a realistic or naturalistic method predominates. The city, dealing with the elementals of our lives, inspires men to a realistic mood." Here is the list of some of our latter-day classics as crowned by Chicago journalism:

Theodore Dreiser in *Sister Carrie* and *The Financier*, Robert Herrick in *The Web*, *The Common Lot*, and *The Memoirs of an American Citizen;* Edgar Lee Masters in *Children of the Market Place* and *Skeeters Kirby*, Henry Kitchell Webster in *An American Family*, Joseph Medill Patterson in *Rebellion* and *A Little Brother of the Rich*, Sherwood Anderson in *Marching Men* and *Winesburg, Ohio;* Ben Hecht in *Erik Dorn*, I. K. Friedman in *By Bread Alone*, Hamlin Garland in *Rose of Dutchers Coolly* and *A Daughter of the Middle Border* and Frank Norris in *The Pit*.

I laid down the book, with its level atmosphere of contempt for "the old household gods whose engraved portraits hang on schoolhouse walls," its hydrophobic rage at the bare mention of "Puritanism," always made synonymous with "Comstockery" and "cant," its youthful cocksureness, and its inference on every page that now for the first time in all history a group of young men had arisen that was telling the truth about human life, the truth—I laid it down in the mood, I fancy, of the Man of Wrath in "Elizabeth and her German Garden":

I very much like to hear you talk together. It is all so young and fresh what you think and what you believe, and not of the least consequence to anyone.

Then suddenly a phrase on the jacket caught my eye and I got a thrill such as nothing in all the many chapters of the book had given me, a shock as from a live spark plug: "These are figures of importance to their own generation." Their own generation thinks these writings are literature; the outpourings of these Chicago candidates for the booby prize their own generation thinks are literature. What does it matter what my own generation—the generation passing from the stage—thinks of these things: my generation does not own the next period and these young men do. Can it be possible that a period is coming in the history of literature when the shot of Hyrtacus is to win the tournament? God help us if it is true.

A tribe larger than that of Hyrtacus, though less noisy and far less cocksure, traces descent back to Mnestheus, No. 2 in the ancient contest. Sensation—to cut the unseen string and send the bird bounding into the sky—what a moment of thrill! Sentiment—the winged thing helplessly fettered to earth set free, cast unharmed into the heavens, its element—what a stroke at the sensibilities! The arrow was kind; it was aimed not to kill, but to free—humanitarianism! Sentimentalism comes from self-pity; it comes from imagination which looks at the butterfly, winged for the heavens, sinking deeper in the mud with every stroke of its beautiful wings, and sees itself; it comes from conviction innate in some men, if not in all, that the great average of men is fundamentally good even as one believes oneself to be good. And the crowd forever delights to sit and watch the joy of the winged thing restored to its native sky, and sometimes, while watching absorbedly this creature of the skies buffeting the winds and surmounting the utmost cloud, it even forgets for a time that its own feet are on the muddy earth. Sentimentalism, sensationalism, art for art's sake, art for mere entertainment's sake, popular romance—these in literature are some of the names for it. *Udolpho*, Laurence Sterne, N. P. Willis, *The Gunmaker of Moscow*, *The Lamplighter*, Mrs. Stowe and *Alton Locke*, E. P. Roe, Dick Davis, *Pollyanna*, O. Henry, and most of the women—this is the tribe of old Mnestheus.

And the heirs of Hyrtacus stand and jeer with a scorn that deplores the poverty of our language in withering adjectives. Sickly sweet sentimentality! "Neruna!"—I forbear— but see Mencken *passim*. In early Victorian days the English Frasers let out on Fenimore Cooper with "He's a liar, a bilious braggart, a full jackass, an insect, a grub, and a reptile." And to a degree there is reason for their scorn. Of all debauchery that of emotion uncoupled with attendant action is the most deadening to the soul of man. William James has said the last word upon it. We remember his aristocrat who wept in the theater over the imaginary woes of the heroine while her own coachman was slowly freezing outside. And sensationalism—the freeing of the bird simply for the momentary thrill of it, again and yet again—is hardly less debauching. Go to the movies and look not at the screen but at the people. Purposeless watching for the cut string and the suddenly bounding bird, weltering in a smother of sentiment and leaving the dishes unwashed at home—castles in the air with no foundations at all upon the earth—continue it long and your soul, if you still have one, withers and dies.

But always Mnestheus wins over Hyrtacus. He caught at least a glimpse of the divine blue; he saw for a moment at least the loosened dove of man's soul mounting into the upper air, and for a moment at least he felt the freedom of the gods—

he was himself a god, with all the boundless sky as his demesne.

The tribe of Eurytion is dubbed by D. H. Lawrence in his amazing new book, *Classical American Literature*, the "killers." With no thought of alluding to Vergil's parable, he has this of James Fenimore Cooper:

> This is Natty, the white forerunner. A killer. As in *Deerslayer*, he shoots the bird that flies in the high, high sky, so that the bird falls out of the invisible into the visible, dead; he symbolizes himself. He will bring the bird of the spirit out of the high air. He is the stoic killer of the old great life.

Good! It is a shot of Eurytion: it hits the mark. Bliss Perry, also with no thought of his Vergil, has voiced the same thought:

> Flaubert once compared our human idealism to the flight of a swallow; at one moment it is soaring towards the sunset, at the next moment some one shoots it and it tumbles into the mud with blood upon its glistening wings. The sudden poignant contrast between light, space, freedom, and the wounded, bleeding bird in the mud is the very essence of tragedy.

The best example is "Don Quixote." Once men dreamed honestly of chivalry and tried to practice it and the whole race took a step in advance; then Cervantes shot the bird down into the barnyard mud and we laugh and jeer. Anatole France in *L'île des Penguins* shoots down the old great life of France and sneers and jeers at the dead bird and they give him the Nobel Prize for his marksmanship. The human soul takes as naturally to the upper air as the winged dove; it is incurably romantic and idealistic, and a Eurytion stands on every street corner shooting at it as if it were an obscene bird. The American Mark Twain sends a Connecticut Yankee into King Arthur's court and we classify his book as humor. He catches a glimpse of the old great life of the passing American frontier—romance with the golden light upon it; a glimpse again of the marvelous romance of Domremy and its peasant saint, and he dies growling curses on "the damned human race." The Puritan tradition deals with one of the loftiest flights of the Anglo-Saxon soul, and no young archer to-day with arrow so blunt that he cannot bring it down into the mud. The typical Eurytion of the younger generation let us call James Cabell. Life is tragedy; a glimpse of heaven and then a nose-dive into the dunghill dead; the "comedy of disenchantment"; let us rather call it the tragedy, the supremest tragedy man knows. I mean Cabell is the tragedy. The man who sees no gods above his clouds is dead and in hell. Prometheus brought down from the Olympic zone fire for the blessing of mortals; Mnestheus also brought down the heavenly thing, but he brought it down dead—not fire, but ashes—and, having delivered this monstrous gift, he stands and sneers: "These are your gods, O Israel." Life is a monstrous joke: look at these ashes.

Yet Eurytion is infinitely more deserving of the prize than Hyrtacus: he at least has looked higher than the muddy earth; he is more deserving than Mnestheus, for he did not stand impotently and dream of the skies. He brought down something out of the unseen, even though he brought it down dead.

And now Acestes. His tribe is almost as small as that of the Mohicans. Even one Acestes in a generation makes a people rich. His gift is to see beyond eyesight, to bring the fire of the gods down alive. Standing with Acestes and looking into the invisible blue, one begins to understand many hard sayings of the philosophers. We catch a glimpse of what Melville meant when speaking of Hawthorne: "Irving is a grasshopper to him—putting the souls of the two men together." Irving was of the tribe of Mnestheus. We jeer no longer at Barrett Wendell's Harvard dictums: "The writings of Irving, of Cooper, of Bryant never dealt with deeply significant matters," and "In the work of Poe nothing was produced that touched seriously on God's eternities." And we understand Thoreau even in such Orphic sayings as: "We should see that our dreams are the solidest facts that we know," and "My actual life is a fact, in view of which I have no occasion to congratulate myself; but for my faith and aspiration I have respect."

Great literature is always an arrow launched into the blue by an archer who sought no prize save that furnished by his own soul, who followed no precedents, but who shot to bring down alive the unseen powers, call them gods or call them what you will. Novalis sought the blue flower; Maeterlinck the bluebird, and they sought it not in the mud of the swamps. Thoreau had lost among other things a dove with wings. His dream was "to discover the sources of the Nile, perchance the Mountains of the Moon." Never was he a naturalist: rather was he a supernaturalist.

Always somewhere in the great classic comes the stage direction, often implied, "Enter the gods." The arrow kindles in the sky and becomes a trail of light for generations to come. Melville wrote *Moby Dick* to suit his own imperious soul and two generations later its trail was burning brighter than when he first shot it. Whitman, not the earlier poet of the body, but the later voicer of the soul, created his splendid *Passage to India* out of his own life without models and without expectation of reward or recognition. Thoreau for years wrote his journal daily for himself and the gods. He had no thought of publication. Emerson's most quoted line is "hitch your wagon to a star," and he holds the commanding place that he does to-day simply because his whole life long he tried for himself to make this celestial connection.

There are those who fear that Acestes is dead and that in America at least he has left no descendants. After reading a book like *Midwest Portraits* one is inclined to agree with them. But if Acestes is dead then is the soul of America dead. Inconceivable! The Cabells and the Andersons and the Dreisers and the Menckens rule the moment by their clatter and their cocksureness, but their day is brief. A donkey braying in the back lot may drown for me the music of the spheres—if I will let it. These creatures of the moment have as little power to realize the possibilities and the harmonies and the winged powers of the human soul, its ability to triumph over the merely physical, compelling as the physical unquestionably is, as they have to wear the shoes of St. Francis. They see but the mud and they bathe in the mud and they cry to the world: "Come on in; the mud is fine. Everybody's in it. Look, here is a sample of it, warranted genuine. You can't stay out anyway, even if you want to." But Acestes looks away from the mud and talks of the glory of man. His eyes are upon the gods beyond the clouds, and when he shoots his mighty arrow becomes a burning pathway across the heavens lighting the race in its groping progress upwards towards the gods.

PREFACE

After wandering far afield and after considering the many and conflicting points of view concerning poetry in general and American poetry in particular, one could do far worse than to come finally to a consideration of poetry as a contributing influence in world civilization. Poetry may seem superfluous to many, and only trivial or moderately important to others; but, in its highest sense, it is akin to philosophy on the one side, and to religion, on the other. Envisioned with beauty and truth, it guides the world onward toward the light.

Mr. Woodberry, in the present essay, has done a real service by lifting poetry thus into the realm of life's higher realities. It is a similar service to that which Matthew Arnold did for his generation through such essays as *The Study of Poetry*.

Mr. Woodberry was born in Massachusetts. He is a graduate of Harvard. He was, for a few years, Professor of English in the University of Nebraska, and later, Professor of Comparative Literature at Columbia University. He is a member of the American Academy of Arts and Letters, and a Fellow of the Royal Society of Literature. He has received honorary degrees from a number of different universities. He has a large number of critical volumes to his credit. These were brought together in his *Collected Essays* (six volumes) in 1921. He has also published a number of volumes of poetry. "The Language of All the World" was first published in *The Torch*, 1905.

THE LANGUAGE OF ALL THE WORLD [1]

By George Woodberry

The language of literature is the language of all the world. It is necessary to divest ourselves at once of the notion of diversified vocal and grammatical speech which constitutes the various tongues of the earth, and conceals the identity of image and logic in the minds of all men. Words are intermediary between thought and things. We express ourselves really not through words, which are only signs, but through what they signify—through things. Literature is the expression of life. The question, then, is—what things has literature found most effectual to express life, and has therefore habitually preferred? and what tradition in consequence of this habit of preference has been built up in all literatures, and obtained currency and authority in this province of the wider realm of all art? It is an interesting question, and fundamental for anyone who desires to appreciate literature understandingly. Perhaps you will permit me to approach it somewhat indirectly.

You are all familiar with something that is called poetic diction—that is, a selected language specially fitted for the uses of poetry; and you are, perhaps, not quite so familiar with the analogous feature in prose, which is now usually termed preciosity, or preciousness of language, that is, a highly refined and æsthetic diction, such as Walter Pater employs. The two are constant products of language that receives any literary cultivation, and they are sometimes called diseases of language. Thus, in both early and late

[1] Reprinted from *The Torch* by permission of Harcourt, Brace and Co.

Greek there sprang up literary styles of expression, involving the preference of certain words, constructions, and even cadences, and the teaching of art in these matters was the business of the Greek rhetorican; so in Italy, Spain, and France, in the Renaissance, similar styles, each departing from the common and habitual speech of the time, grew up, and in England you identify this mode of language in Elizabeth's day as Euphuism. The phenomenon is common, and belongs to the nature of language. Poetic diction, however, you perhaps associate most clearly with the mannerism in language of the eighteenth century in England, when common and so-called vulgar words were exiled from poetry, and Gray, for example, could not speak of the Eton schoolboys as playing hoop, but only as "chasing the rolling circles' speed," and when, to use the stock example, all green things were "verdant." This is fixed in our memory because Wordsworth has the credit of leading an attack on the poetic diction of that period, both critically in his prefaces and practically in his verse; he went to the other extreme, and introduced into his poetry such homely words as "tub," for example; he held that the proper language of poetry is the language of common life. So Emerson in his addresses, you remember, had recourse to the humblest objects for illustration, and shocked the formalism of his time by speaking of "the meal in the firkin, the milk in the pan." He was applying in prose the rule of Wordsworth in poetry. Walt Whitman represents the extreme of this use of the actual language of men. But if you consider the matter, you will see that this choice of the homely word only sets up at last a fashion of homeliness in the place of a fashion of refinement, and breeds, for instance, dialect poets in shoals; and often the choice is really not of the word, but of the homely thing itself as the object of thought and expressive image of it;

and in men so great as Emerson and Wordsworth the practice is a proof of that sympathy with common life which
made them both great democrats. But in addition to the
diction that characterizes an age, you must have observed
that in every original writer there grows up a particular
vocabulary, structure, and rhythm that he affects and that
in the end becomes his mannerism, or distinctive style, so
marked that you recognize his work by its stamp alone, as
in Keats, Browning, and Swinburne in poetry, and in
Arnold in prose. In other words, there is at work in the language of a man, or of an age even, a constant principle of
selection which tends to prefer certain ways and forms of
speech to others, and in the end develops a language characteristic of the age, or of the man.

This principle of selection, whether it works toward refinement or homeliness, operates in the same way. It must
be remembered—and it is too often forgotten—that the
problem of any artistic work is a problem of economy. How
to get into the two hours' traffic of the stage the significance
of a whole life, of a group of lives; how to pack into a sixteen-
line lyric a dramatic situation and there sphere it in its own
emotion; how to rouse passion and pour it in a three-minute
poem, like Shelley's *Indian Air*—all these are problems in
economy, by which speed, condensation, intensity are gained.
Now words in themselves are colorless, except so far as their
musical quality is concerned; but the thing that a word
stands for has a meaning of its own and usually a meaning
charged with associations, and often this associative meaning is the primary and important one in its use. A rose, for
example, is but the most beautiful of flowers in itself, but it
is so charged with association in men's lives, and still more
heavily charged with long use of emotion in literature, that
the very word and mere name of it awakes the heart and sets

a thousand memories unconsciously vibrating. This added meaning is what I am accustomed to term an overtone in words; and it is manifest that, in view of the necessity for economy in poetic art, those words which are the richest and deepest in overtone will be preferred, because of the speed, certainty, and fullness they contain. The question will be what overtones in life appeal most to this or that poet; he will reproduce them in his verse; Pope will use the overtones of a polished society, Wordsworth and Emerson those of humble life. Now our larger question is what overtones are characteristically preferred in great literature, in what objects do they most inhere, and in what way is the authoritative tradition of literature, as respects its means of expression, thus built up?

It goes without saying that all overtones are either of thought or feeling. What modes of expression, then, what material objects, what forms of imagination, what abstract principles of thought, are most deeply charged with ideas and emotions? It will be agreed that, as a mere medium, music expresses pure emotion most directly and richly; music seems to enter the physical frame of the body itself, and move there with the warmth and instancy of blood. The sound of words, therefore, cannot be neglected, and in the melody and echo of poetry sound is a cardinal element; yet, it is here only the veining of the marble, it is not the material itself. In the objects which words summon up, there is sometimes an emotional power as direct and immediate as that of music itself, as for example, in the great features of nature, the mountains, the plains, the ocean, which awe even the savage mind. But, in general, the emotional power of material objects is lent to them by association, that is, by the human use that has been made of them, as on the plain of Marathon, to use Dr. Johnson's old illustration, it is the thought of what happened there that makes the spectator's patriotism "gain force" as he surveys the scene. This human use of the world is the fountain of significance in all imaginative and poetic speech; and in the broad sense history is the story of this human use of the world.

History is so much of past experience as abides in race-memory; and underlies race-literature in the same way that a poet's own experience underlies his expression of life. I do not mean that when a poet unlocks his heart, as Shakespeare did in his sonnets, he necessarily writes his own biography; in the poems he writes there may be much of actual event as in Burns's love-songs, or little as in Dante's *New Life*. Much of a poet's experience takes place in imagination only; the life he tells is oftenest the life that he strongly desires to live, and the power, the purity and height of his utterance may not seldom be the greater because experience here uses the voices of desire. "All I could never be," in Browning's plangent line, has been the mounting strain of the sublimest and the tenderest songs of men. All Ireland could never be, thrills and sorrows on her harp's most resonant string, and is the master-note to which her sweetest music ever returns. All man could never be makes the sad majesty of Vergil's verse. As with a man, what a nation strongly desires is no small part of its life, and is the mark of destiny upon it, whether for failure or success; so the note of world-empire is heard in the latest English verse, and the note of humanity—the service of all men—has always been dominant in our own. History, then, must be thought of, in its relation to literature, as including the desire as well as the performance of the race.

History, however, in the narrowest sense, lies close to the roots of imaginative literature. The great place of history and its inspirational power in the literature of the last century I have already referred to; it is one of the most important elements in the extraordinary reach and range of that splendid outburst of imagination throughout Europe. Aristotle recognized the value of history as an aid to the imagination, at the very moment that he elevated poetry above history. In that necessary economy of art, of which I spoke, it is a great gain to have well-known characters and familiar events, such as Agamemnon and the "Trojan War," in which much is already done for the spectator before the play begins. So our present historical novelists have their stories half-written for them in the minds of their readers, and especially avail themselves of an emotional element there, a patriotism, which they do not have to create. The use of history to the imagination, however, goes farther than merely to spare it the pains of creating character and incident and evoking emotion. It assists a literary movement to begin with race-power much as a poet's or—as in Dickens's case— a novelist's own experience aids him to develop his work, however much that experience may be finally transformed in the work. Thus the novel of the last age really started its great career from Scott's historic sense working out into imaginative expression, and in a lesser degree from so minor a writer as Miss Edgeworth in whose Irish stories—which were contemporary history—Scott courteously professed to find his own starting point. It is worth noting, also, that the Elizabethan drama had the same course. Shakespeare following Marlowe's example developed from the historical English plays, in which he worked in Scott's manner, into his full control of imagination in the purely ideal sphere. History has thus often been the handmaid of imagination, and the foster-mother of great literary ages. Yet to vary Aristotle's phrase—poetry is all history could never be.

It appears to me, nevertheless, that history underlies race-literature in a far more profound and universal way.

History is mortal: it dies. Yet it does not altogether die. Elements, features, fragments of it survive, and enter into the eternal memory of the race, and are there transformed, and—as we say—spiritualized. Literature is the abiding-place of this transforming power, and most profits by it. And to come to the heart of the matter, there have been at least three such cardinal transformations in the past.

The first transformation of history is mythology. I do not mean to enter on the vexed question of the origin of mythologies; and, of course, in referring to history as its ground, I include much more than that hero-worship such as you will find elaborated or invented in Carlyle's essay on Odin, and especially I include all that experience of nature and her association with human toil and moods that you will find delineated with such marvelous subtleness and fullness in Walter Pater's essay on Dionysus. In mythology, mankind preserved from his primitive experience of nature, and his own heroic past therein, all that had any lasting significance, and, although all mythologies have specific features and a particular value of their own, yet the race, coming to its best, as I have said, bore here its perfect blossom in Greek mythology. I know not by what grace of heaven, by what felicity of blend in climate, blood, and the fortune of mortal life, but so it was that the human soul put forth the bud of beauty in the Greek race; and there, at the dawn of our own intellectual civilization and in the first sunrise of our poetry in Homer, was found a world filled with divine—with majestic and lovely figures, which had absorbed into their celestial being and forms the power of nature, the splendor and charm of the material sphere, the fructifying and beneficent operations of the external universe, the providence of the state and the inspiration of all arts and crafts, of games and wars and song; each of these deities was a flashing center of human energy, aspiration, reliance—with a realm and servants of its own; and mingling with them in fair companionship was a company of demigods and heroes, of kings and princes, and of golden youths, significant of the fate of all young life—Adonis, Hippolytus, Orestes. This mythologic world was near to earth, and it mixed with legendary history, such history as the *Iliad* contained, and also with the private and public life of the citizens, being the ceremonial religion of the state. It was all, nevertheless, the transformation that man had accomplished of his own past, his joys and sorrows, his labors, his insights and desires, the deeds of his ancestors, —the human use that he had made of the world. This was the body of idea and emotion to which the poet appealed in that age, precisely as our historical novelists now appeal to our own knowledge of history and preëstablished emotion with regard to it, our patriotism. Here they found a language already full charged with emotion and intelligence, of which they could avail themselves, and speaking which they spoke with the voices of a thousand years. Nevertheless, it was at best a language like others, and subject to change and decay in expressive power. The time came when, the creative impulse in mythology having ceased and its forms being fixed, the mythic world lay behind the mind of the advancing race which had now attained conceptions of the physical universe, and especially ideas of the moral life, which were no longer capable of being held in and expressed by the mythic world, but exceeded the bounds of earlier thought and feeling and broke the ancient molds. Then it was that Plato desired to exile the poets and their mythology from the state. He could not be content, either, with a certain change that had occurred; for the creative power in mythology having long ceased, as I have said, the imagination put forth a new function—a meditative power—and brooding over the old fables of the world of the gods discovered in them, not a record of fact, but an allegorical meaning, a higher truth which the fable contained. Mythology passed thus into an emblematic stage, in which it was again long used by mankind, as a language of universal power. Plato, however, could not free himself from the mythologic habit of imagination so planted in his race, and found the most effective expression for his ideas in the myths of his own invention which he made up by a dexterous and poetic adaptation of the old elements; and others later than Plato have found it hard to disuse the mythologic language; for, although the old religion as a thing of faith and practice died away, it survived as a thing of form and feature in art, as a phase of natural symbolism and of inward loveliness of action and passion in poetry, as a chapter of romance in the history of the race; and the modern literatures of Europe are, in large measure, unintelligible without this key.

The second great transformation of history is chivalry. Here the phenomenon is nearer in time and lies more within the field of observation and knowledge; it is possible to trace the stages of the growth of the story of Roland with some detail and precision; but, on the other hand, the Arthur myth reaches far back into the beginnings of Celtic imagination, and all such race-myths tend to appropriate and embody in themselves the characteristic features both of one another and of whatever is held to be precious and significant in history or even in classical and Eastern legend. The true growth, however, is that feudal culture, which we know as knighthood, working out its own ideal of action and character and sentiment on a basis of bravery, courtesy, and piety, and thereby generating patterns of knighthood, typical careers, and in the end an imaginative interpretation of the purest spiritual life itself in the various legends of the Holy

Grail. As in the pagan world the forms and fables of mythology and their interaction downward with the human world furnished the imaginative interpretation of life as it then was, so for the medieval age, the figures and tales of chivalry and their interaction upward with the spiritual world of Christianity, and also with the magic of diabolism round about, furnished the imaginative interpretation of that later life. It was this new body of ideas and emotion in the minds of men that the medieval poets appealed to, availed themselves of, and so spoke a language of imagery and passion that was a world-language, charged as I have said with the thought and feeling, the tradition, of a long age. What happened to the language of mythology, happened also to this language; it lost the power of reality, and men arose who, being in advance of its conceptions of life, desired to exile it, denounce it or laugh it out of existence, like Ascham in England, and Cervantes in Spain. It also suffered that late change into an allegorical or emblematic meaning, and had a second life in that form, as in the notable instance of Spenser's *Faerie Queene*. It also could not die, but—just as mythology revived in the Alexandrian poets for a season, and fed Theocritus and Vergil—chivalry was reborn in the last century, and in Tennyson's Arthur, and in Wagner's *Parsifal* lived again in two great expressions of ideal life.

The third great transformation of history is contained in the Scriptures. The Bible is, in itself, a singularly complete expression of the whole life of a race in one volume—its faith and history blending in one body of poetry, thought, and imaginative chronicle. It contains a celestial world in association with human events; its patriarchs are like demigods, and it has heroes, legends, tales in good numbers, and much romantic and passionate life, on the human side, besides its great stores of spirituality. In literary power it achieves the highest in the kinds of composition that it uses. It is as a whole, regarded purely from the human point of view, not unfairly to be compared in mass, variety, and scope of expression, with mythology and chivalry as constituting a third great form of imaginative language; nor has its history been dissimilar in the Christian world to which it came with something of that same remoteness in time and reality that belonged equally to mythology and chivalry. It was first used in a positive manner, as a thing of fact and solid belief; but there soon grew up, you remember, in the Christian world that habit of finding a hidden meaning in its historical record, of turning it to a parable, of extracting from it an allegorical signification. It became, not only in parts but as a whole, emblematic, and its interpretation as such was the labor of centuries. This is commonly stated as the source of that universal mood of allegorizing which characterized the medieval world, and was as strongly felt in secular as in religious writers. Its historical tales, its theories of the universe, its cruder morals in the Jewish ages, have been scoffed at, just as was the case with the Greek myth, from the Apostate to Voltaire and later; but how great are its powers as a language is seen in the completeness with which it tyrannized over the Puritan life in England and made its history, its ideas, its emotions the habitual and almost exclusive speech of that strong Cromwellian age. In our country here in New England it gave the mold of imagination to our ancestors for two whole centuries. A book, which contains such power that it can make itself the language of life through so many centuries and in such various peoples is to be reckoned as one of the greatest instruments of race-expression that man possesses.

Mythology, chivalry, the Scriptures are the tongues of the imagination. "It is far more important to know them than to learn French or German or Italian, or Latin or Greek; they are three branches of that universal language which though vainly sought on the lips of men is found in their minds and hearts. To omit these in education is to defraud youth of its inheritance; it is like destroying a long-developed organ of the body, like putting out the eye or silencing the nerves of hearing. Nor is it enough to look them up in encyclopedias and notes, and so obtain a piecemeal information; one must grow familiar with these forms of beauty, forms of honor, forms of righteousness, have something of the same sense of their reality as that felt by Homer and Vergil, by the singer of *Roland* and the chronicler of the *Mort d'Arthur*, by St. Augustine, and St. Thomas. He must form his imagination upon these idealities, and load his heart with them; else many a masterpiece of the human spirit will be lost to him, and most of the rest will be impaired. If one must know vocabulary and grammar before he can understand the speech of the mouth, much more must he know well mythology, chivalry, and Bible-lore before he can take possession of the wisdom that the race-mind has spoken, the beauty it has molded life into, as a thing of passion and action, the economy of lucid power it has achieved for perfect human utterance, in these three fundamental forms of a true world-language. The literature of the last century is permeated with mythology, chivalry, and to a less degree with Scripture, and no one can hope to assimilate it, to receive its message, unless his mind is drenched with these same things; and the further back his tastes and desires lead him into the literature of earlier times, the greater will be his need of this education in the material, the modes, and the forms of past imagination.

It may be that a fourth great tongue of the imagination is now being shaped upon the living lips of men in the present and succeeding ages. If it be so, this will be the work of the democratic idea, which is now still at the beginning of its career; but since mythology and chivalry had their development in living men, it is natural to suppose that the human force is still operative in our own generation as it once was in those of Hellenic and medieval years. The characteristic literature of democracy is that of its ideas, spirtualized in Shelley, and that of the common lot as represented in the sphere of the novel, spiritualized most notably in Victor Hugo. In our own country it is singular to observe that the democratic idea, though efficient in politics, does not yet establish itself in imaginative literature with any great power of brilliancy, does not create great democratic types, or in any way express itself adequately. This democratic idea, in Dickens for example, uses the experience of daily life, that is, contemporary history, or at least it uses an artistic arrangement of such experience: but the novel as a whole has given us in regard to the common lot, rather a description of life in its variety than that concentrated and essential significance of life which we call typical. If democracy in its future course should evolve such a typical and spiritualized embodiment of itself as chivalry found in Arthur and the Round Table, or as the heroic age of Greece found in Achilles and the Trojan War, or as the genius of Rome found in Æneas and his fortunes, then imagination—race-imagination will be enriched by this fourth great instrument; but this is to cast the horoscope of too distant an hour. I introduce the thought only for the sake of including in this broad survey of race-imagination that experience of the present day, that history in the contemporary process of being transformed, out of which the mass of the books of the day are now made.

Let me recur now to that principle of selection which through the cumulative action of repeated preferences of phrase and image fixes a habit of choice which at last stamps the diction of a man, a school, or an age. It is plain that in what I have called the transformation of history, of which literature is the express image, there is the same principle of selection which, working through long periods of race-life, results at last in those idealities of persons and events in which inhere most powerfully those overtones of beauty, honor, and righteousness that the race has found most precious both for idea and emotion; and to these are to be added what I have had no time to include and discuss, the idealities of persons and events found outside mythology, chivalry, and Scripture, in the work of individual genius like Shakespeare, which nevertheless have the same ground in history, in experience, that in them is similarly transformed. Life-experience spiritualized is the formula of all great literature; it may range from the experience of a single life, like Sidney's in his sonnets, to that of an empire in Virgil's *Æneid*, or of a religion in Dante's *Comedy*. In either case the formula which makes it literature is the same. I have illustrated the point by the obvious spiritualizations of history. Race-life, from the point of view of literature, results at last in these molds of imagination, and all else though slowly, yet surely, drops away into oblivion. In truth, it is only by being thus spiritualized that anything human survives from the past. The rose, I said, has been so dipped in human experience that it is less a thing of nature than a thing of passion. In the same way Adonis, Jason and Achilles, Roland and Arthur, Lancelot, Percival and Galahad, Romeo and Hamlet have drawn into themselves such myriads of human lives by admiration and love that from them everything material, contemporary, and mortal has been refined away, and they seem to all of us like figures moving in an immortal air. They have achieved the eternal world. To do this is the work of art. It may seem a fantastic idea, but I will venture the saying of it, since to me it is the truth. Art, I suppose, you think of as the realm and privilege of selected men, of sculptors, painters, musicians, poets, men of genius and having something that has always been called divine in their faculty; but it appears to me that art, like genius, is something that all men share, that it is the stamp of the soul in every one, and constitutes their true and immaterial life. The soul of the race, as it is seen in history and disclosed by history, is an artist soul; its career is an artistic career; its unerring selective power expels from its memory every mortal element and preserves only the essential spirit, and thereof builds its ideal imaginative world through which it finds its true expression; its more perfect comprehension of the world is science, its more perfect comprehension of its own nature is love, its more perfect expression of its remembered life is art. Mankind is the grandest and surest artist of all, and history as it clarifies is, in pure fact, an artistic process, a creation in its fullness of the beautiful soul.

It appears, then, that the language of literature in the race is a perfected nature and a perfected manhood and a perfected divinity, so far as the race at the moment can see toward perfection. The life which literature builds up ideally out of the material of experience is not wholly a past life, but there mingles with it and at last controls it the life that man desires to live. Fullness of life—that fullness of action which is poured in the epic, that fullness of passion which is poured in the drama, that fullness of desire that is poured in the lyric—the life of which man knows himself capable and realizes as the opportunity and hope of life —this is the life that literature enthrones in its dream. You have heard much of the will to believe and of the desire to live: literature is made of these two, warp and woof. Race after race believes in the gods it has come to know and in the heroes it has borne, and in what it wishes to believe of divine and human experience; and the life it thus ascribes to its gods and to its own past is the life it most ardently desires to live. Literature, which records this, is thus the chief witness to the nobility, the constancy and instancy of man's effort for perfection. What wonder, then, if in his sublimest and tenderest song there steals that note of melancholy so often struck by the greatest masters in the crisis and climax of their works, and which, when so struck, has more of the infinite in it, more of the human in it, than any other in the slowly triumphant theme!

To sum up—the language of literature is experience; the language of race-literature is race-experience, or history, the human use that the race has made of the world. The law appears to be that history in this sense is slowly transformed by a refining and spiritualizing process into an imaginative world, such as the world of mythology, chivalry, or the Scriptures, and that this world in turn becomes emblematic and fades away into an expression of abstract truth. The crude beginning of the process is seen in our historical fiction; the height of it in Arthur or in Odin; the end of it in the symbolic or allegoric interpretation of even so human a book as Vergil's *Æneid*. Human desire for the best enters into this process with such force that the record of the past slowly changes into the prophecy of the future, and out of the passing away of what was is built the dream of what shall be; so arises in race-life the creed of what man wishes to believe and the dream of the life he desires to live; this human desire for belief and for life is, in the final analysis, the principle of selection whose operation has been sketched, and on its validity rests the validity and truth of all literature.